汉语病句辨析九百例

Error Analysis of
900 Sample Sentences
—For Chinese Learners from English Speaking Countries

主　编　程美珍
副主编　李　珠

华语教学出版社
北　京
Printed in China

First Edition   1997
Fourth Printing   2009

ISBN 978-7-80052-515-5
Copyright 1997 by Sinolingua
Published by Sinolingua
24 Baiwanzhuang Road, Beijing 100037, China
Tel: (86)10-68320585
Fax: (86)10-68326333
http: //www.sinolingua.com.cn
E-mail: hyjx@sinolingua.com.cn
Printed by Beijing Foreign Languages Printing House
Distributed by China International
Book Trading Corporation
35 Chegongzhuang Xilu, P.O.Box 399
Beijing 100044, China

Printed in the People's Republic of China

序

　　病句是个疑难杂症,它不是那么容易治疗的。庸医固然不行,头疼医头脚疼医脚也不行。遇上良医,手到病除。

　　病句实际上不单纯限于句子,叫它语病或许更恰当一些。从病情上面来说,有的属于语言结构方面出了问题,有的属于其他方面(例如逻辑、事理、习惯、情调等等)出了问题。就语言结构来说,单词、词组、句子、段落等不论哪个环节弄不好都可能闹毛病。因为语言是表达的根本,句子是语言表达的根本,不论语病怎么错综复杂,我们把语病叫成病句,治理也主要抓句子里面各个组成部分,还是完全可以的。

　　要检查学生的语文水平如何,素养深浅,观察能力是否敏锐,有一种办法,人们称之为开"文章病院",各科门诊俱全,修改病句。给这种办法起个简化的叫名儿,称之为"改错儿"。大致是:列出一些句子让学生①指出哪条是病句,如果把无病之句判断为病句,这当然不行;②对病句进行修改,如果把坏牙留下,把好牙拔掉,这当然也不行;③要求修改为健康的句子,如果把阑尾确实割干净了,却把剪子纱布缝在肚子里头,这也照样不行;④说明修改的理由。

　　这种训练对于提高学生语文能力还是有效的,训练方法也比较简明扼要,切实可行,适合于中等学校使用。范围最好是在日常的学习中使用。病句简单的,容易改,只有一种答案;这样的修改,小学也无妨采用。病句复杂的,往往有许多种修改的可能,什么样的改法算是完整的准确的,大家并不一定马上就取得一致意见;还有更麻烦的事,脱离了具体语言环境,没有上下文,你还很难说你所"修改"的"病句"就是改对了的，弄不好，你这"改错儿"很可能反到是改错了哩。这样的修改，高中也无妨多练习，使学生扩展眼界，活跃思路。

修改病句，如果用于高级中学毕业地方性统一"会考"，用于高等学校一年级新生入学考试，我个人认为是不合适的。主要的原因是：题目虽小，较难控制，要求作出唯一、全面、正确的标准答案，并不容易；几十万人考卷乃到几百万人考卷里面出现了意想不到而又是合理的答案是完全可能的。修改病句所得分数有限，牵扯太多，费时费力，实非上策。

以上是就本国学生学习本民族语言文字来说的。有许多人往往把修改病句看成很简单很容易的事，其实它也有很复杂很繁难的。不能小看它。

在第二语言的学习过程中，使用修改病句来提高学生语文水平确是各种最佳方法之中的一种。

这本书精心挑选了900条病句，概括了使用英语的留学生在学习汉语时容易出问题的96个"使用不当"。"误"先列，"正"后出，然后说明修改的理由。

假定这本书的读者看完了《总说》之后，从本书（一）词法方面常见的错误这一部分起，看每条病句的时候，你可先把"正"和修改的理由盖上完全不看，自己修改而且动脑子想为什么要修改的道理，然后再看书，比较一下。你改对了，当然很高兴啦。你改错了，改的理由也站不住，不要泄气，因为你提高了认识，这对你就有很大的帮助，你也学到了正确的修改方法，也很愉快。如果你下定决心，坚持从第1句到第900句都这样认真，那么，我向你表示热烈祝贺，因为：

第一，你真有毅力。有毅力的人，天大的困难也难不倒，高山向你低头，河水为你让路，你会以更大的毅力在许多许多方面获得更大的胜利的。

第二,你以最简捷的途径抓住学习汉语的一些主要关键性问题。

第三,你学会了辨认病句和修改病句的方法。学会方法比学会知识有时或许更重要些。

收获如此之多,还能不向你表示热烈祝贺?

这本书是由程美珍老师发起并邀集李珠老师等很多人齐心协力,分工合作而编写成的。不但这项工作成果重要,这种集体主义的精神也是很可珍贵的。

是为序。

张清常
1996 年 11 月 7 日

FOREWORD

Erroneous sentences are a difficult and complicated case to cope with. Someone like a quack doctor can not help. Neither will the kind of palliative remedies the problem. However, difficulties can be smoothed away in the case of a "good doctor".

The so-called erroneous sentences are actually not merely confined to sentences. Thus, the term faulty wording may be more precise to be used. With respect to the source of error, sometimes the problem lies in linguistic structure, sometimes in other aspects such as logic, reason, convention, or mood etc. So far as language structure is concerned, errors may be found in any level of language —— word, phrase, sentence or paragraph. Language is the base of expression and sentence is the base of language. Hence, however complicated a faulty wording can be, we may refer to it an erroneous sentence and focus our attention on its constituents while making corrections.

There is a method to test how well students have mastered the language and see whether they have keen observation. It is called to open a language hospital which offers all outpatient services for erroneous sentences. We simply call it error correction. That is to require the students 1) to find out the erroneous sentence. If the student takes a right sentence for a wrong one, he certainly fails. 2) to decide where is wrong. It certainly won't do if a good tooth is pulled out with the bad one kept. 3) to change the wrong sentence into a correct one. Removing the appendix but with the scalpel and gauze left inside is not a successful operation. 4) to explain why the correction should be made.

This kind of drill is helpful to develop students' language capacity. As a simple and practical method, it is applicable to secondary schools, but better be kept within the scope of ordinary practice. Exercises of correcting wrong sentences that are easy and have only one possible answer may also be adopted by primary schools. However, complicated sentences may have several possible ways of correction and it is uncertain as to which one is perfect. What is even more bothersome is that without a specific context, one can not rely on his correction which is probably not correct. Nevertheless, this type of exercise may be used extensively in high schools in order to prompt the students to think more creatively.

I personally consider it improper to use error correction for local joint examinations for high school graduates. Neither is it fit for entrance examinations to institutions of higher learning. The main reason is that it is not an easy task to give the only comprehensive and standard answers to such exercises. It is quite possible that other reasonable answers, unexpected, occur among some of the millions of test papers. Additionally, sentence correction involves many factors. It takes time and energy but does not score proportionally. Hence this is not the best way.

So far we have considered things from the viewpoint of students learning native language. Many people tend to regard error correction as an easy matter. But in fact, it is sometimes very complicated and troublesome and should not be overlooked.

For second language learning, error correction proves to be one of the best ways to enhance students' language ability.

The present book has carefully selected 900 erroneous sentences and generalized 96 types of improper use which English-speaking students are likely to have problems with. The wrong example stays above and the correct one comes below and then follows the explanation.

Suppose you start from the section of COMMON ERRORS IN MORPHOLOGY after reading the General View. With each example, you cover the correct sentence and the explanation and try to find an answer using your own head, and then contrast with what is on the book. If you are right, it is very well; if not, don't feel depressed, for you also benefit from the right answer and having learnt a proper method of correcting errors is also a pleasant thing. If you are determined to treat every example attentively, from the 1st to the 900th, then warmly congratulate you for:

1) You have a strong will. No difficulty whatever it is can beat a person of strong will. Even mountains bow to him and rivers make way for him. With greater willpower, you will be able to achieve greater success in many other aspects.

2) You have grasped the keys to some of the major issues of learning Chinese by a most simple and short way.

3) You have obtained the method of identifying and correcting erroneous sentences. To learn method is in a sense more important than to study knowledge.

How shall we not congratulate you when you have achieved such a great deal?

This book has been compiled on the initiative of Prof. Cheng

Meizhen who invited many other teachers, such as Li Zhu, to work in collaboration, with each individual devoted specially to one particular part of the book. Their joint work has not only made an important academic achievement, but also demonstrates the value of collective spirit.

Zhang Qingchang

11. 7, 1996

前　言

　　在长期的对外汉语教学实践中，我们积累了相当数量的病句。不同母语或媒介语的学生，在学习汉语的过程中，出现的错误既有相同之处，又有不同之点，为此，我们专为英语国家地区汉语学习者编写了《汉语病句辨析九百例》。

　　《汉语病句辨析九百例》是针对以英语为母语或媒介语的初学汉语的外国朋友在学习中普遍存在的典型病句进行分析或对比，以期使读者知道哪种说法是错误的，哪种说法是正确的。书后编有病句索引，目的在于说明不同的学习阶段产生的病句是不同的。全书采用汉英对照的形式。以上三点是本书区别于其他有关病句分析书籍的地方。此书供外国朋友自学或研究汉语使用，也可作为从事对外汉语教学的教师教学或编写课本的参考书。

　　书中九百例病句摘自 1964—1989 年的一年制基础汉语教学不同阶段的试卷、作业、课堂练习以及二年级的部分试卷，包括词法、句法及标点符号三个方面。此书在尊重原句意思的前提下，对每个病句不仅修改其谬误，而且指出错误的原因和纠正的方法。力求讲解简明扼要，语言通俗易懂，尽量少用语法术语。编排次序和内容选择都以切合英语国家地区朋友们学习汉语的需要为出发点。

　　全书共五个部分。"第一章总说"是编写此书遵循的几个原则；第二、三、四章是本书的正文，每个句子的排列方式是病句在上边，改正的句子在下边，误正对照，一目了然；第五部分是索引，提示每个病句出现的学习阶段、使用的课本、序号（与正文序号一致），以便使此书更具有实用价值。

本书能愿动词误用由韩玉芳执笔;副词"才"和"就"由朱庆明执笔;连词"和"误用由韩孝平执笔;助词"吗"误用由崔福英执笔;状语误用由胡志英执笔;动量补语误用由杜同蕙、彭志平、李秀清执笔;时量补语和"跟……一样"误用由李成才执笔;假设、条件、因果和转折关系复句的误用由董原执笔;反诘句误用由王秀云执笔;其余的部分由李珠、程美珍执笔。最后由程美珍统稿。

本书的英文翻译:贾钰。

参加资料整理工作的有(按姓氏笔划为序):王珏、刘美琴、刘青、韩焰、满汉英、穆恩龄。

本书在编写过程中得到了许多同志的帮助,不少同志提供了学生的病句,阎得早同志为本书作了大量的准备工作,常宝儒、陈亚川、鲁健骥、赵金铭同志对本书的编写提出了宝贵意见,石佩雯同志审阅了书稿,张清常先生在百忙之中为本书写了序言,在此一并表示衷心的感谢。

由于水平有限,不妥之处在所难免,恳请专家、同行和朋友们批评、指正。

编者　1996.6.10

PREFACE

We have gathered an enormous number of erroneous sentences through the years of teaching Chinese as a foreign language. It has been observed that students from different native or intermediary language backgrounds make the same mistakes in some cases and different in others. This book (which will simply be referred to as *Error Analysis 900*) is intended for English speakers.

In this book, we give contrastive analysis of typical errors frequently committed by Chinese beginners from English-speaking countries, in order to help the readers to distinguish between the correct and incorrect ways of expression. The book is in Chinese-English bilingual form, and with an index at the end showing that types of errors vary with stages of learning. Such characteristics mentioned above differentiate the present book from other books concerning error analysis. We expect it to benefit foreigners in self-study or research work in Chinese language and also serve as a reference book for teaching and textbook compiling.

The 900 illustrative examples of errors were selected from test papers, assignments, class drills of one year elementary Chinese course and some of the test papers for sophomores made between 1964 and 1989. These errors involve three aspects—morphology, syntax and punctuation. In the book, we not only offer the grammatical forms identical in meaning with the original ungrammatical ones, but also give the reason and ways to correction. The explanations were intended to be brief and to the point, through easy language and with grammatical terms reduced to a minimum. The contents were selected and ordered to meet the need of English speakers.

The book has five parts, among which (Ⅱ) (Ⅲ) (Ⅳ) constitute the main body and the first part serves as A General View that states what principles we followed in writing the book. In the main body, the right version is arranged below the wrong one for clear contrast. Ⅴ is the index which makes our book even more practical by suggesting at what stage each type of error tends to appear and the textbook concerned. Sentences are numbered in the index corresponding to the numbering in the main body.

This book is attributed to a group of writers: Errors in the use of Auxiliary Verbs by Han Yufang, Adverb "才" and "就" by Zhou Qingming, Conjunction "和" by Han Xiaoping, Particle "吗" by Cui Fuying, Adverbial Adjuncts by Hu Zhiying, Complements of Frequency by Du Tonghui, Peng Zhiping, Li Xiuqing, Complements of Duration and "跟…一样" by Li Chengcai, Complex Sentences of Suppositional, Conditional, Causative and Adversative Relation by Dong Yuan, Rhetorical Question by Wang Xiuyun, and the rest by Li Zhu, Cheng Meizhen. The work of integrating separate sections into a final whole was performed by Cheng Meizhen.

English translation by: Jia Yu

Those who joined the work of sorting out reference include (listed in stroke order of surname): Wang Jue, Liu Meiqin, Liu Qing, Han Yan, Man Hanying, Mu Enling.

In the course of compilation, we have benefited from the assistance of many comrades among whom some presented errors made by students. Comrade Yan Dezao did a great deal of preparatory work. Comrade Chang Baoru, Chen Yachuan, Lu Jianji and Zhao Jinming provided valuable comments on compiling the book. Comrade Shi Peiwen read through the manuscript. Finally, Mr. Zhang Qinchang tried and found time to write the preface. Here, we extend our hearty thanks to them all.

Due to our limited ability, defects are inevitable. We earnestly request comments and criticism from specialists, colleagues and friends.

Editor

6. 10,1996

目 录
CONTENT

第一章 总说 ·· 1

CHAPTER ONE　A GENERAL VIEW

一、什么叫病句 ·· 1

What Are Erroneous Sentences?

二、病句的范围 ·· 2

The Scope of Erroneous Sentences

三、产生病句的原因 ······································ 5

The Sources of Erroneous Sentences

四、怎样查找病句 ··· 7

Ways to Distinguish Erroneous Sentences

五、汉语的各级语法单位和句子成分 ············· 9

Grammatical Units of Various Levels and Sentence

Elements in Chinese

第二章 词法方面常见的错误 ····················· 13

CHAPTER TWO　COMMON ERRORS IN MORPHOLOGY

一、名词的误用 ··· 13

Errors in the Use of Nouns

1. 普通名词使用不当 ······························· 13

Improper use of common nouns

2. 方位词使用不当 ································· 15

Improper use of locality nouns

3. 时间词使用不当 ……………………………………… 16

Improper use of time nouns

4. 词尾"们"使用不当 ……………………………………… 21

Improper use of suffix "们"

二、代词的误用 …………………………………………… 23

Errors in the Use of Pronouns

1. 人称代词使用不当 ……………………………………… 23

Improper use of personal pronouns

2. 指示代词使用不当 ……………………………………… 25

Improper use of demonstrative pronouns

3. 疑问代词使用不当 ……………………………………… 28

Improper use of interrogative pronouns

三、动词的误用 …………………………………………… 34

Errors in the Use of Verbs

1. 不能带宾语的动词使用不当 …………………………… 34

Improper use of intransitive verbs

2. 带一个宾语的动词使用不当 …………………………… 36

Improper use of verbs taking one object

3. 带两个宾语的动词使用不当 …………………………… 40

Improper use of verbs taking two objects

4. 趋向动词"来""去"使用不当 ………………………… 44

Improper use of directional verbs "来" and "去"

5. 动宾式离合词使用不当 ………………………………… 45

Improper use of verbs in verb-object construction

6. 动词重叠使用不当 ……………………………………… 46

Improper use of reduplications of verbs

四、能愿动词的误用 ……………………………………… 47

Errors in the Use of Auxiliary Verbs

五、形容词的误用······························ 57

Errors in the Use of adjectives

1. 形容词使用不当 ······················· 57

Improper use of adjectives

2. 非谓形容词使用不当 ················· 58

Improper use of non-predicate adjectives

3. 形容词重叠使用不当 ················· 59

Improper use of reduplications of adjectives

六、数词的误用······························· 61

Errors in the Use of Numerals

1. 基数使用不当 ······················· 61

Improper use of cardinal numerals

（1）"二"和"两"······················· 61

"二" and "两"

（2）一百以上的称数法················· 62

Enumeration of numbers above one hundred

（3）俩······························· 63

two

2. 概数使用不当 ······················· 63

Improper use of approximate numbers

（1）相邻的两个数字连用··············· 63

Two adjacent digits used together

（2）"多"表示概数··················· 64

"多" expressing approximate numbers

（3）"几"表示概数··················· 66

"几" expressing approximate numbers

（4）"左右"表示概数················· 67

　　"左右" expressing approximate numbers

　　3. 序数使用不当 ················· 68
　　　　Improper use of ordinal numbers

　　4. 分数使用不当 ················· 69
　　　　Improper use of fractions

　　5. "半"使用不当 ················· 69
　　　　Improper use of "半"

　　6. 人民币的表示方法不当 ········· 70
　　　　Improper ways to read Renminbi

七、量词的误用 ······················· 72
　　Errors in the Use of Measure Words

　　1. 名量词使用不当 ··············· 72
　　　　Improper use of nominal measure words

　　2. 不定量词使用不当 ············· 74
　　　　Improper use of indefinite measure words

八、副词的误用 ······················· 78
　　Errors in the Use of Adverbs

九、介词的误用 ······················· 112
　　Errors in the Use of Prepositions

十、连词的误用 ······················· 129
　　Errors in the Use of Conjunctions

十一、助词的误用 ···················· 134
　　Errors in the Use of Particles

　　1. 动态助词使用不当 ············· 134
　　　　Improper use of aspect particles

　　2. 结构助词使用不当 ············· 142
　　　　Improper use of structural particles

　　3. 语气助词使用不当 ············· 147

Improper use of interjections

第三章　句法方面常见的错误 ·············· 157
CHAPTER THREE　COMMON ERRORS IN SYNTAX

一、词组的误用 ····································· 157
Errors in the Use of Phrases

1. 主谓词组使用不当 ························ 157
Improper use of subject-predicate phrases

2. 动宾词组使用不当 ························ 161
Improper use of verb-object phrases

3. "的"字词组使用不当 ···················· 163
Improper use of the 的-phrase

4. 介宾词组使用不当 ························ 165
Improper use of prepositional phrases

5. 同位词组使用不当 ························ 169
Improper use of appositive phrases

二、句子成分的误用 ······························ 170
Errors in the Use of Sentence Elements

1. 主语使用不当 ···························· 170
Improper use of subjects

2. 谓语使用不当 ···························· 172
Improper use of predicates

3. 宾语使用不当 ···························· 176
Improper use of objects

4. 定语使用不当 ···························· 179
Improper use of attributives

5. 状语使用不当 ···························· 183
Improper use of adverbial adjuncts

6. 补语使用不当 ···························· 189

Improper use of complements

(1) 结果补语 ·· 189
the complement of result

(2) 程度补语 ·· 194
the complement of degree

(3) 简单趋向补语 ·· 197
the simple complement of direction

(4) 复合趋向补语 ·· 200
the compound complement of direction

(5) 可能补语 ·· 205
the complement of potentiality

(6) 时量补语 ·· 208
the complement of duration

(7) 动量补语 ·· 210
the complement of frequency

三、单句的误用 ··· 212
Errors in the Use of Simple Sentences

1. 主谓句使用不当 ··· 212
Improper use of subject-predicate sentences

(1) 名词谓语句 ·· 212
sentences with a noun predicate

(2) 形容词谓语句 ··· 213
sentences with an adjectival predicate

(3) 主谓谓语句 ··· 215
sentences with a subject-predicate (S-P phrase)
predicate

2. 非主谓句使用不当 ·· 217
Improper use of the non-subject-predicate (non-S-P)

sentences

四、几种特殊动词谓语句的误用 ·················· 217

Errors in the Use of Several Special Types of Sentences
with a Verbal Predicate

1. "是"字句使用不当 ························· 218

Improper use of the 是-sentence

2. "有"字句使用不当 ························· 220

Improper use of the 有-sentence

3. 兼语句使用不当 ·························· 223

Improper use of the pivotal sentence

4. 连动句使用不当 ·························· 227

Improper use of sentences with verbal constructions
in series

5. "把"字句使用不当 ························· 230

Improper use of the 把-sentence

6. 意义被动句使用不当 ······················ 241

Improper use of notionally passive sentences

7. "被"字句使用不当 ························· 245

Improper use of the 被-sentence

8. 存在句使用不当 ·························· 250

Improper use of the existential sentences

五、几种比较句的误用 ························ 252

Errors in the Use of Several Types of Comparative
Sentences

1. 用"更"比较的句子使用不当 ················· 252

Improper use of sentences with "更" to express
comparison

2. 用"更加"比较的句子使用不当 ··············· 254

Improper use of sentences with ″更加″ to express
comparison

3. 用"最"比较的句子使用不当 ································· 255
Improper use of sentences with ″最″ to express
comparison

4. 用"比"比较的句子使用不当 ································· 256
Improper use of sentences with ″比″ to express
comparison

5. 用"没有"比较的句子使用不当 ························· 261
Improper use of sentences with ″没有″ to express
comparison

6. 用"不如"比较的句子使用不当 ························· 263
Improper use of sentences with ″不如″ to express
comparison

7. 用"跟……一样"比较的句子使用不当 ··················· 266
Improper use of sentences with ″跟…一样″ to express
comparison

8. 用"有"比较的句子使用不当 ························· 269
Improper use of sentences with ″有″ to express
comparison

9. 用"像"比较的句子使用不当 ························· 271
Improper use of sentences with ″像″ to express
comparison

10. 用"越来越"比较的句子使用不当 ··················· 273
Improper use of sentences with ″越来越″ to express
comparison

六、几种表示强调的句子的误用 ························· 275
Errors in the Use of Emphatic Sentences

1. 反诘句使用不当 ……………………………………… 275
   Improper use of rhetorical questions

2. "是……的"使用不当 ………………………………… 277
   Improper use of "是…的"

3. "连……也……"使用不当 …………………………… 279
   Improper use of "连…也…"

4. "一……也(不、没)……"使用不当 ……………… 281
   Improper use of "一…也(不、没)…"

5. 二次否定使用不当 ………………………………… 282
   Improper use of double-negation

6. 疑问代词活用的句子使用不当 …………………… 283
   Improper use of interrogative pronouns in extended
   meanings

七、复句的误用 ……………………………………………… 285
Errors in the Use of Complex Sentences

1. 并列关系复句使用不当 …………………………… 286
   Improper use of co-ordinate complex sentences

2. 承接关系复句使用不当 …………………………… 293
   Improper use of complex sentences of successive relation

3. 递进关系复句使用不当 …………………………… 296
   Improper use of complex sentences of progressive relation

4. 假设关系复句使用不当 …………………………… 301
   Improper use of complex sentences of suppositional relation

5. 条件关系复句使用不当 …………………………… 305
   Improper use of complex sentences of conditional relation

6. 选择关系复句使用不当 …………………………… 313
   Improper use of complex sentences of alternative relation

7. 因果关系复句使用不当 …………………………… 315

Improper use of complex sentences of causative relation

8. 转折关系复句使用不当 ································· 320
Improper use of complex sentences of adversative relation

第四章　标点符号方面常见的错误·················· 325
CHAPTER FOUR　COMMON ERRORS IN PUNCTUATION

一、点号的误用 ·· 325
Errors in the Use of Dots

1. 句号使用不当 ···································· 325
Improper use of the full stop

2. 问号使用不当 ···································· 327
Improper use of the question mark

3. 感叹号使用不当 ································· 329
Improper use of the exclamation mark

4. 顿号使用不当 ···································· 330
Improper use of the slight-pause mark

5. 逗号使用不当 ···································· 331
Improper use of the comma

6. 冒号使用不当 ···································· 332
Improper use of the colon

二、标号的误用 ·· 333
Errors in the Use of Markers

1. 书名号使用不当 ································· 333
Improper use of the title mark

2. 引号使用不当 ···································· 333
Improper use of the quotation mark

附　录　病句索引·································· 335
Appendices　SENTENCE INDEX

第一章 总 说
CHAPTER ONE   A GENERAL VIEW

在具体地分析修改每一个病句之前,我们先总的谈一下什么是病句、病句的范围以及针对病句产生的原因而采取的相应措施等问题,这些也是本书所遵循的几个基本原则。

Before analysing and revising each individual erroneous sentence, we shall first give a general view of what erroneous sentences are, their scope, source and appropriate ways to prevent them in accordance with the source. These are actually the basic principles followed in the present book.

一、什么叫病句
What Are Erroneous Sentences?

语言是人们交际的工具,任何一种语言都有自己的特点,英语国家地区的朋友们用汉语进行交谈、写文章的时候,应当遵照汉语的语法法则,合乎汉语的规范。那就是看一看每一类词用得是否符合各自的语法特点,词与词的搭配是否得当,词语的排列顺序是否合理,句子的结构和使用的场合是否受到英语的影响,句子内容有无逻辑错误等。如果说出来的话和写出来的句子违背汉语的组合规律或违背客观事物的事理,有碍交际,这样的句子就是病句。

Language is a tool for social communication and each language has its own features. People from English-speaking countries and regions should be guided by the grammatical rules of Chinese language to produce standard Chinese sentences in speaking and writing. That is to make sure that each part of speech is used properly in terms of their grammatical properties, that words are in good collocation and right order, that no interference of English results in wrong sentence structures and use of expressions ill-adapted to specific situation, and that sentences satisfy logical requirements. An utterance is an erroneous sentence if it blocks the way to communication for violating combination rules in the language or runs against the common sense of the objective world.

二、病句的范围
The Scope of Erroneous Sentences

这里所说的病句范围,是指从零起步直到掌握 4000 个常用词、150 个最基本的语法点、母语或媒介语为英语的学生在实践中出现的病句。完成以上所说的学习内容,一般需要 900 学时(每小时 50 分钟),为便于了解病句分布状况,将 900 学时粗略地划分成三个学习阶段:前两个阶段为一年级学习总时数,剩下的为此书选用的二年级病句出现的学习阶段所占用的时间,不同阶段的学习内容有不同的侧重方面。请参看下表:

The scope of erroneous sentences given in this book encircles all sorts of errors made by English speakers from the time they start to learn Chinese till they have gained a mastery of 4,000 daily used words and 1,500 basic grammatical points. To learn such a considerable number of words and grammatical points, it normally takes 900 class hours (one class hour = 50 minutes) which are approximately divided here into three periods of learning for a better understanding of the distribution of erroneous sentences. The first two of the three periods add up to the total class hours of the first school year, while the remaining part accounts for the time of second school year in which errors committed by sophomores as suggested in this book tend to appear. Different periods of learning emphasize different points. Refer to the following table.

学习阶段 学习时数	一 年 级		二 年 级
	第 一 阶 段	第 二 阶 段	第 三 阶 段
	350 学时	350 学时	200 学时
学 习 内 容	以最基本、最常用的实词和语法点为主,适当安排少量的虚词和复句。 此阶段词汇量约1200 个。	逐渐扩大近义词和虚词的数量,增加含有引申意义、比较复杂的语法点、复句和极少量固定词组。 此阶段词汇量约1800 个。	扩大虚词、近义词、多义词、固定词组和复句的数量。 此阶段词汇量约 1000 个。

period of learning class hours	The First Academic Year		The Second Academic Year
	Period I	Period II	Period III
	350	350	200
contents to be learned	The most basic daily used notional words and grammatical points Some function words and complex sentences A vocabulary of nearly 1,200 words	Gradual expansion of function words and synonyms Increase in complicated grammatical points with extended meaning Increase in complex sentences A few set phrases A vocabulary of 1,800 words	Increase in function words, synonyms, polysemants, set phrases and complex sentences A vocabulary of 1,000 words

本书的内容与各院校目前正在学习使用的课本紧密相关，主要是北京语言学院编写的如下各类教材：

The errors discussed in this book are closely related to the textbooks currently used. Here are some teaching materials compiled by Beijing Language Institute：

1. 汉语教科书　　　　（商务印书馆出版）

   Modern Chinese Readers

   Published by the Commercial Press

2. 汉语课本　　　　　（商务印书馆出版）

   Chinese Readers

   Published by the Commercial Press

3. 基础汉语课本　　　（华语教学出版社出版）

   Elementary Chinese Readers

   Published by Sinolingua

4. 普通汉语教程　　　（华语教学出版社出版）

   Introductory Chinese

   Published by Sinolingua

5. 科技汉语教程　　　（华语教学出版社出版）

   A Course in Scientific Chinese

   Published by Sinolingua

6. 初级汉语课本　　　（北京语言学院出版社

   　　　　　　　　　　华语教学出版社　　联合出版）

   Modern Chinese—Beginner's Course

   Co-published by Beijing Language Institute Press and Sinolingua

7. 现代汉语教程　　　（北京语言学院出版社出版）

   A Course in Contemporary Chinese

   Published by Beijing Language Institute Press

8. 现代汉语进修教程　（北京语言学院出版社出版）
   A "Brush Up" Course in Modern Chinese
   Published by Beijing Language Institute Press
9. 初级口语　　　　（北京语言学院出版社出版）
   Everyday Chinese for Beginners
   Published by Beijing Language Institute Press
10. 高级汉语　　　　（北京语言学院）
    Advanced Chinese
    Published by Beijing Language Institute Press
11. 医学汉语　　　　（北京语言学院）
    A Chinese Course for Traditional Chinese
    Published by Beijing Language Institute Press

三、产生病句的原因
The Sources of Erroneous Sentences

　　从大量病句的分析比较中,可以看到出现病句的原因主要有以下几种情况:

　　Analysis and comparison of a large quantity of data show that erroneous sentences mainly derive from the following sources:

　　1. 在语义上、结构特点上、使用场合方面没能很好地掌握汉语规律。尤其是汉语中特有的重叠形式、补语、主谓谓语句、"把"字句等语言现象,学习起来困难更多些,反映在口头表达和笔头作业中确实存在着许许多多这样或那样的问题。

　　Failure to master the semantic, structural and pragmatic features peculiar to the Chinese language. For foreign learners, a number of characteristic items of Chinese are particularly difficult to

5

handle, e. g. reduplicative formulas, complements, sentences with an S-P phrase predicate, 把-sentences. This is a plain fact that a lot of problems concerning such aspects do exist in the utterance and written work of our students.

2. 由于英语习惯的干扰。我们在教学实践中经常看到、听到"我是很忙"、"他复习功课每天"这样的句子,显然是 I am very busy. 和 He reviews lessons everyday. 的直译。前一个句子乍一看,没有什么毛病,但是对于刚刚接触汉语的学生来说,这是一个病句。因为在这个学习阶段,他们并不懂得这个"是"表示"确实""实在"的意思,而是把英语语法照搬到汉语上来。后一个句子的错误很明显,是按照英语词序,混淆了时间词("每天")在汉语与英语中特有的不同语法功能。类似这种英语式的汉语句子,俯拾皆是。

The interfering effects of the established English language habits. We often encounter such sentences as "我是很忙", "他复习功课每天" which are obviously literal interpretation of "I am busy" and "He reviews lessons every day". The first sentence is perfect at a glance, but it is actually a wrong sentence in the case of a Chinese learner who has just begun to get into contact with the language. This is because a beginner naturally does not know the intensifying function of "是" meaning "indeed" or "really", he may mechanically apply the grammatical form in English to Chinese. The second sentence is evidently mal-formed attributable to mis-ordering. The time noun 每天 in Chinese bears different grammatical functions from "every day" in English, but the speaker mixes them up. Such Chinese sentences in patterns of English are highly frequent.

3. 受修辞知识的限制,影响表达的效果。以"雪下得真大,房屋、树木都很白"为例,句中用"都"总括它前边的"房屋、树木",形容被雪覆盖的面积,用"很"表示雪"白"的程度,这种遣词造句的形式是很勉强的。应该将"都很"改成"一片",既写了雪景,又说明了面积范围较大。

Lack of rhetorical skill results in poor expressive effects. Take "雪下得真大,房屋,树木都很白" for example. Referring to both "房屋" and "树木", "都" shows the acreage covered with snow, "很" indicates the degree of white. The presence of these two words makes the sentence sound awkward to a Chinese ear. It would become perfect if we substitute "都很" with "一片" which both depicts a snow scene and demonstrates its width.

四、怎样查找病句
Ways to Distinguish Erroneous Sentences

1. 句子成分分析法
The method of identifying sentence elements

在句法中,汉语把句子成分划分为主要成分(主语、谓语、宾语)和附加成分(定语、状语、补语)。以"她父亲已经写完那篇论文"为例,"父亲"是主语,"写"是谓语,"论文"是宾语,"她"和"那篇"分别作主语和宾语的定语,"已经"是谓语("写")的状语,"完"是谓语("写")的补语。分析句子时,先查主要成分,然后查附加成分,最后检查主要成分同附加成分之间的关系。这样,可以看出来句子是不是有问题,也可以找出来有没有由于受英语影响而出现的错误。

In syntax, sentence elements are classified into central elements (subject, predicate, object) and adjunctive elements (attributive, adverbial adjunct, complement). For instance, in "她父亲已经写

完那篇论文"，"父亲" is the subject，"写" the predicate，"论文" the object，她 and 那篇 serve as the attributives of the subject and the object respectively，and 已经 acts as the adverbial adjunct of the predicate 写，完 is the complement of 写. To analyse a sentence, one should first look for the central elements, then look for the adjunctive elements, and lastly examine the relationship between the central and the adjunctive elements. In this manner, one may decide if a sentence is well-formed or mal-formed and distinguish the errors due to the interference of English language.

2. 语义搭配检验法

The method of checking semantic collocation

虽说构成句子的各种成分是完整无缺的,但是还要进一步检查成分之间在语义上是否配得拢。比如:动词谓语"唱"可以同宾语"歌"结合成动宾词组"唱歌",而同"舞"就配不拢,不能说唱舞。"好"能作"学"的补充成分,可以说"学得很好",而"忙"就不成,不能说"学得很忙"。哪个词可以跟哪个词搭配,哪个词不能跟哪个词搭配,很多情况没有规律可循,需要逐个地死记。即使下很大的工夫,词语搭配不当的现象仍是不可避免的。因此,这也是检查句子时不能忽略的方面。

Although a sentence is complete with every necessary element, it needs further examination guarantee that the elements match semantically. For example, verbal predicate 唱 may take the object 歌 to form a verb-object phrase 唱歌, but it does not go with 舞—we can not say 唱舞. 好 may function as the complement of 学, as in 学得很好, whereas 忙 can not—we can not say 学得很忙. There is no absolute rule as to which words match and which do not. So the learner has to memorize them one by one. Special attention should be paid to word incollocation which is almost inevitable despite of an extreme effort to avoid it.

3. 逻辑审察法

The logical criterion

一个句子如果在语法上找不出问题,那就看看在使用概念进行判断、推理时,是否讲得通。试看下边一个病句,"安娜买了苹果、梨、桔子和很多水果",显而易见,这是由于弄错了概念之间的关系造成的错误。"苹果、梨、桔子"是种概念,"水果"是属概念,误把属种关系的概念当作并列关系的概念。应改"水果"为表示种概念"葡萄""香蕉"一类的词。

In making judgment and inference with concepts, a grammatical sentence needs further inspection to ensure logic. See this sentence,安娜买了苹果,梨,桔子和很多水果. The error results from a misunderstanding of the relationship between concepts. Apple, pear and orange are subsets within the concept of fruit, but the speaker treats them as co-ordinate. "水果" should be replaced with words of concepts subordinate to it and co-ordinate with 苹果……, such as 葡萄 or 香蕉.

五、汉语的各级语法单位和句子成分
Grammatical Units of Various Levels and Sentence Elements in Chinese

为便于辨析,说明语句正误,有必要简要地重复一下汉语里的语法单位和句子成分。

For an efficient analysis and explanation, it is useful to review the grammatical units and sentence elements in Chinese.

1. 汉语的各级语法单位

Grammatical units at all levels in Chinese

（1）词

Word

词是组成句子的最基本的语言单位。现代汉语的词依照组合能力、句法功能和词的意义分成名词（"父亲"）、代词（"她"、"那"）、动词（"写"）、能愿动词（"能"）、形容词（"多"）、数词（"二"）、量词（"篇"）、副词（"已经"）、介词（"在"）、连词（"和"）、助词（"吗"）、叹词、象声词十三类。其中，前七类为实词，后六类为虚词。此外，还有两个附类：词头（"第"）、词尾（"们"）。

Words are the most basic units to make up a sentence. In modern Chinese they are grouped into thirteen classes in terms of combination potentiality, syntactical function and meaning, namely noun （父亲）, pronoun （她，那）, verb （写）, auxiliary verb （能）, adjective （多）, numeral （二）, measure word （篇）, adverb （已经）, preposition （在）, conjunction （和）, particle （吗）, interjection and onomatopoeia. The first seven classes belong to the notional word category, and the rest the function word category. Besides, there are two kinds of affixes, namely, prefix and suffix.

（2）词组

Phrases

词组是词和词按照一定的语法规则组合起来的一组词。按词组的结构划分成并列词组（"她和父亲"）、主谓词组（"父亲写"）、动宾词组（"写论文"）、动补词组（"写完"）、偏正词组（"她父亲"、"已经写"）、"的"字词组（"她的"）、介宾词组（"在北京"）、同位词组等。

A phrase is a combination of words arranged according to certain grammatical rules. Phrases are structurally classified into the following types: the co-ordinate phrase （她和父亲）, the subject-predicate (S-P) phrase （父亲写）, the verb-object (V-O) phrase

（写论文），the verb-complement（V-C）phrase（写完），the endo-centric phrase（她父亲，已经写），the 的-phrase（她的），the prepositional phrase（在北京），the appositive phrase，etc.

（3）句子

Sentences

句子是由词或词组直接组合而成的。汉语的句子可以分单句和复句两大类。单句又有主谓句（"我学习汉语"）和非主谓句（"下雪了"）之分。

Sentences are composed of words or phrases. In Chinese, sentences are divided into two kinds, the simple and the complex. With respect to the former one, a distinction is made between the subject-predicate sentence（我学习汉语）and the non-subject-predicate sentence（下雪了）.

2. 句子成分

Sentence elements

构成句子的词或词组在句中担任的语法职务和所起的作用叫句子成分。汉语的句子成分有六种，即主语、谓语、宾语、定语、状语和补语。句法中的句子成分和词法中的词类是密不可分的。必须掌握各个词的语法特点，尤其是虚词的语法特点，才能正确地组词造句。仍以四、1. 的句子为例：

Grammatical roles or functions performed by words or phrases in a sentence are called sentence elements. Chinese language has six sentence elements, namely, subject, predicate, object, attributive, adverbial adjunct and complement. Sentence elements in syntax are closely related to parts of speech in morphology. A mastery of the grammatical features of words especially those of function words is essential to word usage and sentence making. Let's return to the sentence in 4.1 for illustration：

11

她	父亲	已经	写	完	那篇		论文。
定语	主语	状语	谓语	补语	定语		宾语
代词	名词	副词	动词	动词	代词	量词	名词
她	父亲	已经	写	完	那篇		论文。
attributive	subject	adverbial adjunct	predicate	complement	attributive		object
pronoun	noun	adverb	verb	verb	pronoun（那）	measure word（篇）	noun

第二章 词法方面常见的错误
CHAPTER TWO COMMON ERRORS IN MORPHOLOGY

一、名词的误用
Errors in the Use of Nouns

1. 普通名词使用不当
Improper use of common nouns

例 001

误：他今年二十年，我二十一年。

正：他今年二十岁，我二十一岁。

英语 year 可以表示时间(in the year 1985)，也可以表示年龄 (He is twenty years old)。汉语的"年"则只表示时间。应将受英语影响的"年"改成汉语表示年龄的"岁"。

"Year" in English indicates time (in the year 1985) as well as age (He is twenty years old). But 年 in Chinese only refers to time. 年，the use of which here is the consequence of interference of English language，should be changed into 岁 meaning age.

例 002

误：一个男人和一个女人教我们汉语。

正：一个男老师和一个女老师教我们汉语。

"男人"、"女人"用在这里,与全句的感情色彩不协调,尤其"女人"有时带有嫌恶的意味。原句的"男人"、"女人"指的是老师,汉语的习惯表示法是在表示身份、职业的名词前边分别加上"男"、"女"(如:男学生、女学生、男大夫、女大夫等)。"男人"、"女人"应改成"男老师"、"女老师"。

The presence of 男人 and 女人 is out of tune with the emotional colouring of the sentence. The word 女人 sometimes even carries an overtone of disgust. 男人 and 女人 here refer to teachers. According to Chinese way of expression,男,女 are usually accompanied by nouns showing status or occupation as in 男学生,女学生,男大夫,女大夫. Here,男老师,女老师 should be used instead of 男人,女人.

例 003

误:作者想自己不够爱情自己的妻子。

正:作者想自己不够爱自己的妻子。

"爱情"和"爱"都可以译成 love,但是,在汉语里,"爱情"是名词;"爱"是动词。应改"爱情"为"爱",作谓语。

爱情 and 爱, both expressed by "love" in English, belong to different parts of speech. 爱情 is a noun and 爱 is a verb. Thus, we replace 爱情 with 爱 as the predicate.

例 004

误:结婚以后他们很恩情。

正:结婚以后他们很恩爱。

汉语里,"恩情"是名词。"恩爱"是形容词,指夫妻之间的感情。此句应把"恩情"改成"恩爱"。作谓语。

恩情 is a noun. 恩爱 is an adjective describing the affection between husband and wife. The right word to function as the predicate of the sentence should be 恩爱.

14

2.方位词使用不当

Improper use of locality nouns

例 005

误：现在我在北京里学习汉语。

正：现在我在北京学习汉语。

"北京"是地理名称。它的后边不能再用方位词"里"。

北京 is a proper name of place. It can not be followed by a noun of locality as ″里″ used here.

例 006

误：他把那张画儿挂在屋子的墙里了。

正：他把那张画儿挂在屋子的墙上了。

把画儿挂在墙里，不符合常理。实际上是把那张画儿挂在墙的表面。应改"里"为"上"。

It is against the common sense to ″hang the picture in the wall″. The actual case is ″hang the picture on the wall″. So ″里″ should be used instead of ″上″.

例 007

误：有一条蛇掉进缸。

正：有一条蛇掉进缸里。

"缸"是个表示实体的名词，不能单独用来作"掉进"的宾语。须在"缸"后加上方位词"里"，表示处所。

As a noun denoting entity, ″缸″ can not be the object of ″掉进″ just by itself, but ought to be followed by the noun of locality 里, to show location.

例 008

误：从前有一家里姓姜。

正：从前有一家姓姜。

"家里"表示范围。它和"姜"不是同一关系，不能搭配。可以改

15

"家里"为"家"。"家"是婚姻和血统关系为基础的社会单位。

家里 shows sphere and does not match with 姜. One should substitute 家里 with 家 which stands for the social unit based on marriage and blood relationship.

3. 时间词使用不当

Improper use of time nouns

年	月	日	点钟	小时
year	mouth	date	time of the clock	hour

例 009

误:我9月10日1986年开始学习汉语。

正:我1986年9月10日开始学习汉语。

September 10, 1986是英语日期的表示法,汉语则是由大概念到小概念。应改为1986年9月10日。

"September 10, 1986" is the English way of expressing date. In Chinese language, concepts are arranged in a descending order—from large ones down to smaller ones. Thus, it should be 1986年9月10日.

例 010

误:现在已经5分过12点了。

正:现在已经12点过5分了。

"5分过12点"是 five past twelve 的直译。应按照汉语时间的表示方法改成"12点过5分"。

"5分过12点" is the literal translation of "five past twelve". One should change it into "12点过5分" in line with the Chinese way of expressing time.

例 011

误:她每天学习四点(钟)。

正:她每天学习四个小时(或"四个钟头")。

16

原句是说"学习"占用的时间。应当改"点（钟）"为"小时"。口语里也说"钟头"。表示时段。

The sentence is intended to tell the duration of study. But the right word is "小时" rather than "点（钟）". Another word for time duration is 钟头 which usually occurs in spoken Chinese.

例 012

误：我们上午八小时上课。

正：我们上午八点上课。

原句意是要说明上午什么时间上课。应把"小时"改成"点"，表示时点。

What the sentence means to show is the time when classes begin. 小时 should be replaced with 点 which indicates a point in time.

例 013

误：我们只谈了一半小时。

正：我们只谈了半个小时。

"一半小时"是 a half hour 的直译。按照汉语的说法，应改为"半个小时"。

"一半小时" is the literal interpretation of "a half hour". In Chinese, the proper form is "半个小时".

刚才

just new, a moment ago

例 014

误：特别是刚才毕业的大学生，失业是个大问题。

正：特别是刚毕业的大学生，失业是个大问题。

名词"刚才"指刚过去不久的时间，这里是说"毕业"这种情况发生在不久以前，应改"刚才"为副词"刚"。

The time noun 刚才 refers to a time in the near past. Howev-

17

er, what the sentence implies is that the event of "毕业" took place not long ago. Thus, "刚才" should be replaced by "刚".

今年

this year

例 015

误:去年我是工人,这年我是老师了。

正:去年我是工人,今年我是老师了。

"这年"是 this year 的直译。汉语应当说"今年"。

"这年" is the word-to-word translation of "this year". In Chinese, we say 今年.

⋯⋯的时候

while

例 016

误:我们上课,他走进教室来了。

正:我们上课的时候,他走进教室来了。

句子的原意是,"他走进教室来"发生在"我们上课"这段时间里。在汉语里应把主谓词组"我们上课"用在"⋯⋯的时候"的前边,作时间状语。

The sentence means that "his coming into the classroom occurred during the time we were having class". To express such meaning in Chinese, a subject-predicate phrase such as 我们上课 should be used with "的时候" after it, together serving as the adverbial adjunct of time.

例 017

误:我们出去时候,外边下着雪呢。

正:我们出去的时候,外边下着雪呢。

主谓词组放在"⋯⋯的时候"的前面,作时间状语时,其中"的"字不能缺少,应当在"我们出去"的后面加上"的"。

18

When a subject-predicate phrase, together with 的时候 serves as an adverbial adjunct of time, 的 is an obligatory particle. So 的 must be added.

例 018

误：祥子小的时失去了父母。

正：祥子小（的）时候失去了父母。

由单音节形容词（如"小"）作谓语的主谓词组放在"……的时候"之前，可简说为"时候"，这里应去掉"的"，在"时"的后边加上"候"字。

的时候 may be shortened into 时候 if the predicate of the subject-predicate phrase before it is a monosyllabic adjective. The sentence can be corrected this way：add 候 to 时，and 的 may be omitted.

例 019

误：开始的时，林道静想自己的丈夫很不错。

正：开始（的）时（候），林道静想自己的丈夫很不错。

动词"开始"用在"……的时候"的前边，可简说成"……时"。此句或者在"的时"后边加"候"，或者去掉"的"。

When preceded by the verb 开始，的时候 can be simplified as 时. To revise the sentence，we may either add 候 to 的时 or delete 的.

例 020

误：从上大学的时候以来，他一天假也没有请过。

正：从上大学以来，他一天假也没有请过。

正：上大学的时候，他一天假也没有请过。

两种表示时间的格式"……的时候"和"……以来"相互杂糅，只能取其中的一种说法。

"…的时候" and "…以来" can not occur simultaneously. A

19

choice has to be made between the two patterns.

天

day

例 021

误:今天是10月25天。

正:今天是10月25号(日)。

"天"与"号"混淆,应改成"10月25号",口语里常用。书面语里
还可以用"日"。

The speaker has confused the word "天" with "号" which is
the proper word to be used here. An alternative to 号 is 日. But 号
is frequent in spoken Chinese whereas 日 is often seen in written
Chinese.

以后

after, afterwards, later

例 022

误:没关系,你的病一会儿以后会治好的。

正:没关系,你的病以后会治好的。

"一会儿"和"以后"(指所说某时之后的时间)是两个时间概念
不同的名词,不能混在一起用。根据原意,治病需要时间,应当删去
"一会儿"。

"一会儿" and "以后" signify two distinct time concepts and
must not be mixed up. "以后" refers to the time after a particular
moment. According to what the sentence means, the curing of the
disease takes time. Therefore, "一会儿" should be deleted.

例 023

误:刚结婚以后,他们很幸福。

正:结婚以后,他们很幸福。

副词"刚"与时间名词"以后"就所指的时间来说是不同的,两

个词连用,相互矛盾,可以删去"刚"。

Adverb 刚 and time noun 以后 represent different time concepts. The coexistence of these two words makes the sentence self-contradictory. Thus we delete "刚".

从前

before

例 024

误:我没有来过这儿以前。

正:我以前没有来过这儿。

正:以前,我没有来过这儿。

这句是 I haven't been here before. 的直译,在汉语里,时间名词"从前"应放在主语("我")后边,或放在句首。

This is a literal interpretation of "I haven't been here before." In Chinese, "以前" (a time noun) either follows the subject (我) or occupies the initial position of a sentence.

4. **词尾"们"使用不当**

Improper use of the suffix 们

例 025

误:三个女孩子们把鲜花送给代表了。

正:三个女孩子把鲜花送给代表了。

正:女孩子们把鲜花送给代表了。

英语名词加上-s 表示复数后,名词前边还可以加数词,如 three daughters。在汉语里,指人的名词加表示复数的词尾"们"后,名词前边不能再加确指的数量词,这个句子要么去掉"们",要么删去"三个"。

In English, a noun pluralazed by the suffixes may also be qualified by a numeral, e. g. three daughters. However, in Chinese, a personal noun with a plural suffix 们 can not be modified by a defi-

21

nite numeral-measure word. Thus the above sentence must drop either ″们″ or ″三个″.

例 026

误：我还有几个朋友们要来这儿学习。

正：我还有几个朋友要来这儿学习。

用作概数的"几"充当修饰成分，被修饰的成分后不能再用"们"。应改"朋友们"为"朋友"。

When the approximate numeral ″几″ serves as a modifier, the modified element can not carry ″们″. 们 is redundant here.

例 027

误：我们的老师们是中国人。

正：我们的老师是中国人。

"我们"表示复数，作修饰成分时，被修饰成分不能用复数形式。应删去"老师"后边的"们"。

A head word can not appear in plural form if it is modified by a plural pronoun such as 我们. ″们″ should be deleted.

例 028

误：我们学校的外国留学生们很多。

正：我们学校的外国留学生很多。

汉语中，表示数量多的词语（如"很多"）作谓语，充当句子主语的名词后边不能再加词尾"们"，应把"留学生们"改成"留学生"。

In Chinese, if the predicate of a sentence is a word meaning many or a great deal, the subjective noun can not be suffixed with ″们″. ″们″ must be deleted.

例 029

误：除了阿里以外，别的同学们去旅行了。

正：除了阿里以外，同学们去旅行了。

在已经加"们"的名词前边，不能再用表示个别性的词"别的"。

22

"别的" can not be used in front of a noun with suffix 们.

例 **030**

误:今天的节目演得真好,观众们都热烈地鼓掌。

正:今天的节目演得真好,观众都热烈地鼓掌。

"观众"本身表示复数,不能再加"们"。

"观众" alone implies plural. "们" is unnecessary.

例 **031**

误:人民们对这新生事物表现了极大的兴趣和热情。

正:人们对这新生事物表现了极大的兴趣和热情。

"人民"是泛指性的名词,它不能受数量词或本身含有复数的词语修饰,也不能加"们"。应改"人民们"为"人们"。"人们"是"许多人"的意思。

As a noun of generic reference,"人民" allows no modification of a numeral-measure word or words indicating plural, neither does it allow the addition of "们". The sentence will be correct if 人民 is replaced with "人们" meaning many people.

二、代词的误用
Errors in the Use of Pronouns

1. 人称代词使用不当
Improper use of personal pronouns

例 **032**

误:阿里你别着急,咱们等你。

正:阿里你别着急,我们等你。

"咱们"包括谈话的对方即阿里,而此句不包括谈话的对方。应改"咱们"为"我们"。

"咱们" includes the hearer. But in present sentence, the group of people waiting for 阿里—the hearer certainly does not include him. Thus 我们 rather than 咱们 should be used.

例 033

误:要是我没有汽车,我给你我的。

正:要是你没有汽车,我给你我的。

称代不相符合。前个分句说"我没有汽车",后个分句又说"我给你",前后不一致,应将前个分句"我"改为"你"。

The sentence lacks correspond. The first clause "我没有汽车" does not coherence with the second clause 我给你. "我" in the first clause should be replaced with "你".

例 034

误:我很喜欢我妹妹的两个儿子,我常和他一起玩儿。

正:我很喜欢我妹妹的两个儿子,我常和他们一起玩儿。

"他"指妹妹的两个儿子。"两个儿子"是复数,"他"是单数,前后矛盾。应改"他"为"他们"。

"他" refers to the two sons. "两个儿子" is plural while "他" is singular. To remove the contradiction, we change "他" into "他们".

例 035

误:玛丽和安娜来了,你问问她。

正:玛丽和安娜来了,你问问她们。

"她"指代不清,是问"玛丽"还是问"安娜",看不出来。应改"她"为"她们"。

"她" is ambiguous since it directs at "玛丽" or "安娜" with equal possibility. 她们 should be used.

例 036

误:那个领导不怕我们给自己提意见。

正：那个领导不怕我们给他提意见。

"自己"是指"那个领导"，还是指"我们"，意思不清楚。应将"自己"改成指代"那个领导"的"他"。

It is unclear whether "自己" refers to "那个领导" or "我们". The sentence will be coherent if we use "他" to indicate "那个领导".

例 037

误：我一听，我就明白了。

正：我一听，就明白了。

英语可以说 I got the idea as soon as I heard it。在汉语里，因"一……就……"连接两个紧接着发生的动作，前后两个分句的主语用词重复，应该删去第二个"我"。

In English, it is perfect to say "I got the idea as soon as I heard it". However in the Chinese fixed pattern "一…就…" which joins two events in quick succession, only one among the two clauses requires a subject. "我" in the second clause should be erased.

例 038

误：祥子没有办法，他只好卖他自己的力气了。

正：祥子没有办法，(他)只好卖力气了。

"没有办法"和"卖力气"同属于一个主语（"祥子"），后个分句却又用"他"和"他自己"指代前个分句的主语，全句"他"字太多，显得太不简洁，应当删去多余的定语"他自己"和主语"他"。

The sentence sounds wordy with two "他". "他" and "他自己" in the second clause need not be present since they refer to the same person as the subject of the first clause (祥子).

2. 指示代词使用不当

Improper use of demonstrative pronouns

这　这儿(这里)

this here

例 039

误:丁力让我在这等他。

正:丁力让我在这儿(这里)等他。

"在"的宾语应当是表示处所的词语。"这"是用来指代事物的,不能指代处所。应在"这"后加"儿",或者加"里"。

〃在〃 requires a place object. 〃这〃 refers to thing rather than location. Hence it may not serve as the object of 〃在〃, and must carry 〃儿〃 or 〃里〃 to make a phrase of locality.

例 040

误:他在这儿里的生活非常愉快。

正:他在这儿(这里)的生活非常愉快。

"这儿里"是"这儿"和"这里"的杂糅,或者用"这儿",或者用"这里"。

〃这儿里〃 is a mixture of 〃这儿〃 and 〃这里〃. Use either 〃这儿〃 or 〃这里〃.

那儿

there

例 041

误:请你告诉巴里亚来我那儿。

正:请你告诉巴里亚来我这儿。

远指与近指的混淆。"巴里亚"的行为动作"来"是朝着说话人("我")进行的,距离说话人很近。应当用"这儿"。

The error lies in the confusion of two words of close and distant reference respectively. 那儿 refers to a location further away from the speaker while 这儿 refers to somewhere around the speaker. The action 〃来〃 which is towards the speaker (〃我〃) brings 〃巴里亚〃 close to 〃我〃. Thus 这儿 is the right word.

例 042

误：你去那儿？

正：你去哪儿？

"那儿"读nàr，是指示代词，指"那个地方"。"哪儿"读nǎr，是疑问代词，指"哪个地方"。可以改"那儿"为"哪儿"。

"那儿" pronounced nàr is a demonstrative pronoun denoting "that place"; "哪儿" pronounced nǎr is an interrogative pronoun denoting "which place". Thus "哪儿" should be used instead of "那儿".

例 043

误：明天早上你去朋友吗？

正：明天早上你去朋友那儿吗？

动词"去"的宾语应是表示处所的词语，"朋友"是指人的名词。要在"朋友"后加上"这儿"或"那儿"变为处所词语。由于动作"去"是从所在的地方往远处走，只能用"那儿"。

The object of the verb "去" ought to be a word of locality. "朋友" is a personal noun, but it becomes a phrase of locality with "这儿" or "那儿" added to it. Since "去" represents an action in direction of somewhere further away from the speaker, it requires "那儿" as the head word of its object.

这么　那么

this　that

(so)

例 044

误：这个商店没有那个商店这么大。

正：这个商店没有那个商店那么大。

"那（个商店）"是远指，应该用与"那（个）"顺意的表示程度的"那么"，不能用表近指的"这么"。

"那个商店" is a distant reference. It does not correspond with "这么" which is related to something nearby, but corresponds with "那儿" that relates to something further away.

例 **045**

误:去年的水果产量没有今年的水果产量那么多。

正:去年的水果产量没有今年的水果产量这么多。

这句话是重在说明今年的情况,距离谈话的时间比较近。应改用"这么"。

The sentence is focused on the situation of this year which encloses the moment of utterance. One should use "这么".

例 **046**

误:那么钱一个钟头数得完数不完?

正:那么多钱一个钟头数得完数不完?

"那么"主要用在形容词、动词之前,作状语,不能直接修饰名词("钱")。从原句的意思看,应当在"那么"后加中心语"多"。

"那么" is mainly used before adjectives or verbs, serving as an adverbial adjunct. It can not be an immediate modifier of a noun (like "钱"). In light of what the sentence means, we add the head word "多" to "那么".

3. **疑问代词使用不当**

Improper use of interrogative pronouns

谁

who

例 **047**

误:你等谁人?

正:你等谁?

"谁"是用来询问人的,可以单独作宾语。"人"多余。

"谁" is an interrogative pronoun referring to a person. It can act as an object independently, so "人" is redundant.

例 **048**

误：谁马老师问题？

正：马老师问谁问题？

这是 Whom did teacher Ma. ask the question? 的直译。在汉语里，动词"问"在后面可以带两个宾语，一个指人（"谁"），一个指事物（"问题"）。指人的宾语在前，指事物的宾语在后。

This is the literal translation of "Whom did teacher Ma ask the question?" In Chinese, the verb "问" can take two objects, one denoting person ("谁"), the other denoting object ("问题"), and the former one always goes before the latter.

例 **049**

误：谁是哪国人？

正：他是哪国人？

正：谁是美国人？

在用疑问代词构成的特指问中，通常只有一个疑点。在这个仅有五个字的短句里却有两个疑点（"谁"和"哪"），令人摸不到头脑。或者去掉"谁"，或者去掉"哪"。不论采用哪种改法，原句结构都要稍有变动。

A special question using the interrogative pronoun normally has only one point to be asked. Thus it is senseless for the above sentence of merely five characters to bear two interrogative points. Either "谁" or "哪" is to be deleted. Both two ways require a slight change in the original structure.

什么

what

例 **050**

误：什么你教？

正：你教什么？

这句是 What do you teach?的直译。在汉语里，用"什么"作宾语的疑问句中，"什么"只能放在动词谓语（"教"）的后边。

This is the literal interpretation of "What do you teach?". In Chinese, if "什么" is the object of an interrogative sentence, it must follow the verbal predicate ("教").

例 051

误：星期天很多人去什么玩儿？

正：星期天很多人去什么地方（哪儿）玩儿？

"什么"单用时，用来询问事物。跟在动词"去"后面的，应是表示处所的词语。这个句子有两种改法：或者在"什么"后加上"地方"一类的词；或者删去"什么"，改用"哪儿"。

"什么" alone is used to inquire things. The verb "去" can only take objects of locality. There are two possible ways of correction: put "地方" after "什么", or use "哪儿" instead of "什么".

例 052

误：你家有什么口人？

正：你家有什么人？

"什么"作修饰成分时，与中心语（"人"）之间不能用量词。删去"口"。

No measure word is allowed between "什么" as modifier and its head word ("人"). Delete "口".

例 053

误：对老年妇女什么称呼？

正：对老年妇女怎么称呼？

"什么"是指代人或事物的，不能放在动词（"称呼"）之前作状语。这里是询问称呼方式，应当改用"怎么"。

"什么" refers to persons or things. It can not premodify verbs (such as ″称呼″) as an adverbial adjunct. Here is a question of how to address people. Thus the proper word is ″怎么″.

例 054

　　A：昨天你做什么了？

误：B：昨天我做写信、洗衣服、看朋友了。

正：B：昨天我写信、洗衣服、看朋友了。

　　"做什么"是动宾词组，用来询问进行的活动。在含有"做什么"的疑问句里，疑点应当是"做什么"，答案"写信、洗衣服、看朋友"便是疑问所在。如果疑点仅仅是"什么"，答案自然成了"做写信"，这是错误的。

　　″做什么″ is a verb-object phrase which inquires about an activity. In an interrogative sentence containing ″做什么″, the question lies in ″做什么″ as a whole, to which the answer is ″写信，洗衣服，看朋友″. If the question is considered to lie in ″什么″ alone, the answer naturally turns to be ″做写信″, which is definitely ungrammatical.

几

a few, several

例 055

误：北京语言学院有几个外国留学生？

正：北京语言学院有多少个外国留学生？

　　汉语里，"几"表示大于一而小于十的不定数目。病句用"几"来询问主要承担对外汉语教学任务的北京语言学院的外国留学生的人数，与客观实际情况不符。应改"几"为"多少"。不管问话人本身是否了解北京语言学院的留学生的人数，用"多少"询问，要主动、灵活得多。因为"多少"代表的数目范围很广，可大可小。

　　In Chinese, ″几″ represents a proximate number larger than one and smaller than ten. It is unreasonable to use ″几″ to inquire the number of students in such an institute as Beijing Language Institute. Covering a much wider range of numbers, "多少" proves to be a more efficient, flexible way of asking about number. Thus, we use "多少" instead of "几个".

例 056

误：您要几苹果？

正：您要几个（公斤）苹果？

用"几"询句数量时，"几"与中心语之间一定要用量词。"苹果"的计量单位可以用"个"，也可以用"公斤"。

There must be a measure word between "几" and its head word in a sentence using "几" to inquire number. Apples are usually calculated in units of "个" or "公斤", so either "个" or "公斤" should be added before "苹果".

例 057

误：老大爷，您今年几岁了？

正：老大爷，您今年多大岁数（年纪）了？

"几岁"使用场合不当，在汉语里，询问老人年龄时，要用"多大岁数"或"多大年纪"。问小孩的年龄时才用"几岁"。

The use of "几岁" doesn't fit the context here. In Chinese, to inquire the age of old people, "多大岁数" or "多大年纪" is used. In the case of small children, one should say "几岁".

多少

how many, how much

例 058

误：请问，这种毛衣多少？

正：请问，这种毛衣多少钱？

"多少"用来询问数量。这个句子是问毛衣的件数，还是问毛衣的价钱？要是买毛衣问价格，在"多少"的后边要加上中心语"钱"。

"多少" is for asking about quantity. But it is unclear here whether the sentence is a question about the number or a question about the cost of the sweaters. Such a problem can be solved by putting the head word "钱" after "多少".

例 059

误:长江比黄河多少长公里?

正:长江比黄河长多少公里?

"多少"不能放在谓语之前作状语。通常跟在名词或名词和量词前,作定语。"多少"应移到"公里"的前边。

"多少" normally premodifies a noun or a combination of a noun and a measure word. It can not stay in front of the predicate to serve as an adverbial adjunct. We shift it to the position before "公里".

哪

which

例 060

误:你是从哪地方来的?

正:你是从哪个地方来的?

疑问代词"哪"主要用作定语。"哪"与中心语("地方")之间要用量词。"地方"的计量单位是"个"。改"哪地方"为"哪个地方"。

The interrogative pronoun "哪" mainly serves as an attributive. A measure word is needed between it and its head word ("地方"). The counting unit of "地方" is "个". Thus we insert "个" between "哪" and "地方".

怎么

how

例 061

误:去动物园在怎么地方换332路公共汽车?

正：去动物园在什么地方换332路公共汽车？

"怎么"用来询问方式、状况、原因等。原句是问换车的地方，应当删去"怎么"，改用"什么"。

"怎么" is a word for asking manner, state, reason, etc. The sentence is a question of where to change a bus. Erase "怎么" and use "什么".

例 062

误：这个图书馆怎么书都有。

正：这个图书馆什么书都有。

因为要说明这个图书馆有各种各样的书，应该用表示泛指的疑问代词"什么"代替"怎么"。

In order to express that the library has a variety of books, one should choose "什么"（an interrogative pronoun of generic reference）rather than "怎么".

三、动词的误用
Errors in the Use of Verbs

1. 不带宾语的动词使用不当
Improper use of intransitive verbs

出发

start out

例 063

误：明天早上八点我们出发学校。

正：明天早上八点我们从学校出发。

"出发"是不能带宾语的动词，如果要指明"出发"的地点，应当用表示时空关系的介词"从"，组成介宾词组"从学校"，放在"出发"

的前边，作状语。

"出发" is a verb which does not take the object. To demonstrate the place of departure, one ought to use "从"——a preposition showing a space-time relationship. "从" plus its object "学校" forms a prepositional phrase, preceding "出发" as an adverbial adjunct.

旅行

travel

例 064

误：我想明年再旅行中国。

正：我想明年再来中国旅行。

汉语的"旅行"是到较远的地方去观看名胜、风景，它的后边不能带宾语。应把"旅行中国"改成连动形式"来中国旅行"或"到中国来旅行"。

"旅行", meaning to go to a distant place for sight-seeing, is incapable of taking objects. Two proper substitutes for "旅行中国" are "来中国旅行" and "到中国旅行" which are both verbal constructions in series.

旅游

travel

例 065

误：去年暑假我们旅游了西藏。

正：去年暑假我们到西藏去旅游了。

"旅游"既有旅行又有游览的意思。在用法上与"旅行"相同，它的后边也不能带宾语。"旅游"可以和一些名词组成固定词组，如旅游商品、旅游车、旅游鞋、旅游点等。

"旅游" means to travel and tour. Similar to "旅行" in usage, it does not take objects either. "旅游" can form set phrases with some nouns, e. g. 旅游商品,旅游车,旅游鞋,旅游点.

2. 带一个宾语的动词使用不当

Improper use of verbs taking one object

应用

apply

例 066

误:溶液在工业、农业、医学上有什么重要的应用?

正:溶液在工业、农业、医学上有什么重要的作用?

误用动词为名词,应该把"应用"改为"作用"。

The verb "应用" is misused as a noun. It should be replaced by "作用".

访问

visit

例 067

误:昨天我们访问了一个工厂。

正:昨天我们参观了一个工厂。

在汉语里,"访问"指有目的看望某人并谈话,它的宾语大多是人。有时说"访问中国",意思是不只游览,还要和中国有关人士会谈。句中宾语是"工厂",主要是看工厂的情况,应改"访问"为"参观"。

In Chinese, "访问" means to visit and talk with someone for a purpose. It usually requires a personal noun as its object. To say "visit China" implies not only a tour but also talks or discussions with people concerned. The object of the sentence is "工厂" which in fact indicates the state of the factory. "参观" is the matching word for "工厂".

参观

visit

36

例 068

误：我想参观一个中国工人的家庭。

正：我想访问一个中国工人的家庭。

"参观"是实地观察，它的宾语多是处所词。句中的宾语是"家庭"，一般不会只是去看工人家庭里的东西，主要还是与工人家庭成员交谈，了解情况。应改"参观"为"访问"。

Meaning to watch on the spot，"参观" usually takes a word of locality as its object. To visit a family is not just to look around the house but mainly involves talking with the family members. One should use "访问" in place of "参观".

说定

decide

例 069

误：他决定了参加足球比赛。

正：他决定参加足球比赛。

"决定"的意思是对如何行动作出主张。它可以单独作谓语（如："这件事就这么决定了""考试日期已经决定了"），也可以带宾语，这个句子的宾语是动宾词组"参加足球比赛"。在这种情况下，"决定"的后边不能用动态助词"了"。

"决定" means to decide on an action. It may form a predicate by itself (e. g. 这件事就这么决定了，考试日期已经决定了). It may also take an object as in the present sentence，参加足球比赛 (which is a verb-object phrase). In such case，"决定" can not have aspect particle "了" attached to it.

说

speak

例 070

误：老师常常说我们："你们学习努力，进步很快"。

正:老师常常对我们说:"你们学习努力,进步很快"。

英语可以说 say to us,直译成汉语为"说我们"。汉语中"说我们"有责备、批评的意思,这与后续句"你们学习努力,进步很快"的语义相悖。应改用"对……说"这种格式。

"说我们" is the word-to-word interpretation for "say to us" in English. In Chinese, "说某人" carries the implication of blame and criticism. Thus "说我们" contradicts the meaning of the following clause "你们学习努力,进步很快". The right pattern should be "对…说".

例 071

误:我说他了,下星期学习第三本书。

正:我告诉他了,下星期学习第三本书。

可以理解为谓语动词后边有两个宾语,一个指人("他"),一个是一件事("下星期学习第三本书")。应该把"说"改为"告诉"。

The predicate verb here may be considered to have two objects, with one referring to the person ("他"); the other referring to the event ("下星期学习第三本书"). We replace "说" by "告诉".

例 072

误:昨天我们见过面,我知道他。

正:昨天我们见过面,我认识他。

在汉语中"知道"可以表示头脑中对事实、情况已经认识它的存在;"认识"指跟人相识并来往。既然"昨天我们见过面",应删去"知道",改用"认识"。

"知道" means to be conscious of a fact. "认识" means to be acquainted with somebody. "认识" should be used instead of "知道".

例 073

误:我不太知道中国,我想去看看。

正:我不太了解中国,我想去看看。

是说对中国各方面的情况知道的不多,因此,想通过一定的手段,调查研究。宜用"了解",不能用"知道"。

The speaker means that he does not know much about China and wants to have a look with his own eyes. He ought to use "了解" rather than "知道".

认识

know

例 074

误:我认识这件事的经过。

正:我知道这件事的经过。

正:我了解这件事的经过。

若原句说的是对这件事的经过有所耳闻,则应该用"知道";若强调对这件事的经过知道得很清楚,可改用"了解"。

If the speaker means that he has a general idea of the happening, he ought to use "知道". If he stresses that he knows the whole course of the incident, he ought to use "了解".

要求

require, demand

例 075

误:她被要求去参观了一个工厂。

正:她被邀请去参观了一个工厂。

"要求"有提出具体愿望或条件,希望得到满足或实现的意思,可以说"要求应参观一个工厂"。句中用介词"被",是被人请到工厂去参观,应改成"邀请"。

"要求" is to put forward a proposal or condition in the hope of having it carried out and fulfilled. One can say 要求去参观一个工

厂. With a preposition "被", the meaning of the sentence is that she has been invited to a factory for a visit. The proper word is "邀请".

3. 带两个宾语的动词使用不当

Improper use of verbs taking two objects

告诉

tell

例 076

误：每次去朋友家，他总是告诉一两件有意思的事情。

正：每次去朋友家，他总是告诉我一两件有意思的事情。

"告诉"的使用句型是"告诉某人某件事"。原句"告诉"后缺少告诉的对象（指人的宾语），可在"告诉"的后边补上"我"。

"告诉" is used in the pattern "告诉某人某件事". The error lies in the omission of the receiver of the action "告诉" (the object referring to person). We may use "我" after "告诉" to fill the position of "某人".

例 077

误：他对杏仙告诉，他要走了。

正：他告诉杏仙，他要走了。

正：他对杏仙说，他要走了。

这个句子有两种改法，或者根据"告诉"的表达特点，改成双宾语的句子，或者改成"对……说"格式。

The sentence can be corrected in two ways 1) in accordance with the grammatical characteristic of "告诉", change the sentence into the pattern with double objects—告诉某人某件事；2) use the pattern "对…说" instead.

给

give

例 078

误:他给我很多都助我。

正:他给我很多帮助。

应当把易位的双宾语改为指人的宾语"我"紧靠着动词,指事物的宾语在句末。

The double objects wrongly placed should be rearranged in this order: the object referring to person "我" immediately follows the verb and the object of non-personal reference stays at the end of the sentence.

例 079

误:他常常帮助我,我要给他一个感谢。

正:他常常帮助我,我要感谢他。

在语义上,谓语动词"给"与宾语"感谢"不搭配,数量词"一个"也不能做"感谢"的修饰成分,应该把双宾语的原句改成"感谢他"。

Semantically, the predicate verb "给" does not go with the object "感谢", neither does "一个" (a numeral-measure word phrase) match "感谢" as a modifier. The original sentence with double objects should be replaced by "感谢他".

例 080

误:到北京以后没有立刻给你一封信,请原谅。

正:到北京以后没有立刻给你写信,请原谅。

原意是没有及时把到某地的情况用书信的方式告诉对方。它的正确表达方式应将带双宾语的动词"给"改成介词"给",以引出动作的对象,构成介宾词组"给你"作谓语动词"写"的状语。因为否定了这件事,数词"一"须删去,量词"封"也可不用。

The thought of the sentence is that the speaker did not follow the traditional custom to write the other party a letter. The proper form of expressing such meaning requires a preposition "给" to introduce the receiver of the action, rather than a verb, "给" taking double objects. The prepositional phrase "给你" serves as the adverbial adjunct of the predicate verb. Since the action of writing letter is fully negated, the numeral word "一" and the measure word "封" are not needed.

例 081

误：他一本外文书还图书馆。

正：他还图书馆一本外文书。

指物的宾语位置不当。应将"一本外文书"放到另一个宾语"图书馆"的后边。

The object referring to thing（一本外文书）is in a wrong position. It should be placed after the other object "图书馆".

例 082

误：他要还两本杂志给阅览室。

正：他要还给阅览室两本杂志。

"给"用在由动词"还"组成的带双宾语的句子里，起加强给予语气的作用。应当把"给"移到动词"还"的后边，然后再把"还给"后边的两个错位的宾语调换过来。

In a double-object sentence with verb "还", "给" emphasizes the tone of giving. To produce a grammatical sentence first move "给" to the right of verb "还", then reverse the order of the two wrongly positioned objects following "还给".

例 083

误：阿里借我一本词典。

正：阿里向我借一本词典。

正：阿里借给我一本词典。

"借"的英语翻译有两个词：借进用 borrow，借出用 lend。在汉语里，"借"有借进、借出两种含义。为避免产生歧义，或者在原句里加介词"向",组成介宾词组"向我",作"借"的状语。或者在动词后边加"给"。"向我借"只能理解为借进,"借给我"表示借出。

"借" in Chinese has two implications which are expressed in English by "borrow" and "lend" respectively. To avoid ambiguity, we either use preposition "向" to form the prepositional phrase "向我" as the adverbial adjunct of "借", or add "给" after the verb. The only possible explanation for "向我借" is to borrow, and "借给我" only means to lend.

问

ask

例 084

误:我问他去看电影,他立刻答应了。

正:我请他去看电影,他立刻答应了。

汉语"问"一般译作 ask,而 ask 在英语中既可表示询问(如,ask a question),也可以表示请求(如 May I ask a favour of you?)。在汉语里,"问"没有请求的意思,句中"问",也不是请人解答问题,而是邀请,可以改"问"为"请"。

The English equivalent for "问" in Chinese is "ask", which expresses an inquiry (as in "ask a question") as well as request (as in "May I ask a favour of you?"). However "问" in Chinese never means request. The above sentence is not a request or an answer; it is an invitation. Thus "问" ought to be replaced by "请".

例 085

误:他们经常没有钱,但是不轻易问朋友帮助。

正:他们经常没有钱,但是不轻易问朋友借钱。

正:他们经常没有钱,但是不轻易请(求)朋友帮助。

动词"问"如果表示向某人要东西,可以改"帮助"为"借钱";如果表示说明要求,希望得到满足,应改"问"为"求"或"请求"。

If the verb "问" is used for asking someone for something, one may choose "借钱" to replace "帮助". If the speaker wants to express the meaning of making a request, he ought to use "求" or "请求" in place of "问".

找

give change

例 086

误：同志，给您找五块钱。

正：同志，找（给）您五块钱。

要么参照（81）的改法，删去"给"，再把指人的宾语"您"移到动词"找"的后头，要么参照（82）的改法。

There are two ways of correcting the sentence: one way is to erase "给" and move the object referring to person "您" back after the verb "找", as illustrated in (81); the other way has been illustrated in (82).

4. 趋向动词"来"、"去"使用不当

Improper use of directional verbs "来" and "去"

例 087

误：如果接不到你的信，我就不来你那儿了。

正：如果接不到你的信，我就不去你那儿了。

"来"的意思是从别处到说话人所在地。原句却是说话人由所在地向别处走，应当改"来"为"去"。

"来" implies the direction from a place to where the speaker is. In the sentence above, the motion proceeds away from the speaker. Thus "去" rather than "来" is the right word.

例 088

误：我在北京等你，希望你很快去看我。

正：我在北京等你，希望你很快来看我。

"去"是从所在的地方到别的地方,与原句意相悖,应当把"去"改成"来"。

The action of "去" is from a place to another place further away from the speaker. It contradicts the meaning of the sentence. "去" should be replaced by "来".

5. 动宾式离合词使用不当

Improper use of verbs in verb-object construction

例 089

误:她已经毕业大学了。

正:她已经大学毕业了。

"毕业"本身已有一个直接宾语,如果要指明毕业的学校,则应把"大学"移到谓语"毕业"之前,作状语。

"毕业" already contains a direct object, and can not be followed by another object. "大学" must be placed in front of the predicate 毕业 as an adverbial adjunct to show the place of graduation.

例 090

误:昨天我见面我朋友了。

正:昨天我跟(和、同)我朋友见面了。

"见面"后边不能带对象宾语,为了把受影响的对象表示出来,须凭借介词"跟"(和、同)组成介宾词组"跟我的朋友",放在"见面"的前边,作状语。

"见面" never takes objects. In order to present the other side of the mutual activity, one has to use the preposition "跟" (or 和,同) to make up the prepositional phrase "跟我的朋友" and put it before "见面" as the adverbial adjunct.

例 091

误:请代我问好你的父母亲。

45

正:请代我向你的父母亲问好。

正:请代我问你的父母亲好。

这个句子有两种改法:一是借助介词"向"引出动作行为的方向,"向你的父母亲"应当放在"问好"的前面。二是把离合词拆开,中间插入指人的词语,改成"问你的父母亲好"。

There are two ways of rectification:1)use the preposition "向" to show the direction of the action and place "向你的父母亲" before "问好";2)separate the verb 问好 and insert words indicating the person to produce such a form as "问你的父母亲好".

6. 动词重叠使用不当

Improper use of reduplications of verbs

例 092

误:我到这儿已经两个月了,生活上还不习惯,我想想我的爸爸、妈妈。

正:我到这儿已经两个月了,生活上还不习惯,我想我的爸爸、妈妈。

重叠以后的"想想"表示短时,而思念父母之情是一段时期内不能变更的情感,用重叠形式不妥,应改成"想"。

The reduplicative form of "想"——"想想" implies a temporary state. But the emotion of missing one's parents lasts a period of time. Thus it is wrong to reduplicate the verb. A single "想" is just right.

例 093

误:我送送你一下儿。

正:我送送你。

正:我送你一下儿。

"送送"和"一下儿"所表示的意思重复,要么删去表短暂时间的"一下儿",保留不会持续很久的"送送",要么不用动词重叠形式,保留"一下儿"。

"送送" and "一下儿" carry the same implication of being temporary. Their co-existence results in repetition. A choice has to be made between them.

例 094

误:他知道那件事,可以给我们讲了讲。

正:他知道那件事,可以给我们讲讲。

正:他知道那件事,给我们讲了讲。

"可以"是说具有某种可能性;"了"说明动作已经完成,这两个词语义上相互矛盾,只能取其一。

"可以" expresses possibility, and "了" indicates that an action has been already completed. The two words are in conflict. One inhibits the presence of the other.

例 095

误:我送送你们出去吧。

正:我送你们出去吧。

这是一个连动句。这种句子的第一个动词一般不能重叠,原句的第二个动词"出"是表示动作趋向的,没有重叠形成。谓语部分只能改成"送你们出去"。

This is a sentence with verbal constructions in a series which normally allows no duplication of the first verb. Moreover, the second verb "出" does not have a reduplicative form since it shows the direction of an action. The predicate section of the sentence can only be "送你们出去".

四、能愿动词的误用
Errors in the Use of Auxiliary Verbs

会

can , may

例 096

误:只有有才能的人,才会当大使。

正:只有有才能的人,才能当大使。

"会"和"能"混淆,在汉语中这两个词是有区别的,"能"表示具备某种能力、条件,即先行句说的"有才能的人",这是当大使的必备条件,而后续句"会"没有这个意思。应改"会"为"能",前后才一致。

"会" is confused with "能" here. They are two distinct verbs in Chinese , "能" suggests the possession of a certain capability or qualification. In this sentence , "有才能的人" is a necessary qualification for an ambassador. However "会" can not express this meaning. It must be replaced by "能" to achieve consistency of the whole sentence.

例 097

误:你会什么时候去?

正:你能什么时候去?

"会"和"能"都有一种表示有可能的意思,但是,在疑问句里,"能"可以用于任何人称;"会"多用于第三人称。原句是问听者一方做某事的可能性,要用"能",不能用"会"。

"会" and 能 both carry the meaning of possibility. But in a question , "能" suits all persons whereas "会" generally occurs with the third person. In the above sentence , the subject is the hearer , thus "能" should be used instead of "会".

例 098

误:一个好演员既会跳得好,又会唱得好。

正:一个好演员既要(应该)跳得好,又要(应该)唱得好。

对于一个好演员的要求，从道理上讲应达到"跳得好"、"唱得好"的标准，基于这种想法，句中不能用"会"，需要用表示情理上必须如此的"要"或"应该"。

"跳得好" and "唱得好" are logical requirements for a good actor. Therefore, one should not use "会" but should use "要" or "应该" which denotes logical necessity.

例 099

误：我喜欢说汉语，但是我只说一点儿。

正：我喜欢说汉语，但是我只会说一点儿。

"一点儿"表明通过学习、实践获得和掌握的汉语知识和能力极为有限，通常应在第二个谓语动词"说"的前边加"会"。

"一点儿" is used here to indicate that one's knowledge and competence in the Chinese language acquired through learning and practice is rather limited. "会" is needed before the second predicate verb "说".

例 100

误：以后你汉语说得很好。

正：以后你汉语会说得很好。

肯定未来能够实现或肯定将来能作好某事，要在动词（"说"）的前边加上"会"字。

To affirm the prediction that something will be realized or achieved in the future, "会" is required before the verb ("说").

例 101

误：胜利是不轻易得到的。

正：胜利是不会轻易得到的。

句尾"的"有强调胜利来之不易的意思，一般在谓语动词前头加"会"与之呼应。

"的" at the end of the sentence emphasizes the statement that victory is hard-won. One should use "会" before the predicate verb to go with "的".

例 102

误:太晚了,不会他来了。

正:太晚了,他不会来了。

表示可能性的"会"连同否定词"不"不能放在句首,要放在主语之后,否定动作发生的可能性。

The negative form "不会" denoting impossibility can not occur initially before the subject, but should follow the subject to negate the possibility of an action.

能

can, may

例 103

误:谢力,我用你的自行车吗?

正:谢力,我能(可以)用你的自行车吗?

在这个征求对方意见的句子里,缺少表示允诺的词。应在动词的前头加上"能"或者"可以"。

This sentence of asking the other side for permission lacks a word expressing permission. One should add "能" or "可以" before the verb.

例 104

误:请你把你的词典借我用用,能吗?

正:请你把你的词典借我用用,可以吗?

询问对方是否同意做某事的句子末尾,不能用"能",常常用"可以"("成"、"行")。

"能" is never used at the end of a sentence asking for permission. "可以", "成" and "行" are the words often used.

例 105

误：请问,这儿能不能吸烟?能。

正：请问,这儿能不能吸烟?可以。

"能"和"可以"都有表示许可的意思,但单独回答时,通常用"可以"。

Both "能" and "可以" indicate permission. But they are different in that "可以" forms an answer independently.

例 106

误：阿里在家吗?他现在不能在家。

正：阿里在家吗?他现在不会在家。

正：阿里在家吗?他现在不可能在家。

"不能"表示没有能力或条件;"不会"则表示不具备某种客观的可能性。应改"不能"为"不会",也可以改用"不可能"。

"不能" denotes incapability while "不会" expresses objective impossibility. The proper substitute for "不能" may either be "不会" or "不可能".

例 107

误：你把这件衣服洗干净吗?我洗不干净。

正：你能把这件衣服洗干净吗?我洗不干净。

从后续句可以看出,原意是询问对方是否有能力把衣服洗干净。要在介词"把"的前边补上"能"。

From the follow-up sentence, we know that the speaker asks whether the person is able to wash the clothes. "能" should be added before the preposition "把".

例 108

误：旧的杂志可以能借吗?

正：旧的杂志可以(能)借吗?

"可以"和"能"都是用来询问是否允许做某事,用词重复,只能选用其中的一个。

51

The co-existence of "可以" and "能" both used in asking for permission is an unnecessary repetition. The speaker has to choose between the two possibilities.

例 109

误：你能去不去参观？

正：你能不能去参观？

在含有能愿动词"能"的正反式疑问句里，只能并列"能"的肯定和否定形式，而不能并列别的成分。

In an affirmative-negative question with an auxiliary verb such as "能", it is the affirmative and negative forms of the auxiliary verb, rather than any other sentence element, that are to be placed together.

例 110

误：你把你的学习方法能不能给我们介绍一下儿？

正：你能不能把你的学习方法给我们介绍一下儿？

在"把"字句中，能愿动词要放在"把"字之前，而不能放在由"把"构成的介宾词组之后。

In the 把-sentence, the auxiliary verb always precedes "把". It never appears after the prepositional phrase formed by 把.

可以

can

例 111

误：在十天内，你们可不可以造好箭？

正：在十天内，你们能不能造好箭？

"能"和"可以"混淆。"可以"只强调有能力，"能"既强调有能力，还要有条件。句中询问十天内是否造得好箭，要求不仅造箭的人有能力（技术），还应有某种条件（如，原料、工具等）。此句宜用"能"。

52

Here，"能" is confused with "可以"。"可以" merely stresses capability，but "能" emphasizes the objective conditions as well. In the present sentence，asking whether the arrows can be finished within ten days，to achieve the goal depends not only on the capability (the skill) of the arrow maker，but also on such conditions as material and tools. Thus "能" is the proper word to be chosen.

例 112

误:如果你没有钱,不可以结婚。

正:如果你没有钱,不能结婚。

"可以"的否定形式不能说"不可以",通常用"不能",表示不具备结婚的能力和条件。

The negative form of "可以" is "不能" rather than "不可以"。 "不能结婚" here means "not well prepared for a marriage"。

例 113

误:已经十点了,他可以来吗?

正:已经十点了,他会(能)来吗?

原意是询问"他来"的可能性,也是一种猜测估计,"可以"却没有这种用法,应改用"会"或"能"。

This sentence inquires the possibility of "他来"。 It also involves the making of an assumption. "可以" has no such usage. One should use "会" or "能"。

例 114

误:可以你的词典借用一下儿吗?

正:你的词典可以借用一下儿吗?

"可以"放在句首是受英语疑问句中含助动时的词序影响 (May I use your dictionary? 或 Could you lend me your dictionary?)。在汉语里"可以"只能用于谓语动词之前。

Here，the initial position of "可以" is a consequence of the interference of the word order in a question with an auxiliary verb in English (May I use your dictionary? or Could you lend me your dictionary?). In Chinese ″可以 ' always precedes the predicate verb.

例 115

误：我们跟小朋友可以谈话了。

正：我们可以跟小朋友谈话了。

介宾词组（"跟小朋友"）和能愿动词（"可以"）出现在同一动词之前，它们的排列顺序是：介宾词组靠近动词，其次是能愿动词，应把"跟小朋友"放在"可以"的后头。

Where a prepositional phrase (″跟小朋友″) and an auxiliary verb (″可以″) occur simultaneously before the same verb, the order is: the prepositional phrase immediately precedes the verb, and the auxiliary verb goes before the prepositional phrase. One should place ″跟小朋友″ after ″可以″.

例 116

误：我们痛痛快快地可以玩几天。

正：我们可以痛痛快快地玩几天。

描写性的词语与能愿动词同时用在谓语动词的前边，往往是描写性词语紧挨着动词，其次才是能愿动词。"痛痛快快地"应该移到"可以"的后边。

When both a modifier and an auxiliary verb are used before the predicate verb, it usually occurs that the modifier stays near the verb with the auxiliary verb coming next. Thus, we place ″痛痛快快″ after ″可以″.

能够

will

例 117

误：学校同意他能够上二年级吗？

54

正:学校能够同意他上二年级吗?

"能够"表示许可,要放在动词谓语之前,而不能放在充任宾语的主谓词组的谓语的前边。

″能够″ expresses permission. It should precede the verbal predicate of the whole sentence, not the predicate of the subject-predicate phrase serving as the object.

要

want

例 118

误:我身体不太舒服,今天的晚会我不要参加了。

正:我身体不太舒服,今天的晚会我不想参加了。

"要"表示主观上有做某事的愿望,它的否定形式不能说"不要",而是"不想"。

″要″ expresses a desire to do something. Its negative form is not ″不要″, but should be ″不想″.

例 119

误:阿里去图书馆要借一本书。

正:阿里要去图书馆借一本书。

在表示目的的连动句中,能愿动词一般放在第一个动词的前边。

In a sentence with verbal constructions in series, the auxiliary verb normally precedes the first verb.

应该

should

例 120

误:以后我们一定应该生产更多的机器。

正:以后我们一定要生产更多的机器。

正:以后我们应该生产更多的机器。

"一定"和"应该"是一对感情色彩截然不同的词,不能并用。"一定"经常与顺意的表示主观意愿的"要"连用,表明生产更多机器的意思坚决。或者删去"一定",保留"应该",表示情理上或客观上需要生产更多的机器。

　　″一定″ and ″应该″ are quite different in emotional colouring and can not be used together. ″一定″ often occurs in combination with ″要″ which denotes a subjective desire and match ″一定″ semantically. ″一定要″ here implies the strong will to produce more machines. Or one may delete ″一定″ and retain ″应该″ to express the logical or objective necessity of producing more machines.

　　例 121

　　误:老师说:"你们学习很紧张,还注意身体。"

　　正:老师说:"你们学习很紧张,还应该注意身体。"

　　是说学习固然紧张,但是从事实上或情理上讲,身体更重要,需要注意,因此,谓语动词"注意"的前边须补上"应该"。

　　The sentence means that although study is heavy, health is actually or naturally more essential and should be attached importance to. Therefore, ″应该″ should be added before the predicate verb ″注意″.

　　想

　　want, hope

　　例 122

　　误:他想想学会打球。

　　正:他想学会打球。

　　句中"想"作能愿动词用。能愿动词的语法特点之一是不能叠用,应当把"想想"改成"想"。

　　″想″ in the present sentence functions as an auxiliary verb which can not be reduplicated by characteristic. One ought to substitute "想想" with a single "想".

五、形容词的误用
Errors in the Use of Adjectives

1. 形容词使用不当
Improper use of adjectives

例 123

误：今天天气暖和，很合适到山里去玩儿。

正：今天天气暖和，适合到山里去玩儿。

误用形容词为动词。"合适"是形容词，不能带宾语（"到山里去玩儿"），应当改用与其同义的动词"适合"，表示符合实际情况或客观要求。

Here, the adjective is misused as a verb. "合适" is an adjective which does not take objects ("到山里去玩儿"). To express "in accordance with the actual situation or objective demands", one should use the verb "适合" which is similar to "合适" in meaning.

例 124

误：妈妈比五年前旧多了。

正：妈妈比五年前老多了。

英语可以把"旧"和"老"都译成 old，但是汉语的"旧"是用来指事物经过较长时间或经过使用而发生变化。原句说的是妈妈年岁大了，不能用"旧"，要用"老"。

"旧" and "老" are all translated into "old" in English. But "旧" in Chinese only indicates that things have changed after being used for a long time. The present sentence speaks of advancement in age, thus "老" rather than "旧" should be used.

例 125

误：她们俩的年纪一致。

正：她们俩的年纪相同。

"一致"表示没有分歧，与句子主语"年纪"不搭配，应当改"一致"为"相同"。

"一致" meaning "in agreement" does not match with the subject "年纪". It should be replaced by "相同".

例 126

误：今年来北京语言学院学习的可能有多人。

正：今年来北京语言学院学习的可能有很多人。

句中的"多"不能单独作定语，"多"的前边应当加"很"。一并作中心语"人"的定语。"很"表示程度的意义不明显。

"多" can not act as an attributive in isolation. It must be used in combination with "很" before it to serve as an attributive of the head word ("人"). Here "很" does not hold a definite implication of a high degree.

例 127

误：秋天不刮风，小下雨。

正：秋天不刮风，下小雨。

形容词"小"主要作定语。误用作状语的"小"应移到谓语动词"下"的后边。"小雨"指雨量不大的雨。

The main function of the adjective "小" is to be an attributive. "小" which is used wrongly here as an adverbial adjunct should be shifted backwards after the predicate verb "下". "小雨" means "a light rain".

2. 非谓形容词使用不当

Improper use of non-predicate adjectives

例 128

58

误:她觉得自己的丈夫很私人。

正:她觉得自己的丈夫很自私。

因为要表示她丈夫只顾自己的利益,不考虑别人的这一层意思,用"私人"作谓语,句子讲不通,应改"私人"为"自私"。

The sentence does not make sense with "私人" as the predicate. To express that someone is only concerned for his own interests and does not consider others, one should use "自私" instead of "私人".

例 **129**

误:男要长得好的女朋友,女要文化水平比她高的男朋友。

正:男的要长得好的女朋友,女的要文化水平比她高的男朋友。

"男"和"女"通常不单独作主语。汉语的表示法是在"男"、"女"的后边加上"的",构成"的"字词组,即"男的"、"女的"。

"男" and "女" generally do not serve as subjects independently. "的" is often placed after them to form a "的"-phrase, i. e. "男的", "女的".

例 **130**

误:他们离婚的理由是女不喜欢男,男也不喜欢女。

正:他们离婚的理由是女方不喜欢男方,男方也不喜欢女方。

原意是指离婚的双方,应把误用作主语和宾语的"男"和"女"都改成"男方"和"女方"。也可以改成"男的"和"女的"。

"男" and "女" here are meant to represent the two parties involved in divorce. Improperly used as the subjects and the objects of the sentence, they should be replaced by "男方", "女方" or "男的", "女的".

3. 形容词重叠使用不当

Improper use of reduplications of adjectives

例 131

误：同学很高高兴兴地走出教室去了。

正：同学高高兴兴地走出教室去了。

"高高兴兴"是"高兴"的重叠形式，用作状语，表示动作（"走"）的状态。重叠以后的形容词含有程度加深的意味，不能再接受程度副词"很"的修饰。应当删去"很"。

"高高兴兴" is the reduplicative form of "高兴" serving here as an adverbial adjunct to describe the state of the action ("走"). Reduplicated adjectives express intensification, and can no longer be modified by an adverb of degree like "很". Thus，"很" in the sentence should be deleted.

例 132

误：他的房间收拾得干干净净极了。

正：他的房间收拾得干干净净。

重叠形式的"干干净净"用作程度补语时，它的后面不能再跟表示程度的词语，去掉"极了"。

When the reduplicative form of an adjective such as "干干净净" is used as a degree complement, it can not be followed by other words indicating degree. "极了" must be deleted.

例 133

误：这件工艺品做得细细致致。

正：这件工艺品做得细致。

联合式的合成形容词用来表示事物的性质，一般不能重叠，应改"细细致致"为"细致"。

An incorporate adjective in co-ordinate structure describing the property of a thing can not be reduplicated. We change "细细致致" into "细致".

六、数词的误用

Errors in the Use of Numerals

1. 基数使用不当

Improper use of cardinal numbers

(1) "二"和"两"

"二" and "两"

例 134

误:我们的房间有二个书架。

正:我们的房间有两个书架。

例 135

误:下午二点大家在九楼前边集合。

正:下午两点大家在九楼前边集合。

在普通话里,"二"和"两"所表示的意义相同,但用法有些不同,用在量词之前,而且只是一个个位数时大都用"两"。(134)(135)中的"二"都应改为"两"。

In the common language (known as *putonghua*), "二" and "两" mean the same thing but have different usage. "两" is often used when followed by a measure word and representing a single digit. "二" in (134), (135) should be replaced with "两".

例 136

误:同志,找您两块两毛两。

正:同志,找您两块两毛二。

人民币的计量单位是"块"、"毛"、"分"(或"元"、"角"、"分")。在"两块两毛两"中,最后一个数词"两"后带有量词"分",可以说"两块两毛两分"。"两"后省去量词"分",则只能用"二",在对话中,这种省说"分"的说法更常用。

61

Renminbi is counted in units of "块", "毛", "分" (or "元", "角", "分"). In "两块两毛两", the last numeral "两" should carry the measure word "分". We say "两块两毛两分". But if "分" is absent, "二" must be used. Such expression with "分" omitted is very common in dialogue.

例 137

误:我吃了两两来饭。

正:我吃了二两来饭。

"二"用于表示度量衡单位的量词"两"前,因为读音的关系,不能用"两",只能用"二"。

Before "两" which is also a measure word of weight, "二" rather than "两" is used for pronunciation reason.

例 138

误:今天我们用了两十五块八毛二。

正:今天我们用了二十五块八毛二。

"两十五块八毛二"是个多位数,"2"用在多位数中的十位数上,只能用"二"。应改"两"为"二"。

When "2" occupies the ten's place of a big number such as the one in the present sentence, it must be read "二".

(2) 一百以上的称数法

Enumeration of numbers above one hundred

例 139

误:这是五万零零零八块钱。(50008)

正:这是五万零八块钱。

在这个多位数目字当中,三个"零"并列,汉语的表示法是只读出一个"零",即"五万零八块钱",去掉后两个"零"。

In a big number with more than one "0" juxtaposed, only one is pronounced. The sentence should be read as "五百零八块钱".

例 **140**

误：那个大学有十三千人。

正：那个大学有一万三千人。

"十三千"是 thirteen thousand 的直译。汉语的数目是十进位的，个、十、百、千、万是五个基本整数词。中间是十进位的相加关系。13000应当读做一万三千。

"十三千" is the literal interpretation of "thirteen thousand". In Chinese, the decimal system is used, and "个、十、百、千、万" are the five basic integrals.

（3）俩

two

例 **141**

误：她们俩个今天晚上也动身。

正：她们俩今天晚上也动身。

"俩"的意思是"两个"，既包含数词"两"，又包含量词"个"。"俩"的后面不能再接"个"或者其他量词。

"俩" refers to "两个". As the combination of the numeral "两" and the measure word "个", it can not be followed by any measure word including "个".

2. **概数使用不当**

Improper use of approximate numbers

（1）相邻的两个数字连用

Two adjacent digits used together

例 **142**

误：阿里住院已经十四几天了。

正：阿里住院已经十四五天了。

汉语表示概数的方式之一是相邻的两个数目字连用，表示大概的数量，可以说"十三四"、"四五十"。"几"本身是个概数，不能与定数"四"连用,根据两个相邻数目表示概数的要求,应当删去"几",改成"十四五"。

One way to express approximate numbers in Chinese is to use two adjacent digits together. We can say "十三四","四五十". "几" itself represents an approximate number and never occurs next to a definite number such as "四". According to this rule, we change "几" into "五", i.e. "十四五".

例 143

误:这个礼堂坐得下七百、八百人。

正:这个礼堂坐得下七八百人。

两位以上相邻的两个数目的"位",在汉语里不必一一说出,只需保留第二个数目后边的"位"就可以了。删掉"七"后的"百"。

If two adjacent digits are used together to express an approximate number above ten, only the place of the second numeral needs to be read out. Thus "百" after "七" is redundant.

例 144

误:这课生词我写了九、十遍。

正:这课生词我写了九遍(十遍)。

"九"和"十"这两个数字一般不连在一起,用来表示概数。避免与"九十"相互混淆,或者改成"九遍",或者改成"十遍"。

"九" and "十" are seldom used together to express an approximate number so as not to be confused with "九十". Choose either one of the two 九遍 or 十遍.

(2)"多"表示概数

"多" expressing approximate numbers

例 145

误:我一个月多没有接到家里的信了。

正:我一个多月没有接到家里的信了。

"多"的位置失当。概数"多"与数词、量词连用,表示不确定的零数。句中数字是个个位数"一","多"要跟在量词("个")的后头。

"多" here is misplaced. When used with a numeral and a measure word, the approximate numeral "多" indicates an indefinite odd number. The numeral of the present sentence is a digit ("一"). In this case, "多" must follow the measure word ("个").

例 146

误:今天参加运动会的有三千个多人。

正:今天参加运动会的有三千多个人。

"三千(3000)"是个多位数。"多"应放在量词前头。

"三千(3000)" is a big number. "多" must precede the measure word.

例 147

误:这台机器两多天就修好了。

正:这台机器两天多就修好了。

"天"是一个本身含有量词性的名词,"多"与"天"连用,不能放在"天"的前头,应当跟在"天"的后头。

"天" is a noun of quantity. When used with "天", "多" must follow it rather than precede it.

例 148

误:我还有百多块钱。

正:我还有一百多块钱。

用 在动词后的数词"一"可以省去,单说量词(如,"我买本书")。此句动词"有"后紧跟着的是由"百"和"多"构成的表示钱数的概数词组。"一"要说出来。

The numeral "一" after a verb is understood. One may only read out the measure word (such as "我买本书"). In this sentence, the verb "有" is followed by a phrase with "百" and "多" to indicate an approximate sum of money. Thus ″一″ must be read out.

例 149

误：中午我复习了两多小时。

正：中午我复习了两个多小时。

"多"与数词、量词才能组成表示概数的词语。"两多小时"中缺少量词。应在个位数"两"和"多"的中间补上"个"。

Both a numeral and a measure word are required in forming a phrase with ″多″ to represent an approximate number. In ″两多小时″, the measure word ″个″ should be inserted between ″两″ and ″多″.

(3)"几"表示概数

″几″ expressing approximate numbers

例 150

误：我有几中国朋友。

正：我有几个中国朋友。

"几"表示大于一而小于十的不确定的数目。"几"和量词通常连在一起使用。应在"几"的后边加上"朋友"的计量单位"个"。

″几″ can be substituted for the numbers from two to nine. It is generally used with a measure word. ″个″ which can indicate the u-nit of friends should be added after ″几″.

例 151

误：我还有几多百块钱。

正：我还有几百块钱。

"几"和"多"都表示概数,两种表示概数的手段不能混用在一个数目当中。应删去"多"。

As two distinct ways to express an approximate number，″几″ and ″多″ can not be used together for indicating one number. One should delete "多".

例 152

误：他们学校有几十八个国家的学生。

正：他们学校有几十个国家的学生。

"几十"表示概数，"八"是定数。概数与定数不能混杂在一个数目之内，删去"八"。

"几十" is approximate while "八" is definite. One can not mix an approximate number with a definite one while expressing one number. "八" should be deleted.

(4)"左右"表示概数

左右 expressing approximate numbers

例 153

误：今年那儿的水果产量提高了左右百分之二十。

正：今年那儿的水果产量提高了百分之二十左右。

"左右百分之二十"是 about twenty per cent 的直译。在汉语里，"左右"是也许多一些，也许少一些的意思，表示大约的数目，应放在"百分之二十"的后边。

"左右百分之二十" is the word-to-word interpretation of "about twenty per cent". Meaning "more or less" in Chinese，"左右" is used to indicate a rough number. It must be placed after "百分之二十".

例 154

误：这个大学有两千左右个人。

正：这个大学有两千个人左右。

"左右"与整数"两千"、量词和名词连用，"左右"通常用在整个词组之后。

When "左右" is used in combination with a whole number ("两千") and a measure word with its matching noun, it normally occurs at the end of the entire phrase.

例 155

误：他们到北京整整一年左右了。

正：他们到北京整整一年了。

正：他们到北京一年左右了。

"一年"是定数，前边再用表达整数的"整整"，数目就更加明确了。但是，后面用了表示概数的"左右"，前后矛盾，数目概念不清。要么删去"左右"，要么删去"整整"。

"一年" is a definite number, and is even more precise in the present sentence preceded by "整整" which is used to indicate a whole number. What makes the sentence contradictory is that "一年" modified by "整整" is followed by "左右"—the way to express approximate numbers. The presence of both "整整" and "左右" causes a confusion. "左右" or "整整" is to be deleted.

3. 序数使用不当

Improper use of ordinal numbers

例 156

误：为什么你第一天、二天没来？

正：为什么你第一天、第二天没来？

表示次序的先后，一般要在数词前边用"第"，句中"二(天)"前缺少"第"，应当补上。

To show order, "第" is often required before the numeral. "二(天)" in the sentence should be preceded by "第".

例 157

误：他朋友在北京语言学院第二系第一年级学习汉语。

正：他朋友在北京语言学院二系一年级学习汉语。

表示系级的编号的不用"第"。应当删去句中的两个"第"字。

"第" is not needed before numerals used to distinguish departments or grades. One should delete "第" in the sentence.

4. 分数使用不当

Improper use of fractions

例 158

误：这是二分之三。

正：这是三分之二。

"二分之三"(two-thirds)是受英语分数表示方法的影响。英语要以分子为基数词，分母为序数词，并有复数。汉语的表示方法是先说分母，后说分子，应改成"三分之二"。

"二分之三" (two-thirds) is derived from the English way of showing fractions. In English, the numerator is a cardinal number whereas the denominator is an ordinal number which may appear in the plural form. In Chinese, The denominator always comes before the numerator. Thus it should be "三分之二".

例 159

误：那是二十三分六。

正：那是二十三分之六。

汉语用"……分之……"表示分数。应当在"分"后补上不可少的"之"。

"…分之…" is the formula to indicate fractions in Chinese. "之" is obligatory after "分".

例 160

误：这是百分之九十九点六十四。（99.64%）

正：这是百分之九十九点六四。

小数点后的"位"要省去不说，直接读出每一个数字。

Places after the decimal point need not be read out. Just read out the figures one by one.

5. "半"使用不当

Improper use of "半"

例 **161**

误：我刚才吃了半苹果。

正：我刚才吃了半个苹果。

"半"表示二分之一的意思。"半"同其他数词一样，放在名词前边时，必须有一个量词伴随在一起（本身含量词性的名词除外，如"半年"、"半天"）。应在"苹果"前加上量词"个"。

"半" means "half". Like other numerals, it must be accompanied by a measure word to premodify a noun (except when the noun itself suggests quantity, e. g. "半年", "半天"). The measure word "个" should be added before "苹果".

例 **162**

误：我们到中国已经一半年了。

正：我们到中国已经一年半了。

"一半年"是受 one and a half year 的影响。在汉语里，"半"应放在数量词（"一年"）之后。

The word order of "一半年" is copied from "one and a half year" in English. In Chinese "半" is placed after the numeral-measure word phrase ("一年").

例 **163**

误：我已经学了两半个月的汉语了。

正：我已经学了两个半月的汉语了。

"半"用在由名词"月"构成的名词性词组中。"半"应放在量词"个"后。

"半" must follow the measure word "个" in a nominal phrase with "月" as the head word.

6. 人民币的表示方法不当
Improper ways to read Renminbi

例 **164**

误：一个本子才三十五分。

正：一个本子才三毛五（分钱）。

"三十五分"是英语的表示法。人民币采用"十进制"的计算方法，逢十进位，满十即向左进一。如，十分钱等于一毛钱。"三十五分"只能说"三毛五（分钱）"或"三角五分钱"。

"三十五分" is the English way to count money. In counting the Chinese currency Renminbi, the decimal system is adopted, i. e. ten cents（分）makes one mao（"毛"）, and ten mao makes one yuan. The proper way to express "三十五分" is "三毛五（分钱）" or "三角五分钱".

例 **165**

误：这些邮票一共五块零毛六分（钱）。

正：这些邮票一共五块零六分（钱）。

"五块零毛六分（钱）"是多位数，其中"毛"的前边的数目字是"零"时，"零"字不能缺少，量词"毛"却不能显现出来。

In "五块零毛六分（钱）" which involves all the three units of Renminbi, the figure preceding "毛" is "0". In this case, the word "零" must be present while "毛" must not.

例 **166**

误：这件大衣二百八十块零八。

正：这件大衣二百八十块零八毛。（或二百八十块零八分）

"二百八十块零八"到底是二百八十块零八毛，还是二百八十块零八分？如果把零后一位计量单位说出来，意思就清楚了。要么改成"二百八十块零八毛"，要么改成"二百八十块零八分"，两者任取其一。

The meaning of "二百八十块零八" is obscure in that it may be understood as "二百八十块零八毛" or "二百八十块零八分".

However, it will become clear, if one states the phrase in full without dropping the last counting unit. One should say either "二百八
十块零八毛" or "二百八十块零八分".

例 167

误:这是三百十五块钱。

正:这是三百一十五块钱。

"三百十五块钱"是三位数。在三位或三位以上的多位数,十位
数是"一",汉语普话习惯说法是"一十",而不只是说"十"。

三百十五块钱 is a three-figure number. In a big number with
three or more than three digits, "一" which occupies the ten's place
is habitually read as "一十" instead of "十".

七、量词的误用
Errors in the Use of Measure Words

1. 名量词使用不当
Improper use of nominal measure words

例 168

误:那张词典是我的。

正:那本词典是我的。

量词"张"与"本"混淆。在汉语里哪个量词同哪个名词配合,是
有一定要求的,不能任意使用。量词"张"、"本"与事物的形状有关。
"张"用于平面物体或有平面的物体,如"地图"、"纸"、"报"、"票"、
"条子"、"床"等。"本"用于书籍簿册,如"词典"、"杂志"、"画报"、
"小说"、"字典"等。应当把"张"改成"本"。

"张" is confused with "本" here. In Chinese, it is not arbi-
trary as to which measure word goes with which noun. Measure

words "张" and "本" are related to the shape of objects. "张" is used for flat objects or objects with a flat surface, such as "地图", "纸", "报", "票", "条子", "床", etc. "本" applies to volumes or booklets, such as 词典", "杂志", "画报", "小说", "字典", etc. "张" should be replaced with "本".

例 169

误：一个年有三百六十五天或三百六十六天。

正：一年有三百六十五天或三百六十六天。

"年"是个本身含有量词性的名词，它的前边带有数词时，数词与"年"之间不能再加其他量词。应当删去"个"。

"年" is a noun of quantity. No measure word is allowed between it and the premodifying numeral. "个" must be deleted.

例 170

误：一年有十二月。

正：一年有十二个月。

"十二月"表示次序的先后，指一年里边的最后一个月的名称。此句是说一年内的月数总和，应在"月"前加一量词"个"。"十二个月"是基数，表示数量的多少。

"十二月" with respect to order refers to the last month of the year. But the present sentence speaks of the total number of months in a year, so one should use the measure word "个" in front of "月". "十二个月" is a cardinal number which indicates quantity.

例 171

误：我喝了两个杯牛奶，他喝了一个瓶啤酒。

正：我喝了两杯牛奶，他喝了一瓶啤酒。

在汉语里，一件事物名称前只能用一个表示单位的词。"牛奶"和"啤酒"前分别用了两个量词。删去"个"，还是删去"杯"、"瓶"，主要取决于量词与事物名词是否搭配。"牛奶"、"啤酒"的量词命名通常与使用的容器盛具有关,液体的"牛奶"、"啤酒"常用杯、瓶、碗等器皿,所以"杯"和"瓶"可以用来作名词"牛奶"和"啤酒"的量词。应去掉不能充当这类名词的计量单位"个"。

In Chinese, a noun can carry only one measure word. In the present sentence, there are two measure words before "牛奶" and "啤酒". Whether to delete "个" or "杯" and "瓶" depends on which one of them does not match the two nouns. The measure words for "牛奶" and "啤酒" are often the names of certain containers or vessels. Liquids like "牛奶" and "啤酒" are usually held in such containers as "瓶", "杯", "碗", etc. Thus "杯" and "瓶" are the proper measure words to go with "牛奶" and "啤酒". "个" must be deleted.

例 172

误:我认识那位人。

正:我认识那位老师。

正:我认识那个人。

"位"用于人,带敬意,常用于表示称谓的名词前边。这个句子有两种改法:一是删去"人",改用"老师";二是把量词"位"改成"个"。

"位" is normally used before nouns of appellation to show respect. This sentence may be corrected in two ways: one is to replace "人" by "老师", the other is to replace "位" with "个".

2. 不定量词使用不当

Improper use of indefinite measure words

一点儿

a little

例 173

误:我会说汉语一点儿。

74

正：我会说一点儿汉语。

"（一）点儿"是不定量词，表示少量。可以用在名词前，表示事物的数量很少。句中"一点"应放在"汉语"的前边，表明只会说少量的汉语。

"（一）点儿" is an indefinite measure word showing a small quantity. It may be used before nouns. "一点儿" in the sentence should be placed before "汉语" to mean that the speaker can only speak a little Chinese.

例 174

误：他比我一点儿高。

正：他比我高一点儿。

"一点儿"用在带"比"字的比较句中，指出比较成分之间的差量，当然这个差量是很小的。"一点儿"应该移到形容词"高"的后边，作数量补语。

Used in a comparative sentence with "比", "一点儿" shows that the difference between the two compared elements is very slight. It should go after "高" to serve as a complement of quantity.

例 175

误：哥哥新买的皮鞋一点儿小，送给我了。

正：哥哥新买的皮鞋小一点儿，送给我了。

"一点儿"出现在形容词作谓语的句子里，不能用在形容词前头，应把"一点儿"移到"小"的后头。是指说话人以哥哥合适的鞋为标准，经过比较而得出的判断。

"一点儿" may not precede the predicate adjective of a sentence. One should place "一点儿" after "小". Here, the judgement is made through comparison with the shoes that fit the feet of the speaker's brother.

例 176

误:今天的面条煮点儿硬了。

正:今天的面条煮硬了点儿。

"一点儿"用于由形容词作结果补语的句子,不能放在补语的前边。应把"点儿"移到补语"硬"后边,是说面条煮过以后,没有达到软的要求。

When "一点儿" is used in a sentence with an adjective as the complement of result, it can not occur before the complement. "点儿" should be put after "硬" to indicate that the noodles are not soft enough.

例 177

误:你等我一点儿,我马上就来。

正:你等我一下儿(一会儿),我马上就来。

"一点儿"有时可以放在动词的后边,说明程度不高。句中的动词"等"没有程度及量度的问题,只表明动作"等"的时间短暂,所以不能用"一点儿"。应改为表示时间短的动量词"一下儿"或名词"一会儿"。

"一点儿" sometimes follows a verb to imply a moderate degree. In the verb "等", there exists no question of degree or quantity, but duration of the action. Thus "一点" is impossible here and must be replaced by the verbal measure word "一下儿" or the noun "一会儿" to denote a short time.

例 178

误:让她们来这里避雨一点儿。

正:让她们来这里避一下儿雨(避一会儿雨)。

动词"避"与(177)的动词"等"具有相同的特点,应改"一点儿"为"一下儿"或"一会儿"。又因为宾语是名词"雨","一下儿"或"一会儿"须放在"雨"的前边。

The verb "避" holds the same property as the verb "等". "一

76

点儿" should be replaced with "一下儿" or "一会儿" which must occur before the object "雨" since it is a noun.

（一）些

some

例 179

误：一些巴里亚的衣服放在箱子里。

正：巴里亚的一些衣服放在箱子里。

"一些"是不定量词，表示少量，可以用在名词前边。句中"一些"都用在专有名词"巴里亚"之前，在语文上讲不通。"一些巴里亚的衣服"应改成"巴里亚的一些衣服"，是说衣服量少。

As an indefinite measure word，"一些" may be used before a noun to indicate a limited quantity. This sentence is senseless with "一些" preceding the proper noun "巴里亚". One should use "巴里亚的一些衣服" instead of "一些巴里亚的衣服" to mean that the number of clothes is limited.

例 180

误：他们两个应该作让步一些。

正：他们两个应该作一些让步。

"一些"是修饰由"让步"充当的宾语的，只能放在"让步"的前头。

As the modifier of the object expressed by "让步"，"一些" must occur before it.

例 181

误：我听说过北京一些的情况。

正：我听说过北京的一些情况。

"一些"与被修饰成分之间不能用结构助词"的"。应该把"的"放在"北京"的后边，表示领属关系。

"的" is not allowed between "一些" and the modified element.

It must follow "北京" to show classification.

八、副词的误用
Errors in the Use of Adverbs

不

not

例 182

误：昨天他不去张老师那儿。

正：昨天他没（有）去张老师那儿。

因为要表示某种情况"昨天"未曾发生，应该用否定词"没"或"没有"，不能用"不"。

To express that something did not happen yesterday, one should use the negation word "没" or "没有" rather than "不".

例 183

误：我们法语不说得好。

正：我们法语说得不好。

谓语动词的后边带有程度补语时，否定词"不"不能作谓语的修饰语。应把"不"移到补语（"好"）的前边。说明法语口头表达的水平不高。

When the predicate verb is followed by a degree complement, it can not be premodified by the negation word "不". "不" must be put directly before the complement ("好") to indicate a look of proficiency in spoken French.

例 184

误：到北京以后，他立刻不到学校去。

正：到北京以后，他不立刻到学校去。

时间副词"立刻"与"不"连用,一般"不"在前,"立刻"在后。表示不是在很短的时间内就去做另外一件事("到学校去")。

When the adverb of time "立刻" is used with "不", it usually follows "不" meaning "not to do something ("到学校去") immediately."

例 185

误:今天我不有看报呢。

正:今天我还没有看报呢。

是说"看报"这个动作行为尚未发生,但迟早发生。应改"不有"为"还没有"。

The speaker means that the action of "看报" have not yet taken place, but will sooner or later. He should use "还没有" instead of "不有".

例 186

误:她不会游泳,我不也会游泳。

正:她不会游泳,我也不会游泳。

先行句用"不"否定"她"具备游泳的能力,后续句用"也",说明"我"和"她"一样。"也"应放在"不"的前边。

The anticipatory sentence uses "不" to negate her ability to swim, and the follow-up sentence uses "也" to show the similarity between "我" and "她". "也" should go before "不".

例 187

误:你一定不拒绝我的要求。

正:你一定不要(别)拒绝我的要求。

说的是劝阻对方去做某事,而否定词"不"没有这个用法。应当改用副词"不要"或"别"。

The sentence is to dissuade the other person from doing something, but the negation word "不" can not perform such function, and must be replaced by "不要" or "别".

没有

did not, have not

例 188

误:对不起,我没有去,你们快去吧。

正:对不起,我不去,你们快去吧。

从上下文看,是对带有主观意图的否定,不宜用"没有",改用"不"。

It can be understood from the context that what the speaker negates is the intention, not the occurrence of the action. Thus "不" rather than "没有" should be used.

例 189

误:他俩没愿意去那儿游泳。

正:他俩不愿意去那儿游泳。

否定希望去做某件事的主观想法,不能用"没有",应当用"不"。

To negate the subjective desire to do something, one should not use "没有", not "不".

例 190

误:来中国以前,我没有会说汉语。

正:来中国以前,我不会说汉语。

因要表示未曾学习,尚不具备说汉语的能力。不该用"没有",要用"不"。

To express inability to speak Chinese before starting to learn it, "不" should be used instead of "没有".

例 191

误:大家没有知道他俩结婚的事。

正:大家不知道他俩结婚的事。

行为心理动词"知道"的否定形式通常为"不"。删去"没有"，改用"不"。

To negate the verb 知道，不 should be used. Replace 没有 with 不.

例 192

误：马老师过去没吸烟，也没有喝酒。

正：马老师过去不吸烟，也不喝酒。

用"过去"作时间状语，说明"吸烟、喝酒"是以前的习惯性动作。否定这种习惯性的动作，应当换用"不"。

Serving as an adverbial adjunct of time，"过去" shows that "吸烟"，"喝酒" were habitual actions in the past. "不" should be used instead of "没有" to negate habitual actions.

例 193

误：我每天都没有锻炼身体。

正：我每天都不锻炼身体。

"每天"作状语，表示"锻炼身体"是经常性、有规律性的活动。否定这种动作行为要用"不"，删去"没有"。

"每天" serving as an adverbial adjunct implies that "锻炼身体" is a frequent，regular activity which is to be negated by "不" rather than "没有".

例 194

误：明年暑假他和阿里都没有回国。

正：明年暑假他和阿里都不回国。

"明年"表明"他和阿里回国"是以后的事，并含有"他和阿里"的主观意向，对这样的动作行为作否定时，应当把"没有"改成"不"。

The word "明年" shows that "他和阿里回国" is an event related to the future and is in fact the internal intention of "他和阿

里". To negate such an action, one should use "不" in place of "没有".

例 195

误：如果没有上课，咱们就一起去医院看丁力。

正：如果不上课，咱们就一起去医院看丁力。

否定的是假设的情况，不能用"没有"，应改为"不"。

"没有" can not be used to negate supposition. The proper word is "不".

例 196

误：加里亚没有去上海就来你这儿。

正：加里亚不去上海就来你这儿。

这是个表示"如果……"或"要是……"的紧缩句。显然，是对假设行为的否定，应当删去"没有"，改用"不"。

The sentence is the contracted form of the pattern "如果…" or "要是…". The negation here applies to a suppositional action. Thus one should delete "没有" and use "不".

例 197

误：那种花漂亮，这种花没有漂亮。

正：那种花漂亮，这种花不漂亮。

否定某一个事物具有某种性质，不能用"没有"，应当用"不"。

To negate the property of something, one should not use "没有", but ought to use "不".

例 198

误：我没有看那部电影了。

正：我没有看那部电影。

正：我看那部电影了。

动词前用否定词"没有"，句尾又用语气助词"了"，表示事情已经完成。到底完成了没有，没交待清楚。要么去掉"了"，保留"没有",要么去掉"没有",保留"了"。

The sentence is confusing in that there is the negation word "没有" before the verb and while the interjection "了" at the end indicating completion of the event. One of these two elements must be deleted with the other one left.

别(不要)

do not

例 199

误：别说话吧，广播开始了。

正：别说话了，广播开始了。

"别"有劝阻进行某种活动的意思，句子末尾不宜用语气助词"吧"。应改用语气助词"了"，表示禁止已经发生的行为。

"别" means to stop somebody from doing something. The interjection "吧" is improper here. One should use the interjection "了" with "别" to stop an action that has already taken place.

例 200

误：时间不早了，大家别再讨论。

正：时间不早了，大家别再讨论了。

动词谓语的前边带有表示继续的副词"再"与"别"等，句尾经常用"了"，与之呼应。

When the verbal predicate is preceded by "别" in combination with the adverb "再" which denotes continuity，"了" is usually required at the end of the sentence.

例 201

误：昨天晚上十一点才我回到学校。

正：昨天晚上十一点我才回到学校。

"才"的位置失当，应移到动词"回"的前边。"才"与时间词语"晚上十一点"并用，说明回到学校的时间很晚。

"才" here is improperly positioned and should be moved to the front of the verb "回". Occurring with the time phrase "晚上十一点", it implies that the speaker returned to school very late.

例 202

误:每天八点上课,他常常八点一刻来。

正:每天八点上课,他常常八点一刻才来。

"八点一刻"说明他常常超过规定的时间来上课,所以,应当在"来"的前头加"才",强调来得晚。

"八点一刻" shows that he often comes to class behind schedule, so "才" should be added before "来" to stress unpunctuality.

例 203

误:颐和园不远,但是我们一个小时就到那儿。

正:颐和园不远,但是我们一个小时才到那儿。

说的是路程不远,可是到达颐和园的时间并不早。这样,在表示转折关系的后续句里不能用主观上认为动作发生得早的副词"就",应改用"才"。

The speaker means that they arrived at the Summer Palace rather late despite a short distance. The adverb "就" indicates that an action is thought to have taken place ahead of time. Thus it can not be used in the follow-up sentence above which expresses adverse relation and should be replaced by "才".

就

as soon as, right after

例 204

误:昨天下了课,就他去看朋友了。

正:昨天下了课,他就去看朋友了。

"就"的位置不妥,应移到动词"去"的前边,作状语。说明"下课"、"去"和"看朋友"三个动作紧接着发生。

84

"就" occupies the wrong position in the sentence. It should precede the verb "去" as an adverbial adjunct to indicate that the three events— "下课","去","看朋友" happened in quick succession.

例 205

误:骑自行车十分钟可以到清华大学。

正:骑自行车十分钟就可以到清华大学。

因为要表示说话人主观上认为到达清华大学的时间早,应当在"可以"的前面加上"就"。

"就" should be added before "可以" to express that the speaker subjectively thinks that it only takes a short time to get to Qinghua University.

例 206

误:香山很远,我们一个半小时就到。

正:香山很远,我们一个半小时才到。

说话人("我们")觉得距离远,言外之意,路上用的时间要多,到香山的时间要晚。应当删去"就",改用"才"。

According to the speaker, "香山" is far away and it took them a long time to get there. "才" is the proper word to be used instead of "就".

例 207

误:我就才知道他是大夫。

正:我早就知道他是大夫。

正:我才知道他是大夫。

句中"就"表示"知道"得早,"才"表示"知道"得晚,这两个词不能混用在一起。要么去掉"才",在"就"前加"早","早就"强调很早以前已经知道这件事。要么去掉"就",保留"才"。

"就" implies "early" whereas "才" implies "late", so they can

not occur side by side. There are two ways of correction: delete "才" and add "早" before "就" to emphasize early knowledge; or delete "就" and keep "才".

常常

often

例 208

误:以前常常我去友谊商店买东西。

正:以前我常常去友谊商店买东西。

在汉语里,"常常"不能放在主语的前边,应该把"常常"移到主语"我"与谓语动词"去"之前。

In Chinese, "常常" can not occur before the subject. One should put it between the subject "我" and the predicate verb "去".

例 209

误:现在我们跟中国同学常常说汉语。

正:现在我们常常跟中国同学说汉语。

动词谓语前还有介宾词组"跟中国同学"作状语,用来引进动作"说"的对象。它们的排列次序一般是介宾词组紧挨着动词,其次才是"常常"。

The verbal predicate is preceded by the prepositional phrase "跟中国同学" which serves as an adverbial adjunct to introduce the object of the action "说". The usual order in such a sentence is: the prepositional phrase goes directly before the verb with "常常" coming next.

例 210

误:我不常常跟朋友一起吃饭。

正:我不常跟朋友一起吃饭。

"常常"的否定形式是"不常"。去掉第二个"常"字。

The negative form of "常常" is "不常". The second "常" is to

be deleted.

例 **211**

误:他常常早上在操场跑步了。

正:他常常早上在操场跑步。

"常常"表示动作行为在某段确定时间之内多次发生;语气助词"了"肯定事态变化的完成。在语义上,"常常"与"了"配不拢,应当删去"了"。

"常常" indicates that an action occurs frequently in a certain period. The interjection "了" affirms a change of state. These two words do not match semantically. "了" must be deleted.

例 **212**

误:他希望你以后常常也来玩儿。

正:他希望你以后也常常来玩儿。

"常常"与"也"错位。这两个词连用时,一般是表示"同样"的"也"在前,"常常"在后。

"常常" and "也" are in the wrong order. When these words are used together, "也" meaning "also" normally goes before "常常".

往往

usually

例 **213**

误:我以后往往来看望你。

正:我以后常常来看望你。

"往往"只适用于过去经常发生的情况,此句是指"以后"将发生的事。应改用"常常"。

"往往" only applies to habitual events in the past. But this sentence is about something in the future. Thus "常常" should be used.

例 214

误:他们往往去旅游。

正:他们往往利用假期去旅游。

正:他们往往骑自行车去旅游。

正:他们往往跟老师一起去旅游。

"往往"指某情况的出现带有规律性,一般要指明与动作有关的情况,加以限制。这个句子可以改成"利用假期去旅游",是说旅游的时间经常是假期,而不是别的时间。也可以改成"骑自行车去旅游",表示旅游时使用的工具。还可以改成"跟老师一起去旅游"指出"旅游"的方式。

"往往" indicates regularity about a certain happening. It usually requires a statement to provide relevant information about the main action, for qualification. There are a number of grammatical forms to replace the original wrong one. One can say "利用假期去旅游" to express that the traveling usually took place in vocation rather than any other time. One may say "骑自行车去旅游" to indicate the tool for traveling. One may also say "跟老师一起去旅游" to show the manner of the activity.

曾经

once, used to

例 215

误:他曾经在中国住了两年。

正:他曾经在中国住过两年。

"曾经"经常与动态助词"过"前后照应,表示过去有过某种经验或经历。与表示动作完成的"了"不能混在一起用。应删去"了",改用"过"。

"曾经" often occurs with the aspect particle "过" in correlation to indicate an experience in the past. It can not be used with "了"

88

which denotes completion of an action. "了" should be replaced
with "过".

例 216

误：我的朋友曾经学三年英语。

正：我的朋友曾经学过三年英语。

原句的意思是，我的朋友有学习三年英语的经历。应当在"学"
的后边加"过"。

The speaker means that his friend has the experience of learning English for three years. "过" should be added after "学".

例 217

误：我不曾经去过那儿。

正：我不曾去过那儿。

"曾经"的否定形式是"不曾"，不能说"不曾经"。

The negative form of "曾经" is "不曾". There is no such form
as "不曾经".

例 218

误：我们班曾经不参观过农村。

正：我们班不曾参观过农村。

"曾经"与否定词"不"词序颠倒，应颠倒过来。由于"曾经"的否
定形式为"不曾"，须删去"经"字。

"曾经" and the negation word "不" are in reverse order and
must be transposed. Since the negative form of "曾经" is "不曾",
"经" should be deleted.

例 219

误：我过去已经去过好几次故宫。

正：我过去曾经去过好几次故宫。

"已经"和"曾经"混淆。"已经"所指的时间可以延续到说话时，
并且所指相关的事件可能还要延续下去，而"曾经"所限定的动作

行为（"去故宫"）早已结束。应该用"曾经"代替"已经"。

Here "已经" is confused with "曾经". The time that "已经" refers to may last until the point of utterance, and the relevant incident will probably continue. On the contrary, the action modified by "曾经" finished long ago. "曾经" should be used instead of "已经".

例 **220**

误：我在北京语言文化大学的学习已经快要结束了。

正：我在北京语言文化大学的学习已经结束了。

正：我在北京语言文化大学的学习快要结束了。

"已经"表示事情完成或时间过去，"快要"表示在很短的时间以内就要出现某种情况。在语义上，这两个词相互矛盾，可以任取其一。

"已经" indicates completion of an event or passing of time. "快要" suggests that something will happen soon. These two words are contradictory in meaning. One can only choose one of them.

例 **221**

误：已经我们研究（了）那个问题了。

正：我们已经研究（了）那个问题了。

在汉语里，"已经"应放在动词谓语的前边，作修饰成分。把"已经我们"改成"我们已经研究"。

In Chinese, "已经" premodifies the verbal predicate. One should change "已经我们" into "我们已经".

例 **222**

误：她已经身体好了。

正：她身体已经好了。

"已经"用在主谓谓语句中，不能作谓语"身体好"的修饰成分。应该移到小谓语"好"的前头。

When "已经" is used in a sentence with a S-P (subject-predicate) phrase predicate, it can not precede the predicate "身体好" as the modifier. One should move it to the front of the predicate of the S-P phrase —"好".

都

all

例 223

误：下课的时候都我们去外边休息。

正：下课的时候我们都去外边休息。

"都"与它前边的表示复数的词语相联系，起总括前边成分的作用，说明后边的动作行为没有例外。这种用法的"都"不能放在主语"我们"的前边，应在主语的后边。作状语。

"都" is used to sum up the preceding elements which are words indicating plural to express that there is no exception. It can not go before the subject "我们" but should stay behind as an adverbial adjunct.

例 224

误：我们都去国际俱乐部，只有阿里去友谊商店。

正：除了阿里去友谊商店，我们都去国际俱乐部。

既然用"都"表示"我们"的行动是一致的，怎么又提出阿里的行为动作与"我们"不同？前后矛盾，应将动词词组"只有"改成介词"除了"。

Where "都" is used to express that "我们" all went to the same place, there should not be another statement saying that "阿里" went to a different place. The sentence lacks consistency. One should replace the verbal phrase "只有" with the preposition "除了".

例 225

误:大家为他学习上的进步都感到高兴。

正:大家都为他学习上的进步感到高兴。

"都"所总括的成分不是由"为"构成的介宾词组,不是"大家"。应该把副词"都"提到"为他学习上的进步"之前。

"都" refers to "大家" rather than the prepositional phrase formed by "为". It should be placed before "为他学习上的进步".

例 226

误:你们都学习汉语,他们都也学习汉语。

正:你们都学习汉语,他们也都学习汉语。

"都"和"也"词序颠倒,必须对调位置,表示"你们"和"他们"的动作行为("学习汉语")一样。

"都" and "也" are in the wrong order and should be reversed to indicate that "你们" also learn Chinese as "他们" do.

例 227

误:这个班有十个学生,都不是非洲的,还有亚洲的。

正:这个班有十个学生,不都是非洲的,还有亚洲的。

"都不"和"不都"混淆。"都不"是否定全部事物,"不都"是否定部分事物。在语义上,前后两个分句是矛盾的。既然用"都不"否定这个班的学生全部不是非洲的,就没有必要而且也不应该再用"还"补充说明另外一部分亚洲学生。如要保留"还",应改用"不都"。表示一部分是非洲的学生,一部分是亚洲学生。

Here "都不" is confused with "不都". "都不" applies to all in a whole while "不都" applies to only part of a whole. The two clauses are semantically contradictory. Since "都不" has already suggested that no student in the class is from Africa, it is unnecessary and wrong to add with "还" that others are from Asia. If "还" is to be kept, one should use "不都" to indicate that some are African students and some are Asian students.

例 228

A：星期天你都作什么？

误 B：星期天我都洗衣服、写信、去看朋友了。

正 B：星期天我洗衣服、写信、去看朋友了。

"都"用在含有疑问代词（"什么"）构成的特指问中，强调它后边的疑问词所能表示的范围，从答案中可以看出，星期天作的每一件事情"洗衣服"、"写信"、"看朋友"就是"都"所指的内容，为此，在陈述句中"都"不能重现。该句应当删去"都"。

In a special question formed with an interrogative pronoun ("什么"), "都" stresses the scope of reference covered by the interrogative word. It can be understood from the answer that "都" refers to all the activities on Sunday including "洗衣服", "写信", "看朋友". Thus it can not occur in the answer and should be deleted.

多么

how

例 229

误：她汉语多么说得好啊！

正：她汉语说得多么好啊！

"多么"不能用在表示动作的动词"说"的前边，只能限制补语"好"。赞叹她的汉语口头表达能力。

"多么" can not precede the action verb "说". It can only premodifies the complement "好" to express admiration at her spoken ability in Chinese.

例 230

误：老师多么工作认真啊！

正：老师工作多么认真啊！

句子主干是"老师工作认真"，"工作认真"是主谓词组，作谓语,在这种句子里,"多么"不能修饰谓语,应当移到由形容词"认真"充当的小谓语之前,作修饰语,赞美老师的工作态度。

The main part of the sentence is "老师工作认真" in which "工作认真" is a subject-predicate (S-P) phrase serving as the predicate. In this type of sentence,"多么" can not premodify the predicate. It must be shifted to the front of the predicate of the S-P phrase expressed in the present sentence by the adjective "认真" to be the modifier. The speaker praises the working attitude of the teacher.

例 231

误:虽然天气多么冷啊!可是他还是坚持锻炼身体。

正:虽然天气很冷,可是他还是坚持锻炼身体。

"虽然"和"可是"是表示转折关系的关联词,是用来陈述事实的,前个分句却是个感叹句;应该用"很"代表"多么",用逗号代替感叹号,并删去语气词"啊"。

"虽然" and "可是" which are correlative words expressing adverse relation are used in statements. The first clause is an exclamation. One should change it into a statement. That is, use "很" instead of "多么", substitute a comma for the exclamation mark and delete the interjection "啊".

例 232

误:今天的天气多么很暖和啊!

正:今天的天气多么暖和啊!

正:今天的天气很暖和。

"多么"和"很"都是表示程度的副词,"多么"只能用于感叹句,"很"只能用于陈述句,这两个用途不同的词不能混在一起用。原句是感叹句,应当去掉"很"。如要保留"跟",则应删去"多么"和"啊",改成陈述句,句尾的感叹号改用句号。

Both "多么" and "很" are degree adverbs. "多么" is used in an exclamatory sentence while "很" is not. These two words of different uses should not be mixed up together. The original sentence is an exclamation, and can not have "很". If "很" is to be kept, the sentence must be converted into a statement by dropping "多么" and "啊" and ending up with a period instead of an exclamation mark.

例 233

误:他的房间多么干干净净啊!

正:他的房间多么干净啊!

"干干净净"是形容词"干净"的重叠形式,表示程度加深。因此,不能受"多么"的修饰,必须把重叠的"干干净净"改用它的原形"干净",才能与"多么"搭配使用。

"干干净净" is the reduplicative form of the adjective "干净" implying a high degree of cleanliness. Thus it can not be modified by "多么". It must revert to its simple form "干净" to go with "多么".

刚

just

例 234

误:刚到语言学院以后就上课了。

正:刚到语言学院就上课了。

"就"与"刚"呼应,强调两个动作"到"和"上课"相隔时间很短;"以后"表示动作时间的延续,就时间来说先后有矛盾。应当删去"以后"。

"就" and "刚" go together to emphasize that the two actions "到" and "上课" happened in quick succession. "以后" refers to any time after a particular point. It makes the sentence incoherent and must be deleted.

例 235

误:他们刚是北京大学的学生。

正:他们刚成为北京大学的学生。

副词"刚"强调情况或行动发生的时间和当时很贴近,用来修饰动词。但不修饰表示判断的动词"是"。应改"是"为"成为"。

The adverb "刚" stresses that a state or an action comes into being just before the present time. It is used to modify verbs, with the exception of verb "是" which expresses judgement. One should replace "是" with "成为".

还

still

例 236

误:这个电影太好了,我想看一遍。

正:这个电影太好了,我还想看一遍。

是说"这个电影太好了",所以"我"产生了看第二遍的想法。应当在"我"的后边加"还",表示未然动作的重复。

The speaker considers the movie very good, so he wants to watch it for the second time. "还" should be added after "我" to indicate the possible repetition of an action.

例 237

误:他们班上星期去长城了,我们班下星期还要去。

正:他们班上星期去长城了,我们班下星期也要去。

因为要表示在"去长城"的行为活动方面,"我们班"同"他们班"是类同的。应当把"还"改成"也"。

To express that our class will also go to the Great Wall as their class did; one should use "也" rather than "还".

例 238

96

误:大夫,我还这儿疼。

正:大夫,我这儿还疼。

由主谓词组"这儿疼"作谓语的句子里,"还"不能放在大谓语"这儿疼"前,只能放在小谓语"疼"前,作状语,表示"依旧"。

In this sentence, the subject-predicate (S-P) phrase "这儿疼" serves as the predicate. "还" can not occur before it, but should precede its predicate "疼", meaning "still".

例 239

误:你借给我的那本书,我没还看。

正:你借给我的那本书,我还没看呢。

原句的意思是,你借给我的那本书,我现在没看,但是迟早是要看的,一般用"还没……(呢)"表示。把错位的"没还"调换过来就可以了。

The meaning of the sentence is, I haven't read the book borrowed from you, but will sooner or later. This is usually expressed with "还没…呢". One should reverse the word order of "没还".

也

too

例 240

误:我喜欢游泳,他喜欢游泳。

正:我喜欢游泳,他也喜欢游泳。

两个分句的主语"我"和"他"喜欢的是同一类体育活动("游泳"),只有在后个分句动词前加"也",句子才通顺。

"我" and "他" like the same kind of sport ("游泳"). To express the meaning of "also", "也" should be used after the verb of the second clause.

例 241

误:我看画报,也我看杂志。

正：我看画报，我也看杂志。

"也"不能放在主语的前边。应移到主语"我"的后边，作谓语动词"看"的状语。

"也" can not precede the subject. It should follow the subject as an adverbial adjunct of the predicate verb ("看").

例 242

误：你去哪儿，我们都也去哪儿。

正：你去哪儿，我们也都去哪儿。

动词前，"也"和"都"连用，"都"不能用在"也"的前边。须将"都"移到"也"的后边。

When "也" and "都" are both used before the verb, "都" follows "也" rather than precede it.

例 243

误：北京的冬天不但很冷，而且也常常刮风。

正：北京的冬天(不但)很冷，(而且)还常常刮风。

因为要说"冷"是北京冬天的特征，"常常刮风"是北京冬天的另一特征，所以要改"也"为有所补充的"还"。

To express that "常常刮风" is another characteristic of winter in Beijing besides "冷", "也" should be replaced by "还" which means "in addition".

例 244

误：愚公说："我死了以后有儿子，儿子死了也有孙子……"

正：愚公说："我死了以后有儿子，儿子死了还有孙子……"

"儿子、孙子"都是指的一家人，但是不是相同的辈份，不具同一性。不能用"也"。"儿子、孙子"是增加的人口，要用"还"。

"儿子"and "孙子" are members from the same clan belong to different generations, so "也" can not be used here. One should use "还" to emphasize continuity of the clan.

例 245

误：他的中文水平提高得很快，甚至鲁迅的小说能看了。

正：他的中文水平提高得很快，甚至鲁迅的小说也能看了。

这个句子中表示同一的事物没有都出现，隐去了前一个，只出现了表示同一的后一个："鲁迅的小说能看了"。如果把前一个补出来就更清楚了："他的中文水平提高得很快，可以看中文报，甚至鲁迅的小说也能看了"。句中用"甚至"表示强调同一性。

Add "也" before "能". The sentence has not presented both of the two elements belonging to the identical category（看中文书报）. Only one is present —"鲁迅的小说能看了". It will be more clear if we supply the other one — "他的中文水平提高得很快，可·以·看·中文报，甚至鲁迅的小说也能看了". "甚至" is used to intensify iden-·tity·.

很

very

例 246

误：最近我们比较很忙。

正：最近我们很忙。

正：最近我们比较忙。

"很"和"比较"是两个程度上具有差别的词，不能连用，只能取其中的一个。

"很" and "比较" are two words different in degree. One can not use both, but should make a choice.

例 247

误：那里天气很冷，还常很刮风。

正：那里天气很冷，还常刮大风。

句中用"很"，是要强调风力大，而"很"同其他表示程度的副词一样，不能修饰表示动作的动词"刮"。应改"很刮风"为"刮大风"。

The speaker uses "很" to indicate that the wind is strong. But like other degree adverbs, "很" can not modify such action verbs as "刮". "很刮风" should be changed into "刮大风".

例 248

误:这条裤子很合适不合适?

正:这条裤子合适不合适?

由于询问的是说话人所不了解的情况,所以采用正反式提问。只能并列形容词的原形("合适不合适"),应当删去"很"。

The affirmative negative question is used here to inquire what the speaker does not know. In such a question, the affirmative and negative forms of the adjective are placed together. "很" must be deleted.

极(了)

extremely, so

例 249

误:这个展览很好看极了。

正:这个展览好看极了。

在同一个句子里,不能用两个表示程度高的词语,可以任选其一。"极了"含夸张意味,口语中常用。

A sentence can not have two intensifying words. One must choose between "很" and "极了". "极了" implying an exaggerated overtone is common in spoken Chinese.

例 250

误:公园里的人多极了不多极了?

正:公园里的人多不多?

因为询问的是说话人所不了解的某种情况,所以用正反式提问。谓语后边不能带表示程度的补语"极了"。

The speaker uses an affirmative-negative question to ask what he does not know. The predicate of the question can not carry a degree complement ("极了").

究竟

on earth

例 251

误：你究竟去天津学习专业吗？

正：你究竟去不去天津学习专业？

正：你去天津学习专业吗？

用"吗"的疑问句只要求听话的人表示肯定或者否定，而"究竟"表示追究，希望知道真实的情况。这两个词不能混杂在一起，或者删去"吗"，改成"究竟去不去天津学习专业"，或者删去"究竟"。

An interrogative sentence in which "吗" is used merely expects an affirmative or a negative answer. But "究竟" is used in a detailed inquiry to ask for the actual situation. "吗" and "究竟" can not be used together. One may delete "吗" and change the sentence into "究竟去不去天津学习专业？" or delete "究竟".

决心

determine, determination

例 252

误：听了医生的话，我决心了锻炼身体。

正：听了医生的话，我决心锻炼身体。

正：听了医生的话，我下决心锻炼身体。

"决心"是副词，常用在动词谓语前，作状语。"决心"也可以是名词，常组成"下决心""有决心"，后面往往还带有动宾词组。此句或者删去"了"，改成"决心锻炼身体"，或者改成"下决心锻炼身体"。

"决心" is an adverb. It normally precedes the predicate as an adverbial adjunct. It is also a noun which often forms the phrases

"下决心"，"有决心"，and usually followed by a verb-object phrase in a sentence. One may delete "了" and say "决心锻炼身体". One may also say "下决心锻炼身体".

恐怕

be afraid that

例 253

误：我恐怕天要下大雨了。

正：恐怕（天）要下大雨了。

"恐怕"表示人们主观上对自然现象的估计，可能要下雨。在这种句子里，第一人称的"我"不必出现。

"恐怕" here implies the subjective prediction about a natural phenomenon, i.e. there is going to be a heavy rain. In this kind of sentence, "我" denoting the first person singular need not be present.

例 254

误：我恐怕他要生病了。

正：恐怕他要生病了。

这里"恐怕"表示估计而兼担心将会怎么样的意思。如果是本人对自己的估计和担心，可以说"我恐怕要生病了"或"恐怕我要生病了"。对他人情况的估计，担心时，不能用第一人称，要直接用其他人称。这个句子可以改成"恐怕他要生病了"。

Here "恐怕" expresses the prediction as well as worries about an occurrence. If the prediction is about the speaker himself, one may say "我恐怕要生病了" or "恐怕我要生病了". If it is about other people, one can not use the first person "我". Only words indicating other people should be used. One may say "恐怕他要生病了".

快要

soon

例 255

误:快要下雨,我们赶快回学校吧!

正:快要下雨了,我们赶快回学校吧!

由"快要"构成的格式不完整,应加语气助词"了"与之呼应。"快要……了"表示在很短的时间之内就要出现某种情况。

The above sentence beginning with "快要" is incomplete. The interjection "了" should be used to go with "快要". "快要…了" indicates that an event is likely to happen soon.

例 256

误:我们已经快要毕业了。

正:我们快要毕业了。

正:我们已经毕业了。

"已经"和"快要"这两个表示时间范围截然不同的词杂糅在一起了。或者删去"已经",保留"快要",表示即将毕业。或者删去"快要",保留"已经",表示"毕业"成为事实。

"已经" and "快要" are of different temporal reference and can not be used together. To express graduation is at hand, one should delete "已经" and use "快要". If graduation is already a reality, one should delete "快要" and retain "已经".

例 257

误:快要大风了,快关上窗户吧!

正:快要刮大风了,快关上窗户吧!

"快要"是副词,应该用在谓语前作状语。联系上下文,应在"快要"之后加上谓词动词"刮"。

"快要" is an adverb. It occurs before the predicate as an adverbial adjunct. According to the context, we add "刮" after "快要" to be the predicate verb.

例 258

误:现在六点五十五分了,快要音乐会开始了。

正:现在六点五十五分了,音乐会快要开始了。

"快要"不能放在主语"音乐会"前,只能放在其后,作谓语动词"开始"的修饰成分。表示时间紧迫。

"快要" may not precede the subject "音乐会", but can only follow it as a modifier of the predicate verb "开始", meaning "to be about to".

一定

certainly, surely

例 259

误:我一定知道他对跳舞不感兴趣。

正:我知道他一定对跳舞不感兴趣。

句中"一定"表示对某种行为事物确实无疑,但不能用于第一人称,因不合事理。可用于其他人称。

"一定" here means that something is definitely a fact in somebody's eyes. In this case it is unreasonable for "一定" to occur with the first person. It only occurs with the second or the third person.

例 260

误:这些是学过的生词,我一定记住了。

正:这些是学过的生词,我一定记住。

"一定"也可以表示一个人主观意愿要求。在这种情况下可以用于第一人称。既是主观的意愿,肯定动作行为是未实现的,"记住"后不能用表示事情已经完成的"了"。

"一定" can also be used to indicate one's subjective will. In this case, it can occur with the first person. A subjective will is something unrealized, thus "记住" here can not be followed by

104

″了″ which denotes completion of an action.

例 261

误：我们能学好中文一定。

正：我们一定能学好中文。

"一定"不能放在句尾，要移到主语之后。

″一定″ can not be used at the end of a sentence，but must be put after the subject.

例 262

误：他说明天可能有事，一定不来。

正：他说明天可能有事，不一定来。

"一定不"与"不一定"混淆。"一定不"表示坚决、否定的态度，而"不一定"表示情况不能肯定，是对行为动作的估计。根据原句意，应当改为"不一定"。

Here ″一定不″ is confused with ″不一定″. ″一定不″ indicates a firm attitude of negation，while ″不一定″ indicates uncertainty and also carries a tone of conjecture. According to the original meaning，one should use ″不一定″.

例 263

误：你放心，我不一定会忘记给你买书。

正：你放心，我一定不会忘记给你买书。

主语用第一人称"我"，在这种情况下，"一定"的否定形式要用"一定不"。有肯定记住的意思。

The subject is the first person ″我″. In this case，the negation of ″一定″ is ″一定不″. ″一定不会忘记″ means ″will certainly remember″.

例 264

误：你一定不告诉他这件事。

正：你一定不要(别)告诉他这件事。

主语用第二人称"你",否定式应当用"一定别"、"一定不要"、"一定不能"等,含劝阻的意思。

The subject is the second person "你". In this case, the negation of "一定别", or "一定不要" or "一定不能" etc. to indicate dissuasion.

例 265

误:一年来我的汉字一定写得比以前好。

正:一年来我的汉字确实(的确)写得比以前好。

英语中的 Surely,可译成"一定、确实、的确"等词。此句意在肯定某种既成的事实,强调确定不疑的判断,应删去"一定",改用"确实"、"的确"等表示判断的词语。

"Surely" in English can be translated into Chinese as "一定", "确实", "的确" etc. The speaker wants to affirm an accomplished fact and to stress that the judgement is beyond doubt. He ought to use "确实", "的确" or other words expressing judgement instead of "一定".

又

again

例 266

误:他想下星期又去一次友谊商店。

正:他想下星期再去一次友谊商店。

"想"说明重复的行为动作("去友谊商店")并未实现,后边的"又"却表示重复的行为动作已经成为事实,前后矛盾。应改"又"为"再"。

"想" implies that the repetition of the action "去友谊商店" has not been accomplished. At the opposite pole, "又" shows that the repetition of the action is already a fait accompli. Therefore, the sentence is inconsistent. "又" should be replaced with "再".

106

再

once again

例 267

误：这个电影前天我再看了一遍。

正：这个电影前天我又看了一遍。

"看了"表明重复的动作行为已经实现（已然）。要用表示已然的"又"，不能用"再"。

"看了" indicates that the action has already been repeated (a fait accompli). Thus "又" should be used instead of "再".

例 268

误：我听不懂，你告诉我再一遍。

正：我听不懂，你再说一遍。

因为我听不懂，请求对方再说（讲）一遍，所以应改动词"告诉"为"说"或"讲"。又因"再"的后边不能直接跟数量词，还应把"再"移到动词"说"的前边。

The hearer does not understand the speaker and asks him to repeat what he said. On such occasion, he should use "说" or "讲" instead of "告诉". Moreover, "再" can not be followed immediately by a numeral-measure word phrase. It must precede the verb "说".

例 269

误：我去买啤酒，咱们跟他一块儿再喝。

正：我去买啤酒，咱们再跟他一块儿喝。

谓语动词的前边有其他修饰成分，应当把"再"放在其他修饰成分"跟他"和"一块儿"的前头。

When the predicate verb is preceded by other modifiers besides "再", such as "跟他" and "一块儿" in the present sentence, "再" is usually put in front of them.

例 270

误:他照了几张相后,再不照了,留下几张明天照。

正:他照了几张相后,不再照了,留下几张明天照。

"再不"与"不再"混淆。"再不"表示坚决或永远不会如何,"不再"表示某个动作不重复或继续下去。原句说"留下几张明天照"。显而易见,没有永远不照相的意思,应改"再不"为"不再"。

Here "再不" is confused with "不再". "再不" indicates one's resolution not to do something or simply "will forever not...". "不再" expresses that an action will not repeat or continue. In the present sentence, "留下几张明天照" obviously shows that the speaker does not mean "他" will no longer take photographs". Thus "不再" is the proper word.

例 271

误:他要永远留在她身边,不再走了。

正:他要永远留在她身边,再不走了。

明确表示"要永远留在她身边"。应改"不再"为"再不"。

One should use "再不" rather than "不再" to show his resolution to stay by her side.

例 272

误:来这儿以后,我跟我的朋友再有联系。

正:来这儿以后,我跟我的朋友还有联系。

"我"跟朋友之间的联系没有因为"我来这儿以后"有什么变化。应当把"再"改为行为继续进行的"还"。

The speaker means that he has kept in contact with his friends though he came here. "还" should be used instead of "再" to indicate continuity.

例 273

误:虽然比较忙,但是再有时间复习。

正:虽然比较忙,但是还有时间复习。

"虽然比较忙",但"有时间复习"的情况并没有改变。"再"应当改用"还"。

We prefer "还" rather than "再" to indicate that there is no change in the situation, i. e. one still has time of revision though busy.

例 274

误:他看完了电影再走了。

正:他看完了电影就走了。

要强调两个已经实现的动作("看"和"走")相继发生,不宜用"再",应改用"就"。

To emphasize that two completed actions took place one after another, "再" must be replaced by "就".

例 275

误:明天再是星期天了。

正:明天又是星期天了。

表示周期性的重复,应当用"又",删去"再"。

To indicate periodic repetition, "又" rather than "再" should be used here.

在(正、正在)

in course of

例 276

误:你去看他,他正在什么呢?

正:你去看他,他正在做什么呢?

"正在"是副词,放在谓语动词前作状语,表示动作在进行之中。句中"正在"后缺少谓语,联系上下文,应补上动词"做"。询问"正在"从事的活动。

"正在" is an adverb which precedes the predicate verb as an

adverbial adjunct to express that an action is in progress. This sentence has lost the predicate verb. We add verb "做" in accordance with the context to ask about the activity in progress.

例 277

误：别叫阿里了，正他准备考试呢。

正：别叫阿里了，他正准备考试呢。

"正"不能放在主语之前，要把"正"放到主语"他"后，作谓语动词"准备"的修饰成分。

"正" can not precede the subject 他 but must follow it as a modifier of the predicate verb ("准备").

例 278

误：我们早上五点出发的，你可能正在睡觉了。

正：我们早上五点出发的，你可能正在睡觉呢。

"正在" expresses that an action is in progress whereas "了" at the end of a sentence indicates completion of an action or change of state. They do not go together. One should delete "了" and use "呢".

例 279

误：我在要打电话找你，你来了。

正：我正要打电话找你，你来了。

是说就在准备给对方打电话的时候，恰好对方来了。不该用"在"，而应该用"正"。

The speaker means that just as he was about to make a telephone call the person he wanted came. "正" rather than "在" should be used.

例 280

误：快走吧，大家已经正等着你呢。

正：快走吧，大家正等着你呢。

110

"正"着重指动作进行的时间;"已经"指动作行为在这个时间之前发生,相互矛盾。根据上下文,删去"已经"。

"正" and "已经" are two contradictory concepts in that "正" means "in the course of an action" and "已经" indicates that an action occurred before a certain time. We delete "已经" according to the context.

只

only

例 281

误:我问只一个问题。

正:我只问一个问题。

副词"只"必须放在动词"问"前,"只"的作用就是限定宾语("问题")前的数量"一个",强调与动作行为有关数量的有限性。

The adverb "只" must precede the verb "问". Its function is to qualify the measure word "一个" before the object ("问题"), to show that the quantity in relation to an action is limited.

例 282

误:他们有中文书,英文书,没只有阿文书。

正:他们有中文书,英文书,只没有阿文书。

原句意表明他们有各种文字的书,没有的只是阿文书。"只"修饰的是"没有",应放在"没有"前。

The sentence means that they have books in various languages except Arabic. What "只" modifies is "没有". Hence it should be put before "没有".

例 283

误:只努力学习,才能取得好成绩。

正:只有努力学习,才能取得好成绩。

说明表示"取得好成绩"的唯一条件是"努力学习"。因此要用连词"只有"，不能用副词"只"。

To express that a prerequisite for "取得好成绩" is "努力学习", one should use the conjunction "只有" rather than the adverb "只".

九、介词的误用
Errors in the Use of Prepositions

按照

as，according to

例 284

误：按照天气预报，明天有大雨。

正：根据天气预报，明天有大雨。

"按照"与"根据"混淆。"按照"强调以某种事物为依据，不折不扣照着办。而"明天有大雨"这一判断是以科学（即天气预报）为基础。不能用"按照"，应改用"根据"。

Here "按照" is confused with "根据". "按照" stresses to act exactly as something suggests. The judgement that "明天有大雨" is made on scientific grounds (i. e. the weather report). One can not use "按照" but should use "根据".

例 285

误：按照他说，下个月我们该去上海学习专业了。

正：按照他说的，下个月我们该去上海学习专业了。

"按照"的宾语须是名词性的。把"他说"改为"他说的"或者"他说的话"都可以。

"按照" always takes a noun as its object. "他说" should be changed into "他说的" or "他说的话".

例 286

误：我们都作作业，按照老师的方法。

正：我们都按照老师的方法作作业。

根据本句的实际，由"按照"构成的介宾词组可以移到"都"与"作"之间，表示主语"我们"的动作行为没有例外。

This sentence requires the prepositional phrase formed by "按照" to go between "都" and the predicate verb "作".

根据

in line with, according to

例 287

误：根据学校的规定，我们早上八点上课。

正：按照学校的规定，我们早上八点上课。

原句有照着去办的意思，应改"根据"为"按照"。

To mean "following the school regulation", one should use "按照" instead of "根据".

跟

with

例 288

误：地主逼林道静住在一起跟一个有钱的人。

正：地主逼林道静跟一个有钱的人住在一起。

在汉语里，用介词"跟"组成的介宾词组不能放在句尾，只能放在谓语动词的前边，用来引进动作的对象。应把"跟一个有钱的人"移到"住"的前头。

In Chinese, a prepositional phrase formed by the preposition "跟" and its object can not be put at the end of a sentence. It must precede the predicate verb to introduce the partner (s) or opponent(s) engaged in an action together with the subject. "跟一个有钱的人" should be moved to the front of "住".

从

from

例 289

误：你哪个国家来的？

正：你从哪个国家来的？

要说明动作"来"以"哪个国家"做起点，一般须用介词"从"，应当在"哪个国家"的前边加上"从"字。

The preposition "从" should be used before "哪个国家" to introduce it as the starting point of action "来".

例 290

误：他从上课回宿舍去。

正：他从上课的教室（地方）回宿舍去。

作为表示空间起点的"从"，它的宾语必须是处所词语，应把"上课"改成"上课的教室"、"上课的地方"等。

"从" which introduces the starting point of an action requires words denoting locality as its objects. "上课" should be replaced with "上课的教室" or "上课的地方".

例 291

误：丁力从他朋友去大使馆。

正：丁力从他朋友那儿去大使馆。

"从"的宾语"他朋友"不表示处所，应改成"他朋友这儿（近指）"或者"他朋友那儿（远指）"。

In this sentence, the object of "从"—"他朋友" does not indicate locality. It must take "这儿" or "那儿" to be "他朋友这儿 (close reference)" and "他朋友那儿 (distant reference)".

例 292

误：阿里买来一个录音机从上海。

正：阿里从上海买来一个录音机。

在汉语里，由"从"构成的介宾词组不能放在句子末尾，应当提到谓语动词之前。把"从上海"改在"买"的前面。

In Chinese, the prepositional phrase formed by "从" and its object can not occur at the end of a sentence. It must precede the predicate verb. Put "从上海" before "买".

例 293

误：他从操场上跑步。

正：他在操场上跑步。

"操场上"指动作发生的处所。不能用介词"从"，应改用"在"。

"操场上" denotes place of an action. It may not be preceded by "从". One should use "在".

例 294

误：她妈每天从家去工厂早晨六点钟。

正：她妈每天早上六点钟从家去工厂。

句中出现表示时间起点和处所起点的词语。按汉语表达方式，表地点起点的词语应靠近动词，其次是表时间的词语。

When two words which denote starting points in time and in place respectively occur in the identical sentence, the former should precede the latter which is closer to the verb.

例 295

误：车一停，他很快地车上跑下来。

正：车一停，他很快地从车上跑下来。

充当状语的处所词语"车上"与表示随着动作离开高处到达低处的"跑下来"在语义上配不拢，应在"车上"的前边加上表示起点的"从"，改"车上"为"从车上"。

The locality phrase "车上" used here as an adverbial adjunct does not go with the verbal phrase "跑下来" which denotes a motion proceeding from an upper position to a lower position. "从" is needed before "车上".

例 296

误:老人说:狼小路逃走了。

正:老人说:狼从小路逃走了。

用作状语的处所词"小路"与谓语动词"逃"不搭配,应在"小路"的前边加上"从",表示经过的地方。

The locality phrase "小路" does not match with the predicate verb "逃" as its adverbial adjunct. "从" should be put before "小路" to mean "by way of".

例 297

误:到了十字路口,从右拐就行了。

正:到了十字路口,往右拐就行了。

"拐"有转变方向的意思,句中用表示起点的"从"不妥,应当改成表示方向的介词"往"或"向"。

"拐" involves a change of direction. Hence "从" used to indicate starting point is improper here. It should be replaced by the preposition "往" or "向" to express direction.

自从

since, from the time

例 298

误:他自从上海去广州。

正:他从上海去广州。

"自从"一般只能用来表示时间的起点,句中说的是"去"的起点,不能用"自从",改用"从"。也可说"自上海去广州",但多用于书面语。

"自从" only denotes a starting point in time. But departure of "去" is a place. Thus one should use "从" instead of "自从". One may also say "自上海去广州" which occurs in written Chinese.

116

例 **299**

误：我自从1986年学习汉语。

正：自从1986年来北京后我开始学习汉语。

"自从"往往以某一事件发生的时间为起点，常和主谓词组、动宾词组结合，不能用单个时间词。"1986年"应改为"1986年来北京后"。由"自从"构成的词组要放在主语"我"的前边。

"自从" is usually combined with a subject-predicate phrase or an verb-object phrase to indicate that an occurrence is the starting point of a state. It never takes a single time noun as its object. One should say "1986年来北京后" instead of just "1986年". The phrase starting with "自从" must precede the subject "我".

例 **300**

误：自从明年起，我要到清华大学学习专业。

正：从明年起，我要到清华大学学习专业。

"自从"所表示的时间起点只能是过去的，因此，不能说"自从明年起"，改为"从明年起"。

The starting point introduced by "自从" is always a time in the past. Thus, one may not say "自从明年起". "从明年起" is the right form.

当

while，when

例 **301**

误：当我学习上遇到困难，就请老师都助我。

正：当我学习上遇到困难的时候，就请老师都助我。

"当"经常与"的时候"或"时"前后照应，构成格式"当……（的）时（候）"，作时间状语，表示"正在……的时候"。应在"困难"后边加上"（的）时（候）"。

"当" is often used in correlation with "的时候" or "时" to

form the pattern "当…(的)时(候)" which serves as adverbial adjunct of time, meaning "at the time when...." "(的)时(候)" should be added after "困难".

例 302

误：当我们来到北京语言学院的时候，热情地欢迎我们。

正：当我们来到北京语言学院的时候，中国朋友热情地欢迎我们。

"当……的时候"是时间状语，全句缺少主语。谁"热情地欢迎我们"？可以理解为中国朋友、中国老师。应当明确地补上主语。

"当…的时候" is an adverbial adjunct of time. The subject is missing. We do not know who "热情地欢迎我们". One should add the subject, such as "中国朋友" or "中国老师".

对

toward(s)

例 303

误：他不太礼貌对老师。

正：他对老师不太礼貌。

正：对老师，他不太礼貌。

表示人际间的对待关系时，"对老师"可放在谓语前，也可以放在主语前。如果用在主语"他"前边的时候，句中要有停顿。

When "对" with its object is used to indicate attitude or treatment towards people, it may precede the predicate or the subject but with a pause in between.

例 304

误：小王不对他很热情。

正：小王对他不很热情。

在用"对"表示人与人之间关系的句子里，如果谓语之前带有"很"一类程度副词，"不"否定的不是"对"，而是"很"。应改"不对"

118

为"不很"，表示"热情"的程度减弱。

In a sentence using "对" to show interpersonal relation, the element negated by "不" is not "对", but the degree adverb proceeding the predicate, like "很" here. Thus, it should be "不很" rather than "不对" that expresses a lower degree of "热情".

例 305

误：我已经对大家通知了。

正：我已经通知大家了。

动词"通知"的用法通常是"通知某人"或"通知某人某事"。删去介词"对"，改成"通知大家"就可以了。

The verb "通知" is generally used in the pattern "通知某人" or "通知某人某事". One should delete the preposition "对" and just say "通知大家".

例 306

误：京剧对他俩很感兴趣。

正：他俩对京剧很感兴趣。

"对"介绍的对象弄错了，应调换"京剧"和"他俩"的位置，改成"他俩感兴趣"。"京剧"是"感兴趣"的对象。

"对" has introduced the wrong object. By exchanging the positions of "京剧" and "他俩", we make "他俩" the subject of the sentence, and "京剧" the object of "感兴趣" introduced by "对".

对于

to, toward(s)

例 307

误：他对于我们很热情。

正：他对我们很热情。

因为要表示"他"对待"我们"的态度，所以不能用"对于"，只能用"对"。

"对" rather than "对于" should be used to express one's attitude towards others.

例 308

误:这种药说话有副作用。

正:这种药对于说话有副作用。

为进一步表明"这种药有副作用"的指向,应当在动宾词组"说话"前边加上介词"对于"。

The preposition "对于" must be added before the verb-object phrase "说话" to introduce it as the object of "有副作用".

例 309

误:我们要对于这个问题进行研究。

正:我们要对这个问题进行研究。

"对于"的前边一般不能用能愿动词,应删去多余的"于"。

Auxiliary verbs are impossible before the preposition "对于". "于" is redundant and should be deleted.

例 310

误:他们都对于这件事感兴趣。

正:他们都对这件事感兴趣。

介词"对于"通常不受副词的修饰,可以把"对于"改成"对"。

It is unusual for the preposition "对于" to be modified by adverbs. "对" is the proper word.

关于

concerning, about, with respect to

例 311

误:对于去南方旅行的路线,我想听听大家的意见。

正:关于去南方旅行的路线,我想听听大家的意见。

"对于"指出动作的对象,"关于"表示关涉的事物。"听听"涉及到"去南方旅行的路线"的意见,要用"关于"代替"对于"。

"对于" introduces the object of an action, and "关于" brings forward the matters concerned. The content of "听听" is opinions concerning "去南方旅行的路线", so one should use "关于" instead of "对于".

例 312

误:他们正在讨论一些问题关于汉语语法。

正:他们正在讨论一些关于汉语语法的问题。

这个句子是 They are discussing something about Chinese grammar 的直译。汉语的表达方式是把"关于汉语语法"提到"问题"的前边,同时加"的",作修饰成分。

This sentence is the literal interpretation of "They are discussing something about Chinese grammar" in English. In Chinese, "关于汉语语法" with the structural particle "的" attached to it should be put before "问题" as an attributive.

给

give

例 313

误:老师讲语法给我们。

正:老师给我们讲语法。

用"给"引进动作对象"我们"组成的介宾词组,要移到动词谓语"讲"前,作状语。

The prepositional phrase composed of "给" and the object "我们" should be shifted to the front of the verbal predicate "讲" to serve as an adverbial adjunct.

例 314

误:来中国以后没立刻写信你们,请原谅!

正:来中国以后没立刻给你们写信,请原谅!

动词"写"后只能跟一个宾语,不能再带别的宾语。"你们"是动作"写"的对象,必须借用介词"给"构成介宾词组"给你们",提到动词"写"前,作修饰成分。

The verb "写" can carry only one object. "你们" which is the receiver of "写" must be introduced by the preposition "给" to form the prepositional phrase "给你们" serving as a premodifier of the verb.

例 315

误:在端午节的时候,为了给神鱼感谢,人们把粽子扔到江里去。

正:在端午节的时候,为了感谢神鱼,人们把粽子扔到江里去。

"感谢"是可以带宾语的动词,可以说"感谢神鱼"。句中又塞进引进动作对象的介词"给"作状语,自然是错误的,应删去。

"感谢" is a verb which takes an object. One can say "感谢神鱼". It is wrong to use the prepositional phrase "给神鱼" as the adverbial adjunct to introduce the object of the action.

例 316

误:玛丽给我告诉明天参观的事儿。

正:玛丽告诉我明天参观的事儿。

按照"告诉"的用法,改成为带双宾语的句子。删去硬加的介词"给"。

According to the usage of "告诉", we change the sentence into one with double objects and delete the preposition "给".

离

from

例 317

误:我们离语言学院,坐331路汽车可以到。

正:我们这儿离语言学院不远,坐331路汽车可以到。

句子结构不完整,缺少谓语,根据句意可以加"不远"或"很

122

近"。主语"我们"不是处所词,还要在"我们"后加"这儿",改为两地相距的距离。

The sentence structure is incomplete with the predicate absent. We add ″不远″ or ″很近″ according to the context. The subject ″我们″ does not indicate locality, so it must take ″这儿″ after it.

例 318

误:那个商店离我们睡觉不太远。

正:那个商店离我们睡觉的地方不太远。

"我们睡觉"不表示处所,应改为表示地点的词语"睡觉的地方"。

″我们睡觉″ does not indicate locality and should be replaced with ″睡觉的地方″ to denote place.

例 319

误:从他的家离马老师的家很近。

正:他的家离马老师的家很近。

只是表示"他的家"与"马老师家"的距离,应当删去表示起点的介词"从"。

The preposition ″从″ is not needed here to show the distance between ″他的家″ and ″马老师家″.

例 320

误:阿里去学校比较远的地方照相。

正:阿里去离学校比较远的地方照相。

是说阿里去某个地方照相,而这个地方与学校相距很远,因此要在"学校"前加"离"。

″离″ should be added before ″学校″ to express that the place where ″阿里″ is going to take photographs is far away from the school.

例 321

误：古时候有个人住在城里很远的村子里。

正：古时候有个人住在离城里很远的村子里。

句子的主干是：古时候有个人住在村子里，"城里很远"是"村子里"的定语，不成话。应在"城里"前加介词"离"，改成"离城里很远"，点明空间的距离。

The main part of the sentence is：古时候有个人住在村子里. "城里很远" is the attributive of "村子里", but "城里很远的村子里" does not make sense. One should add the preposition "离" before "城里" to indicate distance.

往

to

例 322

误：那儿往1路车站很近。

正：那儿离1路车站很近。

"往"表示动作方向。原句是说"那儿"与"1路车站"两地的距离，要用"离"，不能用"往"。

"往" indicates direction of an action. To express the distance between "那儿" and "1路车站", one should use "离" rather than "往".

例 323

误：您从这儿走往北。

正：您从这儿往北走。

语序有误。介宾词组"往北"应移到谓语动词"走"前，指明动作的方向。

The sentence is disordered. The prepositional phrase "往北" should precede the predicate verb "走" to indicate direction of the action.

为了

in order to, for

例 **324**

误：她为了身体不好，每天早上坚持锻炼。

正：她因为身体不好，每天早上坚持锻炼。

"为了"表示动作行为的目的，而"身体不好"是"每天早上坚持锻炼"的原因，应改"为了"为"因为"。

"为了" is used to show purpose of an action. But "身体不好" is the reason for "每天早上坚持锻炼". Thus one should replace "为了" with "因为".

例 **325**

误：我以后要为了我的国家贡献力量。

正：我以后要为我的国家贡献力量。

"国家"是"贡献力量"的对象，而不是"贡献力量"的目的，要用表示行为对象的"为"替代表示目的的"为了"。

"国家" is the beneficiary rather than the purpose of "贡献力量". "为了" indicating purpose must be replaced by "为" which shows the beneficiary of an action.

例 **326**

误：我们现在努力学习汉语为了以后学好专业。

正：我们现在努力学习汉语是为了以后学好专业。

正：为了以后学习专业，我们现在努力学习汉语。

介宾词组"为了以后学好专业"不能单独作谓语，通常用在表示判断的句子中，作宾语。应在"为了"前加上动词"是"或者把"为了以后学习专业"放在"我们"前，表示目的。

The prepositional phrase "为了以后学好专业" can not serve as a predicate independently. It usually functions as the object in a sentence making judgement. One should use the verb "是" before "为了". One may also put "为了以后学好专业" before "我们" to indicate purpose.

向

toward

例 327

误：来往的汽车很多，向公路上跑着。

正：来往的汽车很多，在公路上跑着。

介词"向"表示动作的方向，这里说的是汽车行驶的处所，应由"在"代替"向"。

The preposition "向" indicates direction of an action. To express place where vehicles run, "在" should be used in place of "向".

例 328

误：玛丽，今天是你的生日，我们表示向你祝贺。

正：玛丽，今天是你的生日，我们向你表示祝贺。

说明动作对象的"向你"应放在谓语动词前，作状语。"向……表示祝贺"是固定的搭配形式。

"向你" which introduces the object of action must precede the predicate verb as an adverbial adjunct. "向…表示祝贺" is a fixed pattern.

沿着

along

例 329

误：那条小路两旁都是树，我们常常晚饭后，沿着小路。

正：那条小路两旁都是树，我们常常晚饭后，沿着小路散步。

误用"沿着"为动词。根据句子的需要，应在介宾词组"沿着小路"后补上动词谓语"散步"。"沿着小路"是处所状语。

"沿着" is misused as a verb. To complete the sentence, one may use "散步" as the verb predicate after the prepositional phrase

"沿着小路" which consequently becomes the adverbial adjunct of place.

例 330

误：您沿这条路一直往前走。

正：您沿着这条路一直往前走。

介词"沿"后通常带"着"，表示动作经过的地方兼表遵循的方向，句中缺少"着"，应加在"沿"及其宾语"这条路"之间。

The preposition ″沿″ normally carries ″着″ to indicate course or direction of a movement. ″着″ which is absent should go between ″沿″ and the object ″这条路″.

由于

because

例 331

误：他的汉语水平提高了由于朋友的帮助下。

正：由于朋友的帮助他的汉语水平提高了。

正：在朋友的帮助下他的汉语水平提高了。

"由于"与"下"不搭配。这个句子有两种改法：或者删去"下"，把"由于朋友的帮助"提到"他"前，表示原因。或者改"由于"为"在"，构成"在……下"，表示条件。都用作状语。

″由于″ and ″下″ do not go together. To correct the sentence, one may delete ″下″ and put ″由于朋友的帮助″ indicating reason in front of ″他″. The other way is to replace ″由于″ with ″在″ to form the phrase ″在…下″ which denotes condition. ″由于朋友的帮助″ and ″在朋友的帮助下″ both serve as adverbial adjuncts.

在

in, at

例 332

误：你这儿作什么？

正：你在这儿作什么？

在动词谓语句中，如果说明动作发生的地点，要用介词"在"引进处所词语。应在"这儿"的前头加"在"。

In a sentence with a verbal predicate, the preposition "在" is required in order to introduce the word of locality which shows the place of an occurrence. "在" must be added before "这儿".

例 333

误：他在书包里拿出来一本新书。

正：他从书包里拿出来一本新书。

"书包里"表示动作涉及的对象所存在的地方，应改"在"为"从"。

"书包里" is the place where the object of the action comes from. Thus, "从" should be used instead of "在".

例 334

误：在这个地方你们踢足球吗？

正：你们在这个地方踢足球吗？

例 335

误：去动物园换车在哪儿？

正：去动物园在哪儿换车？

（334）（335）由"在"构成的处所状语易位，应把误放在句首的"在这个地方"和句末的"在哪儿"分别移到谓语动词"踢"和"换"的前边。

In (334) and (335), the two adverbial adjuncts of place containing "在" are out of position. "在这个地方" and "在哪儿" which are misplaced at the beginning and the end of the two sentence should be moved to the front of the respective predicate verbs—"踢" and "换".

例 336

误：明天下午在两点我去找你。

正：明天下午两点我去找你。

"在两点"是英语 at two o'clock 的直译。在汉语里表示时点的词语一般不用"在"。

"在两点" is the word-to-word interpretation of "at two o'clock" in English. In Chinese, words indicating times of the clock are not normally preceded by "在".

例 337

误：刚才玛丽在我的房间来过。

正：刚才玛丽到我的房间来过。

"在"和处语词语（"我的房间"）的后边，不能带趋向动词"来"。介词"在"应该改为"到"。

"在" and other words denoting locality can not be followed by the directional verb "来". The preposition "在" should be replaced by "到".

十、连词的误用
Errors in the Use of Conjunctions

而且

and

例 338

误：他们买到了飞机票，座位不错。

正：他们买到了飞机票，而且座位不错。

这是表示递进关系的复句，但句中缺少表示递进意义的关联词，应当在后个分句前加上"而且"。

This is a complex sentence of progressive relation. But it lacks a proper correlative to express such relation. One should add ″而且″ at the beginning of the second clause.

还是

or

例 339

误:请你把这张票给阿里还是巴里亚。

正:请你把这张票给阿里或者巴里亚。

原句是表示选择的陈述句,在汉语里,不能用"还是",只能用没有疑问语气的"或者",是说这张票给两个人当中的哪一位都可以。

The sentence is a statement of alternative relation. ″或者″ which carries no interrogative mood should be used instead of ″还是″ to express that the ticket may be given to either of the two persons.

例 340

误:你姐姐是大夫,还是是工程师?

正:你姐姐是大夫,还是工程师?

"还是"连接的是由动词"是"构成的动宾词组"是大夫"、"是工程师"。为使句子简洁,避免音节重复,只能出现一个"是"。

What ″还是″ connects here are two verb-object phrases formed by the verb ″是″, (″是大夫″, ″是工程师″). In order to avoid repetition and keep the sentence concise, only one ″是″ should occur in the second clause.

或者

or

例 341

误:晚上你们看杂技或者看京剧?

正:晚上你们看杂技还是看京剧?

130

在汉语中,表示选择的疑问句,不能用'或者",只能用带有疑问语气的"还是",要求在两种活动中选择一项。在英语里,"还是"、"或者"都是 or。

With an alternative question, one should use "还是" which imparts an interrogative mood instead of "或者" to ask which one of the two items is to be selected. "或者" is unsuitable here. However, both "还是" and "或者" are expressed by "or" in English.

和

and

例 342

误:诸葛亮叫船上的士兵大声喊叫和擂起鼓来。

正:诸葛亮叫船上的士兵大声喊叫、擂起鼓来。

谓语部分是并列的动词词组,后一个是单音节动词"擂"后附加宾语"鼓"和趋向补语"起来",前一个是双音节动词"喊叫"前附加状语"大声",由于这两个词组的结构不同,中间不宜用"和"。应当删掉"和",改为顿号。

The predicate section consists of two co-ordinate verb phrases. The second one is formed by the monosyllabic verb "擂" with an object "鼓" and the directional complement "起来". The first one is a disyllabic verb "喊叫" premodified by "大声". These two verb phrases are in different constructions, hence may not be joined by "和". A pause mark should take its place.

例 343

误:每一事物与周围其他事物都联系着和互相影响。

正:每一事物与周围其他事物都互相联系着和影响着。

虽然谓语动词都是双音节的,但它们的附加成分不同,一个是"都",一个是"互相";一个动词之后有"着",一个没有。应当改成具有共同的附加成分的动词词组,才能用连词"和"连接。

131

The two predicate verbs carry different adjuncts though they are both disyllabic. "联系" is premodified by "都" and followed by "着". "影响" is preceded by "互相". Only with identical adjuncts can two verbal phrases connected by the conjunction "和".

例 **344**

误:我们的教室很大和很干净。

正:我们的教室很大而且很干净。

在两个形容词词组之间不宜用"和",应把"和"改为"而且"。

"和" is not allowed between two adjectival phrases. It should be replaced with "而且".

例 **345**

误:我去他家和他来我家。

正:我去他家,他(也)来我家。

英语可以用 and 连接两个句子,I went to his house and he came to mine,汉语"和"则不能这样用,应删去"和",换用逗号,改成两个分句。还可以在第二个分句"来"的前边加上"也",表示不同的事物发出相同性质的行为。

"And" in English can join two sentences, like "I went to his house and he came to mine", but "和" in Chinese can not. "和" in the above sentence should be deleted, besides which, "也" is needed before the predicate "来" in the second clause to show identity in action.

例 **346**

误:我们复习旧课和我们预习新课。

正:我们复习旧课,预习新课。

"和"不能用来连接句子"我们复习旧课"与"我们预习新课"。因为它们的主语相同,可以删去第二个"我们",再把"和"改用逗号,变成并列动宾词组作谓语的句子。

"我们复习旧课" and "我们预习新课" are two clauses which can not be connected by "和". Since their subjects are identical, the second one should not occur. We change the sentence into one with a predicate of two coordinate verb-object phrases joined by a pause mark.

可见

it is clear that

例 347

误：群众的欢迎，可见这个工厂生产出来的无线电质量很好。

正：群众欢迎这个工厂生产出来的无线电，可见它的质量很好。

连词"可见"是连接句子或段落的，"群众的欢迎"只是一个词组，需改为句子。

The conjunction "可见" is used to join sentences and paragraphs. "群众的欢迎" is a phrase. One should change it into a sentence.

可是(但是)

but

例 348

误：他学习很努力，进步不快。

正：他学习很努力，可是(但是)进步不快。

这是表示转折关系的复句，但是，句子里没有相应的表示转折意义的连词，应在后个分句前加"可是"或"但是"。

This is a complex sentence of adverse relation, but there is no adverse conjunction. "可是" or "但是" should be used at the beginning of the second clause.

所以(因此)

so, therefore

例 349

误：她每天下午打球、跑步，然而身体越来越好。

正：她每天下午打球、跑步，所以(因此)身体越来越好。

这是表示因果关系的复句，"然而"表示转折，在这里使用不妥。应改"然而"为"所以"或"因此"。

This is a complex sentence of causative relation. "然而" which indicates adverse relation is improper here. It should be replaced by "所以" or "因此".

十一、助词的误用
Errors in the Use of Particles

1. 动态助词使用不当
Improper use of aspect particles

了

le

例 350

误：上星期天我们去几个公园。

正：上星期天我们去了几个公园。

"上星期天"指明"去几个公园"发生在过去，应在动词"去"后加上动态助词"了"。着重说明动作已经完成。

"上星期天" shows that "去几个公园" happened in the past. The aspect particle "了" should be added after the verb "去" to affirm that the action has already completed.

例 351

误：楼下有了一个人叫你。

正：楼下有一个人叫你(呢)。

在第一个动词为"有",第二个动词是"叫"的表示动作正在进行的兼语句中,不宜再用表示动作完成的"了"。如果需用助词的话,只能在句尾换用语气助词"呢",表示动作在继续。

A pivotal sentence which expresses an action in progress should not carry "了" denoting completion of an action. However, one may use the interjection "呢" at the end of the sentence to imply that the action is in progress.

例 **352**

误:我一定要记住了这些生词。

正:我一定要记住这些生词。

"要"用在动词前,只表示一种意愿,并未成为现实。根据需要,可以删去"了"。

"要" used before verbs expresses unaccomplished desires. According to the meaning "了" here must be deleted.

例 **353**

误:我没有看了这本历史书了。

正:我没有看这本历史书。

正:我看了这本历史书了。

"没有"是否定"看这本历史书"的行为发生过,"了"则肯定动作行为"看"已经完成,前后矛盾。要么删去"了",保留"没有";要么去掉"没有",保留"了"。

"没有" negates the occurrence of the action "看这本历史书", whereas "了" affirms its completion. The sentence is contradictory with both words present. One of them is to be deleted.

例 **354**

误:我每天复习了一个小时的旧课。

正:我每天复习一个小时的旧课。

"每天"表示"复习"是习惯性的动作。在这个句子中不再用表示动作已经完成的"了"。

"每天" implies that "复习" is a habitual action. Thus "了" denoting completion of an action can not be used.

例 355

误：我和我的朋友喜欢了这个学校。

正：我和我的朋友喜欢这个学校了。

动词"喜欢"是本身含有持续意义的表示心理活动的动词，它的后边一般不用动态助词"了"。可以在句子末尾换用表示变化的语气助词"了"。

The aspect particle "了" can not be attached to verbs which indicate mental state and contain a continuous aspect，such as "喜欢". However，interjection "了" denoting change of state may be used at the end of the sentence.

例 356

误：昨天晚上杜朗去了国际俱乐部看电影。

正：昨天晚上杜朗去国际俱乐部看电影了。

在后一个动作说明前一个动作目的的连动句中，一般只用语气助词"了"，表示"去国际俱乐部看电影"这件事已经完成，应删去动词"去"后边的动态助词"了"，在句末加上语气助词"了"。

This sentence contains two verbal constructions，in which the second action is the purpose of the first one. Interjection "了" should be used to suggest that "去国际俱乐部看电影" has accomplished. One should delete aspect particle "了" after the verb "去" and add interjection "了" at the end of the sentence.

例 357

误：早上我吃早饭了，就来教室了。

正：早上我吃了早饭，就来教室了。

用副词"就"连接"吃"和"来"两个已经紧接着发生的动作的复

句中,前个分句末尾不能用表示事情完成的语气助词"了",要改成说明前一个动作完成的动态助词"了"。

In a complex sentence with ″就″ to join two actions that happened in quick succession (″吃″, ″来″), interjection ″了″ which suggests accomplishment of a whole event can not be used at the end of the first clause. We prefer an aspect particle ″了″ to show completion of the first action.

例 358

误:巴里亚的衣服放了在箱子里。

正:巴里亚的衣服放在了箱子里。

动词后边带着补语"在"和动态助词"了",通常"在"紧跟着动词,"了"在动词和补语之后。应把"放了在"改成"放在了",是说衣服放在箱子里的行为已经完成。

When a verb is followed by the complement ″在″ and the aspect particle ″了″, normally ″在″ stays immediately after the verb with ″了″ coming next. ″放了在″ should be changed into ″放在了″ which means the action of putting the clothes into the case has finished.

例 359

误:以前我吃了烤鸭,我还想吃一次。

正:以前我吃过烤鸭,我还想吃一次。

"了"和"过"混淆。"吃了烤鸭"指完成的时间是确定的,而"吃过烤鸭"因表示过去的经历,一般用于过去时段中的一个不确定的时点,句中用来作状语的"以前"是不确定的时点。所以要用"过"替代"了"。

″了″ is confused with ″过″. ″吃了烤鸭″ implies that the action was completed at a specific moment. ″吃过烤鸭″ shows the past experience and is related to a non-specific time in the past. ″以

前" serving as the adverbial adjunct in the sentence is non-specific. Thus it requires "过" to go with it.

着

zhe

例 360

误：他的箱子很重，阿里要替他拿着。

正：他的箱子很重，阿里要替他拿。

能愿动词后边的动词性词组中的动词不能用动态助词"着"。"着"字应当去掉。

The aspect particle "着" can not be attached to verbs which take before them an auxiliary verb. It should be deleted.

例 361

误：李波拿很多东西走进宿舍去了。

正：李波拿着很多东西走进宿舍去了。

第一个动作（"拿"）是说明第二个动作（"走"）进行的情况的，需要在第一个动词"拿"后加上"着"字。

When the first action ("拿") shows the state of the second action ("走"), "着" should be attached to the first verb.

例 362

误：我的姐姐以前曾经在学校教着书。

正：我的姐姐以前曾经在学校教过书。

"着"表示动作在持续，"以前"表示"教书"是过去的事情。"曾经"与"着"不能前后照应。应改"着"为"过"。指过去有教书的经历。

"着" indicates continuity of the action but "以前" shows "教书" to be a past experience. "着" does not correspond with "曾经" and should be replaced by "过", meaning to have the experience of teaching.

例 363

138

误：他们班的同学站着十楼前边。

正：他们班的同学在十楼前边站着（或"站在十楼前边"）。

处所词语不能跟在动态助词"着"的后边，应借助表示空间关系的介词"在"引进处所词，作状语，"在十楼前边"可以移到动词"站"的前边。或者把"着"改成"在"。

Words of locality can not follow aspect particle "着". With the preposition "在" to introduce the noun phrase denoting locality, a prepositional phrase（在十楼前边"）can be formed and serves as an adverbial adjunct before the verb "站". One may also replace "着" with "在" and say "站在十楼前边".

例 364

误：安娜把衣服挂着在墙上了。

正：安娜把衣服挂在墙上了。

"墙上"是处所词，同表示空间关系的介词"在"相吻合，可以结合成"在墙上"，作补语。删去多余的"着"。

"墙上" denotes location and "在" is the preposition referring to a special relation of space. These two words can form "在墙上" to serve as the complement. "着" is redundant and should be deleted.

例 365

误：我喜欢着我的父亲、母亲。

正：我喜欢我的父亲、母亲。

"着"主要用在表动作的动词之后，表示动作或状态的持续。"喜欢"是本身含有持续意义的表心理活动的动词，后边不能用"着"。

"着" is mainly used after action verbs to indicate continuity of an action or a state. "喜欢" refers to mental state and contains continuous aspect. It can not be followed by "着".

例 366

误:人民的生活水平提高着。

正:人民的生活水平提高了。

"提高"是指人民的生活水平比原来高,它的后边不能用"着",可以用"了",表示变化。

"提高" here means that the people's living standard is higher than before. "着" can not be used after it. One may use "了" to show change of state.

例 367

误:他在北京的很多地方工作,去年才回国。

正:他在北京的很多地方工作过,去年才回国。

句中动词"工作"表示经常性的动作行为,但是后续句说"去年才回国",显而易见,说的是去年以前"工作"已经结束,并没有延续到现在。应在动词"工作"的后边加"过",强调他有在北京工作的经历。

"工作" refers to a regular activity. "去年才回国" obviously shows that "在北京的很多地方工作" is a past event earlier than last year and no longer exists at present. "过" should be added after "工作" to stress that he has the experience of working in Beijing.

例 368

误:祥子没上大学,他对社会上的事情不感兴趣。

正:祥子没上过大学,他对社会上的事情不感兴趣。

说的是祥子所以对社会上的事情不感兴趣,是因为他没有上大学的阅历。应当在动词"上"的后面加"过"。

The sentence means that "祥子" was not interested in social affairs just because he had no college experience. "过" should be added after the verb "上".

例 369

误:这星期我进城过三次。

140

正：这星期我进过三次城。

误把动宾词组"进城"当作动词,因此造成动量补语位置失当的毛病。动词和"过"的后边带有处所宾语和补语,补语要放在宾语前边,把"进城过三次"改成"进过三次城"。

The verb-object phrase "进城" is mistaken for a verb, which leads to the error of misplacing the complement of frequency. If a verb with "过" is followed by a place object and a complement, the latter must precede the former. We change "进城过三次" into "进过三次城".

例 370

误：他在北京大学三年学习过汉语。

正：他在北京大学学习过三年汉语。

句中动词和"过"后边带宾语和时量补语,补语应放在宾语的前边,改成"学习过三年汉语"。

If a verb with "过" is followed by object and a complement of duration, the latter should precede the former. One should say "学习过三年汉语".

例 371

误：他在八个月里已经有过不少进步。

正：他在八个月里已经有了不少进步。

句中有表示过去某一个确定的时段词语("在八个月里"),又因为动作"已经"完成产生了某种结果("不少进步")。应当改"过"为"了"。

In this sentence, "在八个月里" refers to a definite period of time. Furthermore, the action has already accomplished a certain result ("不少进步"). Thus, "了" should be used instead of "过".

例 372

误：他开始过工作不久,又没有工作了。

正:他开始工作不久,又没有工作了。

表示起始终结的动词后边不能带"过"。显然动词"开始"后的"过"字用得不合适,应当删去"过"。

Verbs meaning "begin" and "end" can not take "过". Thus "过" should not be used after the verb "开始" and must be deleted.

例 373

误:我过去知道过这件事情。

正:我过去知道这件事情。

动词"知道"是表示认知意义的词,它后边不能带表示过去有过某种经验或经历的动态助词。"过"字须去掉。

The verb "知道" indicates intellectual state and can not take after it the aspect particle "过" which implies having an experience in the past. "过" should be deleted.

例 374

误:来中国以前我看过介绍北京的书,我的朋友也给我介绍。

正:来中国以前我看过介绍北京的书,我的朋友也给我介绍过。

在第二个动词谓语的后边缺少动态助词"过",应当补上。

The aspect particle "过" is needed after the second verb predicate.

2. 结构助词使用不当

Improper use of structural particles

的

de

例 375

误:谁朋友是英国人?

正:谁的朋友是英国人?

"谁"是中心语"朋友"的定语,但"谁"与"朋友"这间缺少"的"

字。应该加上，表示领属关系。

"谁" is the attributive of the head word "朋友", "的" which is missing must be added in between to indicate category.

例 376

误：她有一双非常漂亮布鞋。

正：她有一双非常漂亮的布鞋。

句子的主干是"她有布鞋"。"一双"、"漂亮"以及"漂亮"的修饰成分"非常"都是"布鞋"的定语，可是在这个复杂的定语与中心语之间缺少联系，应当补上"的"字。

The main part of the sentence is "她有布鞋", "一双", "漂亮" and "非常" which is the modifier of "漂亮" are all attributives of "布鞋". "的" is required between such a complex attributive and its head.

例 377

误：我买了一张《人民的日报》。

正：我买了一张《人民日报》。

"人民"和"日报"结合起来，成为一种报纸的名称，不好说成领属关系。"人民"与"日报"之间不能用"的"。

"人民" and "日报" are put together to be the title of a newspaper. They have no possessive relation and "的" is impossible between them.

例 378

误：谢力踢足球踢的不错。

正：谢力踢足球踢得不错。

形容词"不错"跟在动词"踢"的后边，作补语，说明动作达到的程度。应当把"的"改为补语的标志"得"。

The adjective "不错" follows the verb "踢" as a complement to show the degree that the action reaches. One should replace "的"

with ″得″—the marker of complements.

地

de

例 379

误:我们大家都很认真学习。

正:我们大家都很认真地学习。

复杂状语与动词谓语之间缺少结构助词,应当在"都很认真"与"学习"当中加状语的标志"地"。

A structural particle is needed between the complex adverbial adjunct and the verb predicate. One should use ″地″—the marker of adverbial adjuncts between ″都很认真″ and ″学习″.

例 380

误:我非常地喜欢这个城市。

正:我非常喜欢这个城市。

表示程度的副词"非常"用在动词谓语前,作状语,"非常"后不用"地",须删去。

The degree adverb ″非常″ precedes the verb predicate as an adverbial adjunct. One should delete ″地″ which can not be attached to ″非常″.

例 381

误:这是阿里买来地中文小说。

正:这是阿里买来的中文小说。

主谓词组"阿里买来"是"小说"的修饰成分,不能用状语的标志"地"。应该用"的"来代替"地"。

As the modifier of ″小说″, the subject-predicate phrase ″阿里买来″ may not carry ″地″ which is the mark of adverbial adjuncts. ″地″ must be replaced by ″的″.

例 382

误:不努力发展生产,就不能有幸福地生活。

正:不努力发展生产,就不能有幸福的生活。

"幸福"用来作"生活"的定语,不能够用"地",应改用"的"。

"的" rather than "地" should be used after "幸福" which serves as the attributive of "生活".

例 383

误:我汉语说得不够流利,还差地远呢!

正:我汉语说得不够流利,还差得远呢!

由"差地"作状语,语义上讲不通,应该"地"为"得"。"远"作"差"的程度补语,是说达到流利的程度,还有很大距离。

Serving as an adverbial adjunct, "差地" makes no sense. To express that there is still a long way to go before acquiring fluency, one should use "得" instead of "地" to make "远" the degree complement of "差".

得

de

例 384

误:安娜写汉字写很好。

正:安娜写汉字写得很好。

形容词词组"很好"用在动词谓语"写"的后边,作程度补语,但是,动词与补语之间缺少起连接作用的成分。应当加上结构助词"得",说明写的汉字达到很好的程度。

The adjective phrase "很好" after the verb predicate "写" serves as the degree complement. But there is no conjunctive element in between. One should add the structural particle "得".

例 385

误:这课课文很难,我看得不懂。

正:这课课文很难,我看不懂。

先行句说"这课课文很难"，后续句自然该用可能补语的否定形式"看不懂"。应删去用作可能补语肯定形式的标志"得"。

"这课课文很难" in the anticipatory sentence demands that the negative form of the potential complement—"看不懂" be used in the follow-up sentence. One should delete "得" which is the marker of the affirmative form of the potential complement.

例 386

误：同学们都积极得参加运动会。

正：同学们都积极地参加运动会。

"都"和"积极"用于动词谓语之前，作状语。状语的标志应是"地"，而不是"得"。

"都" and "积极" here precede the verb predicate as adverbial adjuncts the marker of which is "地" rather than "得".

例 387

误：水蒸发的快慢与温度得高低有关。

正：水蒸发的快慢与温度的高低有关。

"快慢"和"高低"都是名词，分别作主语和介词"与"的宾语。主谓词组"水蒸发"和名词"温度"分别是"快慢"和"高低"的定语。应改"得"为"的"。

"快慢" and "高低" are both nouns serving respectively as the subject of the sentence and the object of the preposition "与". Their corresponding attributives are the subject-predicate phrase—"水蒸发" and the noun—"温度". "得" must be replaced with "的".

所

suo

例 388

误：这次我们所休息的地方很安静。

正：这次我们休息的地方很安静。

146

结构助词"所"通常用在做定语的主谓词组的动词前边,表示中心语是受事者,如"校长所说的话很重要"。句中的"休息"是不能带宾语的动词,中心语"地方"不是"休息"的受事者,"所"使用不妥,应删去。

The aspect particle "所" is normally used before the verb in a subject-predicate phrase which serves as an attributive. It implies that the head word is the object of the verb, such as in "校长所说的话很重要". However, "休息" is an intransitive verb and can not take the head word "地方" as its object. Thus "所" is improper here and should be deleted.

3. **语气助词使用不当**

Improper use of interjections

吧

ba

例 389

误:快下雨了,咱们赶快到那边躲一躲了。

正:快下雨了,咱们赶快到那边躲一躲吧。

此句含有催促的语气,应改"了"为"吧"。

The sentence carries a tone of urging. One should use "吧" instead of "了".

例 390

误:让我们高高兴兴地过个节。

正:让我们高高兴兴地过个节吧!

原句要表示请求或号召,应该用"让……吧",但是句中的这一格式不完整,须在句子末尾加语气助词"吧"。

"让…吧" is a pattern to express request or appeal. The interjection "吧" is missing from the sentence and should be added in the final position.

例 **391**

误:我们等一会儿再去书店,好吧?

正:我们等一会儿再去书店,好吗?

"好吧"表示同意。而原意是说出自己的想法来征求对方的意见,应该用"好吗"。

"好吧" shows agreement. But the speaker expresses his opinion in order to expect an answer. One should say "好吗" rather than "好吧".

的

de

例 **392**

误:妈妈的病很快就会好。

正:妈妈的病很快就会好的。

"会"用来估计"妈妈的病"有"很快"痊愈的可能性,句尾应加"的"字,与之呼应。"的"有"一定如此"的意思。

"会" indicates the estimated possibility that mother will soon recover from illness. "的" should be added at the end of the sentence to go with "会". It means "definitely so".

例 **393**

误:老师,布置会场的任务由我们负责的。

正:老师,布置会场的任务由我们负责吧。

表示请求的祈使句句尾不能用"的",应改用"吧",语气显得缓和。

"的" is impossible at the end of an imperative sentence expressing request. We prefer "吧" to indicate a mild tone.

例 **394**

误:运动场上站着很多人的。

正:运动场上站着很多人。

这是叙述某处存在着某人的存在句,句尾不能用"的"。应删去多余的"的"字。

Here is an existential sentence stating the existence of someone. "的" may not occur in the final position and must be deleted.

了

le

例 395

误:老马的病好多。

正:老马的病好多了。

谓语形容词"好"带有比较的意思。"多"作补语,是说"老马"的病情同过去相比,有较大好转。一般还应在句末加"了",表示变化。

Adjective "好" as predicate implies comparison. "多" acts as the complement here to show that the patient is much better than before. Normally, "了" is needed at the end of the sentence to indicate change of state.

例 396

误:这件事我们都知道了,你别再说。

正:这件事我们都知道了,你别再说了。

"别"和"再"用在动词谓语("说")前,有禁止行为动作继续下去的意思。句子末尾该补上"了"。

"别" and "再" are used before the verb predicate ("说") to prohibit the continuity of an action. "了" should be added at the end of the sentence.

例 397

误:昨天他吃了晚饭,就去朋友那儿。

正:昨天他吃了晚饭,就去朋友那儿了。

"昨天"指明"吃晚饭"和"去朋友哪儿"两个动作紧接着发生,事情已经全部结束,应该在后续句末尾加"了"。

"昨天" suggests that "吃晚饭" and "去朋友哪儿" have already finished. Thus the follow-up sentence should end up with "了".

例 **398**

误:我们请张老师教我们中国歌,他教我们。

正:我们请张老师教我们中国歌,他教我们了。

"他教我们"是教了还是没教?不清楚。句尾加上"了",明确已经教完中国歌。

With only "他教我们", the speaker has not made clear whether he taught or not. One should use "了" at the end of the sentence to affirm the accomplishment of the event—"教中国歌".

例 **399**

误:你的身体好不好了?

正:你的身体好不好?

这是一个正反式疑问句,在这种问句的末尾不能用"了",应当去掉。

This is an affirmative-negative question which can not have the interjection "了".

例 **400**

误:我分析得完那几个句子了。

正:我分析得完那几个句子。

"分析得完"是说有分析完那几个句子的可能,而"了"表示完成或变化,前后矛盾,应当删去"了"。

"分析得完" indicates the possibility of completing the analysis of those several sentences. "了" shows completion or change. It makes the sentence incoherent and must be deleted.

例 **401**

误:明天他俩结婚了。

正：明天他俩要结婚了。

正：他俩结婚了。

"明天"说明还没有结婚，"了"肯定已经结婚，究竟结婚了没有，令人摸不到头脑。要么在"结婚"前加上"要"与"了"相照应，表示很快就要结婚。要么删去"明天"，保留"了"，表示事情已经完结。

The sentence is senseless in having ″明天″ to imply unaccomplishment of the marriage and ″了″ at the same time to affirm its completion. One should use ″要″ before ″结婚″ to go with ″了″ to suggest that the marriage is near. One may also delete ″明天″ and keep ″了″ to show the completion of the event.

例 402

误：我天天晚上都复习旧课、预习新课了。

正：我天天晚上都复习旧课、预习新课。

"天天"说明"复习旧课、预习新课"是习惯性的行为动作，句子末尾不该用"了"。

″天天″ shows ″复习旧课、预习新课″ are habitual actions. ″了″ can not be used at the end of the sentence.

例 403

误：我正想看书，忽然有人在敲门了。

正：我正想看书，忽然有人在敲门。

副词"在"表示动作处于进行状态，"了"表示完成。句中误用了"了"，应该删去。

The adverb ″在″ indicates that the action is in progress. ″了″ which shows completion should be deleted.

例 404

误：下一次旅行，我们不是去上海，就是去广州了。

正：下一次旅行，我们不是去上海，就是去广州。

句首用"下一次"表示对于未来"去上海"还是"去广州旅行"进

行选择,为此,句末不宜用"了",应去掉。

"下一次" at the beginning of the sentence implies that the choice made between "去上海" and "去广州旅行" is in the future. Thus it is improper to use "了" here.

例 405

误:狼对老人说,他这样做,不是要闷死我了。

正:狼对老人说,他这样做,不是要闷死我吗?

"不是"经常与"吗"构成反诘句。"不是……吗"这个格式形式上是否定,意义上表示肯定。"不是要闷死我吗"意思是"要把我闷死"。应改"了"为"吗"。

"不是" often goes with "吗" to form the rhetorical question—"不是…吗", which is negative in form but affirmative in meaning. "不是要闷死我吗" means "要把我闷死". "吗" should be used instead of "了".

例 406

误:你给我介绍的那本书我还没有看了。

正:你给我介绍的那本书我还没有看呢。

"还没有"和"呢"常常前后呼应,构成"还没有……呢","呢"带有指明事实的意思。句尾不该用"了",应换用"呢"。

"还没有" is often used with "呢" to form "还没有…呢". "呢" carries the implication of showing someone the fact. We replace "了" by "呢".

例 407

误:现在玛丽能用汉语跟中国朋友谈了话。

正:现在玛丽能用汉语跟中国朋友谈话了。

原意是说,玛丽以前不能用汉语跟中国朋友谈话,现在的情况不同了。应改动态助词"了"为语气助词"了"。

The speaker means, Mary could not talk with her Chinese

friends in their language before, but this is no longer the case. To express such meaning, one should use the interjection ″了″ rather than the aspect particle ″了″.

吗

ma

例 **408**

误：你是什么时候来北京的吗？

正：你是什么时候来北京的？

正：你是上个月来北京的吗？

用"什么"，构成的是特指问，要求对方就疑点作出回答。用"吗"，构成的是是非问，仅仅要求听话人表示肯定或否定。这是两种结构不同的提问形式。不能混用在一个句子里，或者删去"吗"，保留"什么时候"，或者保留"吗"，将"什么时候"改成具体的时间词语"上个月"。

With ″什么″, one constituents a special question which requires the other part to give an answer to what is questioned. With ″吗″, one constituents a question which merely expects an affirmative or a negative answer. These two types of questions are different in structure and can not be blended into one sentence. One may either delete ″吗″ and keep ″什么″ or keep ″吗″ and replace ″什么″ with words denoting a specific time.

例 **409**

误：你们看得见看不见黑板上的字吗？

正：你们看得见看不见黑板上的字？

正：你们看得见黑板上的字吗？

"看得见看不见"是正反问，要求对方在提出的肯定和否定的内容中选择答案。用"吗"构成的是是非问，这两种结构不同的疑问句，同样不能凑在一个句子里。一种改法是去掉"吗"，保留正反问。

另一种改法是保留"吗",但是,句子构造要略有改变。

"看得见看不见" is an affirmative-negative question which requires the other side to choose between the affirmative and negative forms of the predicate. "吗" is used to form a yes-no question. These two types of questions with distinct structures should not be mixed up together in one sentence. One way of rectification is to delete "吗", and the other way is to retain "吗" and make a change in the sentence structure.

例 410

误:明天(还是)你们来,还是我们去吗?

正:明天(还是)你们来,还是我们去?

"(还是)……还是……"构成的是选择句,要求在并列的可供选择的几项中选择答案。选择问与用"吗"构成的是非问的结构不同,不能同时出现在一个句子之内,应当删去"吗"。

"(还是)…还是…" is the formula of the alternative question in which a choice has to be made among several paralleled alternatives. It can not occur in the identical sentence with "吗" which is used in a question expecting a yes-or-no. One should delete "吗".

例 411

误:你去图书馆吗?还是去教室呢?

正:你去图书馆(呢),还是去教室呢?

联系上下文,这是选择问,不是是非问,除了改"吗"为"呢"以外,还应该把前边的问号改为逗号。

From the context, we can tell this is an alternative question, not a yes-or-no question. In addition to the replacement of "吗" with "呢", one should change the first question mark into a comma.

例 412

误:她接到信了,一定高兴了吗!

正:她接到信了,一定高兴了吧!

这是对情况的推测,而不表示疑问,句尾"吗"是表示疑问的,应当删去"吗",改用语气助词"吧"。

The speaker is making an estimate rather than a question, "吗" which indicates interrogation should be replaced by the interjection "吧".

呢

ne

例 413

误:要是明天下雨,我就不去美术馆呢。

正:要是明天下雨,我就不去美术馆了。

是说假如下雨的话,就改变原来去美术馆的计划。语气助词"呢"没有"表示变化"的这种用法,应改成"了"。

The speaker means he will change the plan of going to the Art Gallery in case it rains. The interjection "呢" has no implication of change of state and thus should be replaced with "了".

例 414

误:她不在,正在出去呢。

正:她不在,出去了。

"出"是趋向动词,不能受表示进行状态的"正在"的修饰。同样,句子末尾也不能用表示动作正在继续的"呢"。可以改"呢"为"了",表示完成。

"出" is a directional verb and can not be modified by "正在" which indicates "in the progress of". Neither can one use "呢" with similar implication. One should use "了" to show completion.

例 415

误:他只学过两个多月的英语,怎么能看懂英文杂志了。

正：他只学过两个多月的英语，怎么能看懂英文杂志呢。

"怎么能"经常与"呢"构成"怎么能……呢"，表示反诘。"怎么能看懂英文杂志呢"意思是"不能看懂"。"怎么能"同"了"不搭配，应改用"呢"。

"怎么能" often occurs in correlation with "呢" to form "怎么能…呢" which is a rhetorical question. "怎么能看懂英文杂志呢" means "不能看懂". "了" does not go with "怎么能" and must be replaced with "呢".

例 416

误：明天你们还有课呢？

正：明天你们还有课吗？

回答问题时，只要点头或摇头就可以了，显然，原句是个是非问。句尾不宜用"呢"，应改用"吗"。

This is obviously a yes-or-no question in that either a nod or a shake of the head will be the answer. One should use "吗" rather than "呢".

例 417

误：大家汉语学得好呢。

正：大家汉语学得好着呢。

动词谓语"学"后由形容词"好"作程度补语，不仅肯定学习达到"好"的程度，而且带有夸张的感情色彩，应改"呢"为"着呢"。"着呢"表示程度深，多用在形容词后。口语中常用。

Here the adjective "好" follows the verb predicate "学" as the degree complement. The speaker not only affirms that they learn very well, but also wants to express an emotional colouring of exaggeration. "着呢" should be used instead of "呢". Frequently occurring in speaking, it follows adjectives to show a high degree.

第三章 句法方面常见的错误
CHAPTER THREE COMMON ERRORS IN SYNTAX

一、词组的误用
Errors in the Use of Phrases

1. 主谓词组使用不当
Improper use of subject-predicate phrases

例 418

误：借我看一下杂志你借来，好吗？

正：借我看一下你借来的杂志，好吗？

此句是受英语语法的影响，把由主谓词组"你借来"充任的定语放在中心语"杂志"之后。按照汉语的表达方式，应把这两个成分的位置调换一下，同时在由主谓词组"你借来"用作定语的后边，加上结构助词"的"。这样句子结构才合理。

Influenced by English grammar, the speaker misplaces the attributive which is indicated by a subject-predicate phrase (″你借来″) after the head noun (″杂志″). According to the Chinese ways, the order of these two elements should be reversed and the structural particle ″的″ should be attached to ″你借来″.

例 419

误:他们买东西很便宜。

正:他们买的东西很便宜。

为了避免产生歧义,在充当定语的主谓词组"他们买"后加上结构助词"的",表明"东西"是主语,"便宜"是谓语。改成一个由形容词"便宜"作谓语的形容词谓语句。

The subject-predicate phrase "他们买" serves as an attributive in the sentence. To avoid ambiguity, the structural pariticle "的" is required after it to indicate that "东西" is the subject, and "便宜" the predicate. In this way, we get a sentence with an adjectival predicate expressed by "便宜".

例 420

误:我想他们的决心完成这个任务。

正:我想他们有决心完成这个任务。

"想"的宾语是一个主谓词组。根据句子的实际情况,结构助词"的"应改成动词"有",与"决心"构成主谓词组"他们有决心",表示坚定的意志。只有这样,动宾词组"完成这个任务"才能跟在"他们有决心"的后头。

The object of "想" is a subject-predicate phrase. Considering the sentence structure, we replace the structural particle "的" with the verb "有", in order to form the subject-predicate phrase "他们有决心" which expresses their firm will. Only in this way, can the verb-object phrase 完成这个任务" comes after "决心".

例 421

误:妈妈的希望我有一个好工作。

正:妈妈希望我有一个好工作。

这个句子有两种改法。一是在主语"希望"和宾语"我有一个好工作"之间加表示判断的动词"是"构成"是"字句,说明"是"前后的两个成分属于同一关系。二是删去"的",改成由"希望"作谓语的动词谓语句,"我有一个好工作"是"希望"的宾语。

There are two ways to correct the sentence. One way is to build a 是-sentence by inserting the verb "是" denoting judgement between the subject "希望" and the object "我有一个好工作" "是" shows the identical relation between two elements. The other way is to delete "的" and thus elicit a sentence in which "希望" is the verb predicate and "我有一个好工作" is the object of "希望".

例 422

误:他说的话,大家很感动。

正:他说的话使大家很感动。

"他说的话"怎么样?没有讲,后面就转移到陈述的角度"大家很感动",前后不连贯。加上一个动词"使",就把偏正词组"他说的话"和主谓词组"大家很感动"组合成的一个符合兼语句结构特点的句子了。

This sentence is incoherent with no word to link the topic "他说的话" (an endocentric phrase) and the comment "大家很感动" (a subject-predicate phrase). Verb "使" may be used to join the two phrases into a pivotal sentence.

例 423

误:王进喜参加开采新油田国家宣布大会战。

正:王进喜参加国家宣布的开采新油田的大会战。

此句主干是:"王进喜参加大会战"。动宾词组"开采新油田"和主谓词组"国家宣布"是宾语"大会战"的定语,但这两个词组的位置颠倒了,动宾词组"开采新油田"应靠近中心语"大会战",其次才是主谓词组"国家宣布"。不论动宾词组"开采新油田"还是主谓词组"国家宣布"作定语,定语与中心语之间都要加上"的"字。

The main part of the sentence is:"王进喜参加大会战". The verb-object phrase "开采新油田" and the subject-predicate phrase

"国家宣布" both serving as attributives are in reverse order. "开采新油田" should stay close to the head word "大会战", and the subject-predicate "国家宣布" should come next. Both of them should be followed by "的".

例 424

误：我还没看完你给我介绍那本小说呢！

正：我还没看完你给我介绍的那本小说呢！

句中用作定语的成分后边，应该用结构助词"的"而没有用，使得结构不清，意思不明。此句主干是："我看小说"。主谓词组"你给我介绍"和指量词"那本"都是宾语"小说"的定语，应在主谓词组"你给我介绍"后加上定语标志"的"。

We find no structural particle "的" after certain attributives where there should be. This makes the sentence structure and meaning unclear. "我看小说" is the main body of the sentence. The subject-predicate phrase "你给我介绍" and the demonstrative measure-word phrase are both attributives of the object "小说". The attributive marker "的" should be attached to the subject-predicate phrase "你给我介绍".

例 425

误：工厂领导希望我们给他们的工作意见。

正：工厂领导希望我们给他们的工作提意见。

主谓词组"我们给他们的工作意见"是谓语动词"希望"的宾语。但是在这个主谓词组中缺少动词。为使结构完整，只有加动词"提"，才能和"意见"搭配。"给他们的工作"是介宾词组，用来作谓语"提"的状语。

The object of the predicate verb "希望" is the subject-predicate phrase "我们给他们的工作意见" where the verb is missing. To complete the structure the verb "提" should be used to go with "意

见". The prepositional phrase "给他们的工作" acts as the adverbial adjunct of the predicate "提".

2. 动宾词组使用不当
Improper use of verb-object phrases

例 426

误：现在人等车的很多。

正：现在等车的人很多。

此句受英语词序的影响，把由动宾词组"等车"充当的定语和结构助词"的"放在主语"人"的后头。汉语里，要把定语"等车"和结构助词"的"一同放在主语"人"的前头。

Influenced by the word order in English, the speaker puts the attributive expressed by the verb-object phrase "等车" plus the structural particle "的" after the subject "人". According to Chinese grammar, this order must be reversed.

例 427

误：外面下雨很多。

正：外面雨水很多。

形容词"多"作谓语时，与其搭配的主语一般是指人或事物的词语，表示量大。根据原句意，应改动宾词组"下雨"为名词"雨水"。是说外面由降雨而积的水多。

When the adjective "多" serves as the predicate to suggest a great quantity, the subject usually refers to persons or things. In line with the sentence meaning, we change the verb-object phrase "下雨" into the noun phrase "雨水" to express that the rainfall has caused a lot of water on the ground.

例 428

误：昨天的开会进行了五十五分钟。

正：昨天的会进行了五十五分钟。

动宾词组"开会"指活动,并不指事物,不能用作谓语动词"进行"的主语。应改"开会"为"会"。全句改成意义上的被动句。

The verb-object phrase "开会" indicates an activity rather than a thing. Thus it can not be the subject of the predicate verb "进行". One should replace it with "会" and by doing so change the sentence into a notionally passive sentence.

例 429

误:昨天下了课,我就去看朋友有病的了。

正:昨天下了课,我就去看有病的朋友了。

句子的主干是"我去看朋友"。动宾词组"有病"是宾语"朋友"的定语。按照汉语的词序,要把定语"有病"和结构助词"的"一并移到宾语"朋友"的前边。

The main body of the sentence is "我去看朋友". The verb-object phrase "有病" serves as the attributive of the object "朋友". According to the word order in Chinese, "有病" together with the structural particle "的" should be moved to the front of the object "朋友".

例 430

误:那位是教留学生汉语老师。

正:那位是教留学生汉语的老师。

句子的主干是:"那位是老师"由动词"教"及其宾语——"留学生"和"汉语"构成的动宾词组,作宾语"老师"的定语。应该在这个用来作定语的复杂词组的后边加结构助词"的"。

"那位是老师" is the main body of the sentence in which the verb "教" with its objects "留学生" and "汉语" forms a verb-object phrase functioning as the attributive of "老师" the object of the whole sentence. Such a complex phrase as an attributive must take after it the structural particle "的".

162

例 431

误：去火车站接朋友人多极了。

正：去火车站接朋友的人多极了。

句子的主干是："人多"。由两个动宾词组"去火车站"和"接朋友"组成的连动词组作主语"人"的定语。但在定语"去火车站接朋友"与主语"人"之间缺少"的"字，一定要补上这个必不可少的成分。

The main part of the sentence is ″人多″. The verb-object phrases ″去火车站″ and ″接朋友″ are two verbal constructions in series as the attributive of the subject ″人″. The missing structural particle ″的″ should be added between ″以″ and its attributive.

例 432

误：凡是老师都喜欢他。

正：凡是教过他的老师都喜欢他。

此句有只要是都是老师就喜欢他的意思。这与事理相悖。应当在主语"老师"的前边补上由动宾词组"教过他"充当的定语和定语的标志"的"。这样结构才完整，意思才准确。

It is unreasonable to say ″All teachers like him″. To make sense, the sentence may carry before the subject ″老师″ an attributive expressed by the verb-object phrase ″教过他″ plus the attributive marker ″的″.

3."的"字词组使用不当

Improper use of the 的-phrase

例 433

误：那本词典是我。

正：那本词典是我的。

名词"词典"是主语，指物体。代词"我"，指代人，是宾语，谓语为"是"。"词典"怎么能是"我"呢？显然主语、宾语搭配不当。在宾语

163

"我"的后边加上"的",使宾语成为"的"字词组"我的"。"的"附在代词后,合起来表示事物的名称,即"我的词典"。这样,主语、宾语所指的就是同类事物了。

The noun ″词典″ serving as the subject refers to a thing while the pronoun ″我″ serving as the object refers to a person. The predicate is ″是″. How can one say ″The dictionary is me″. Obviously, the subject and the object do not correspond. The object ″我″ should carry ″的″ to form the 的-phrase ″我的″ which refers to ″我的词典″. Thus, the subject and the object are correspondent in referring to things of the same category.

例 434

误:那件毛衣不是黄,是绿。

正:那件毛衣不是黄的,是绿的。

名词"毛衣"是主语,指物件。形容词"黄"和"绿"是宾语,指颜色。此句主语、宾语不同类。应分别在宾语"黄"和"绿"的后头加"的",使宾语改成"黄的"="黄的毛衣";"绿的"="绿的毛衣"。"的"附着在形容词"黄"和"绿"后,合起来有表示事物名称的作用。

The noun ″毛衣″ which is the subject refers to a thing. The adjectives ″黄″ and ″绿″ which are the objects refer to colours. The subject and the objects belong to different categories. Both ″黄″ and ″绿″ should carry ″的″ to form ″黄的″ and ″绿的″ to indicate ″黄的毛衣″ and ″绿的毛衣″ respectively. Adjectives followed by ″的″ may be used to name objects.

例 435

误:去滑冰多极了。

正:去滑冰的多极了。

"去滑冰"是动宾词组,作主语。指一种行为活动。形容词谓语"多"表示事物的性质。主语与谓语不搭配。必须在主语"去滑冰"后

164

加"的"，使主语成为"的"字词组，"去滑冰的"＝去滑冰的人"。"的"附在动宾词组"去滑冰"后，也有表示人的名称的作用。

"去滑冰" is a verb-object phrase serving as the subject. It refers to an activity. The adjectival predicate "多" indicates property of things. The subject does not correspond with the predicate. One should use "的" after "去滑冰" to make the subject a 的-phrase. "去滑冰" with "的" attached to it can refer to a person.

例 **436**

误：今天晚上的电影是谁的？

正：今天晚上的电影是哪国的？

此句"的"字词组中误用疑问代词"谁"，意思讲不通，应改"谁"为"哪国"。

The misuse of the interrogative pronoun "谁" in the "的"-phrase makes the sentence senseless. "谁" should be replaced with "哪国".

4. 介宾词组使用不当

Improper use of prepositional phrases

从……到……

from…to…

例 **437**

误：我们每天上午有课从八点到十二点。

正：我们每天上午从八点到十二点有课。

"从八点到十二点"由于受英语词序的影响误放到句尾。汉语则应把"从八点到十二点"提到动词谓语"有"前，作时间状语，表示"从什么时候开始到什么时候止"。

Placing "从八点到十二点" at the end of the sentence is a consequence of applying English grammar to Chinese word structure. In Chinese, "从八点到十二点" must precede the verb predicate

"有" as the adverbial adjunct of time to express "from the time …
till …".

从……起

from…on

例 438

误:我每天下午复习从三点起。

正:我每天下午从三点起复习。

句子中的"从……起"出现在句子末尾,这是英语的表示方法。汉语"从三点起"一定要放在谓语动词"复习"之前,作时间状语,表示"从什么时候开始"的意思。

To put "从…起" at the end of the sentence is the English way of expressing the same meaning of "从三点起". In Chinese, it must occur before the predicate verb "复习" to serve as an adverbial adjunct of time, meaning "from the time".

例 439

误:他从中学学习法语和英语。

正:他从中学起学习法语和英语。

"从……"结构不完整。"从"可以表示时间为起点,但时间是延续的,当指出某一时间起点后,时间还是不停地向前延续着,为表延续性,时间词后要加"起"(或"以来""以后"等词)。构成"从……起"等格式。"从……起"的位置也可在主语前。此句也可改成"从中学起他学习法语和英语"。

In this sentence, the phrase starting with "从" is incomplete in structure. "从" is used to indicate a starting point in time. However, time is continuous. It proceeds after any particular point. To show this continuity,起(in some cases it is "以来" or "以后" etc.) is required after the noun that expresses time to form such patterns as "从…起". "从…起" may also precede the subject. Thus one can say "从中学起他学习法语和英语".

对……来说

as far as … is concerned

例 440

误:对日常生活,水十分重要。

正:水对日常生活十分重要。

正:对日常生活来说,水是十分重要的。

对表示事物与事物之间的对待关系时,"对"一般都要放在主语后,谓语动词前。如要把"对"提到主语前,必须把"对"改成"对……来说",强调从某个角度看问题。

To express the effect of something on something else, "对" normally follows the subject before the predicate verb. But it may precede the subject when used in the pattern "对…来说" which stresses "from the angle of".

在……方面

in, with respect to

例 441

误:工业各部门无论在产品的产量、质量和品种都跃进了一大步。

正:工业各部门无论在产品的产量、质量和品种各方面都跃进了一大步。

介词"在"与名词"方面"搭配,表示范围。此句缺少"方面",应当补在谓语部分"都"的前边。

The preposition "在" is often used in combination with the noun "方面" to denote scope. "方面" which is absent should be added before "都" in the predicate section.

在……上

on, in

例 442

误:考试方法还要看学生在困难上解决问题的水平。

正:考试方法还要看学生解决问题的水平。

"学生在困难上解决问题"是宾语"水平"的定语。这个定语里的"问题"是指难于判断的问题,与"在困难上"所表示的意思部分重复。删去"在困难上"。

"学生在困难上解决问题" is the attributive of the object "水平", "问题" refers to problems difficult to handle, so it partially reduplicates the meaning imparted by "在困难上". One should delete "在困难上" which is redundant.

在……下

under

例 443

误:在老师和同学们帮助下,他进步很快。

正:在老师和同学们的帮助下,他进步很快。

"在……下"之间不能插入主谓词组("老师和同学们帮助"),多是偏正词组,即改成"老师和同学们的帮助"。"在……下"通常放在句首,表示"他进步很快"的条件。

"在…下" can not have a subject-predicate phrase ("老师和同学们帮助") inserted in between. It should take an endocentric phrase, i. e. "老师和同学们的帮助". "在…下"occurs at the beginning of the sentence showing the condition of "他进步很快".

在……中

in

例 444

误:参加劳动和社会活动中,他们两个人的感情越来越深了。

正:在参加劳动和社会活动中,他们两个人的感情越来越深了。

168

介词"在"与方位词"中"相互呼应,构成格式"在……中"。一般放在主语之前作状语。此句"在……中"不完整,应补上介词"在",表示促使两个人感情越来越深的环境。

The preposition "在" is often used with "中"—a noun of locality to form the pattern "在…中" which normally precedes the subject as an adverbial adjunct. In the present sentence, the pattern is incomplete. One should add "在" to indicate the surroundings that bring the two people closer to one another.

5. 同位词组使用不当

Improper use of appositive phrases

例 445

误:小王都我买了一本《家》书。

正:小王都我买了一本书《家》。

两个名词"《家》""书"指同一样事物,这是同位词组作宾语。但,带有注释性的名词"《家》"不能放在"书"前,只能放在"书"后。

The two nouns "《家》" and "书" refer to the same thing. They form an appositive phrase serving as the object. "《家》" is the specific annotation to "书" and must be put after it.

例 446

误:他们什么时候两个进城的?

正:他们两个什么时候进城的?

代词"他们"和数量词"两个"指同样的人,"他们两个"是同位词组作主语。"什么时候"只能移到谓语动词"进"前,作时间状语,而不能插在同位词组之间。

Referring to the same people, the pronoun "他们" and the numeral measure-word phrase "两个" are an appositive phrase serving as the subject. "什么时候" can not be inserted between the two constituents of the appositive phrase and must be moved to the front of the predicate verb "进".

二、句子成分的误用
Errors in the Use of Sentence Elements

1. 主语使用不当
Improper use of subjects

例 447

误：他个子很结实。

正：他身体很结实。

主语"个子"指人的身材，与"高"、"矮"有关。"结实"指"身体健壮"。改"个子"为"身体"。

The subject "个子" refers to someone's height. It goes with "高" and "矮". "结实" means stout. Thus one should use "身体" rather than "个子".

例 448

误：他一起抚养这个孩子。

正：他们一起抚养这个孩子。

"一起"前边的主语须是表示复数的词语，主语"他"是单数，应改成"他们"或"他和他朋友"等。

The subject before "一起" must be plural. "他" in the above sentence is singular. One should replace it with "他们" or "他和他朋友" etc.

例 449

误：这个商店的前没有工厂。

正：这个商店的前边没有工厂。

带有复杂定语的单纯的方位词"前"不能单独作主语，应当用

170

合成的方位词。在"前"的后头加"边",改为"前边"。

With a complex attributive, a simple noun of locality like "前" can not serve as the subject. It must be replaced by a compound locality noun. One should add "边" after "前" to form "前边".

例 **450**

误:经过一年的努力,使他的汉语水平提高了。

正:经过一年的努力,他的汉语水平提高了。

由于不适当地用了"使",句中缺少应有的主语。删去了"使","水平"就成为主语了。

The sentence lacks a subject due to the use of "使". However, if "使" is deleted, "水平" will become the subject.

例 **451**

误:在学习上给了我很大的帮助。

正:在学习上谢力给了我很大的帮助。

"在学习上"是介词词组,在句中只能作状语,不能作主语。必须在谓语动词"给"前补上不可少的主语,像"谢力"一类的词语。

"在学习上" is a prepositional phrase which can never be a subject but only serves as an adverbial adjunct. One must add a subject such as "谢力" before the predicate verb "给".

例 **452**

误:运动员走进会场的时候,热烈地鼓掌。

正:运动员走进会场的时候,观众热烈地鼓掌。

"运动员走进会场的时候"是时间状语,全句没有主语。谁"热烈地鼓掌",显然是"观众"。应加在主语的位置上。

"运动员走进会场的时候" is an adverbial adjunct of time. The sentence has no subject. But obviously it was the audience which loudly applauded. One should fill the subject position with "观众".

例 **453**

误:这个电影不错,很多看的人。

正:这个电影不错,看的人很多。

"很多看的人"是词组,不是句子,把它们的语序调整一下,就成为由形容词"多"作谓语的句子了。

"很多看的人" is a phrase rather than a sentence. However, a change in order will turn it into a sentence with the adjective "多" as the predicate.

2. 谓语使用不当

Improper use of predicates

例 454

误:今天天气很美,不过我必须准备考试。

正:今天天气很好,不过我必须准备考试。

谓语形容词"美"侧重于形态的匀称、优美,多形容服装、容貌以及风景等,与主语"天气"不搭配,可以改"美"为"好"。

The adjective "美" stresses the symmetry and grace of shape and is mainly used to describe costumes, looks, scenes. It does not match with "weather". One may replace it with "好".

例 455

误:我刚上车,车就开始了。

正:我刚上车,车就开了。

"开始"表示从头起。这里主语是"车",应当改成"使……发动"的动词"开"。

"开始" means "start from the beginning". The verb "开" meaning to start an engine is the proper word to match "车".

例 456

误:她的丈夫要她在家里办家务。

正:她的丈夫要她在家里操持家务。

动词"办"强调做某件事,而宾词为"家务",指家庭事物,与

"办"不搭配。应改用"操持",强调亲手去做,含有辛辛苦苦地劳动的意味。

The verb "办" means to do something. "家务" which serves as the object and refers in particular to housework, and it does not match with "办". Instead of "办", one should use "操持" to imply doing a toilsome job with one's own hands.

例 457

误:他天天在田里做工作。

正:他天天在田里干活儿。

状语"在田里"表示"他"所从事的是体力劳动,与"做工作"不搭配,应改为"干活儿"。

The adverbial adjunct "在田里" indicates what he does is physical labour. One should use "干活儿" instead of "做工作" to go with "在田里".

例 458

误:这种情况没有使工人失望,反而提高了他们的精神。

正:这种情况没有使工人失望,反而振奋了他们的精神。

动词"提高"是指"位置、水平、数量、质量等方面比原来高",但"提高"与宾语"精神"配不拢。应改为"振奋",使人精神旺盛、情绪高涨的意思。

The verb "提高" refers to arise in position, level, quantity and quality. It does not match "精神". The proper word is "振奋" which means to uplift spirit and morale.

例 459

误:我们好久没见了,没想到你这儿。

正:我们好久没见了,没想到你在这儿。

"想到"后边的宾语缺少动词"在",补上这个必不可少的词,表示某人存在于某处。

Here, the object of "想到" should use the verb "在" to indicate that someone exists somewhere.

例 460

误:我已经完了今天的作业了。

正:我已经写完了今天的作业了。

只说"完了今天的作业"语意不完整,这是因为没有把谓语动词"写"写出来造成的。应该明确地加在谓语的位置上。动词"完"用在谓语动词"写"的后边,表示动作完成以后产生的具体结果。

Only with "完了今天的作业" the meaning of the sentence is incomplete since the predicate verb "写" is absent "写" should be placed in the predicate position followed by the verb "完" which shows the substantial result of the action.

例 461

误:老师让我通知大家明天欢送会。

正:老师让我通知大家明天开欢送会。

动词"通知"可以带两个宾语,通常一个指人,另一个可以指做某一件事。此句两个宾语却是"大家"和"欢送会",讲不通,根据需要,在"欢送会"前边加动词"开"。

The verb "通知" may take two objects with one referring to person(s) and one referring to event(s). The present sentence is meaningless with "欢送会" as one of its objects. The verb "开" should be added before "欢送会".

例 462

误:下一次旅行,我不是去上海,就是广州。

正:下一次旅行,我不是去上海,就是去广州。

"不是……就是"连接的一般是类别、结构相同或近似的成分。后一个分句中缺少动词,须在"就是"与"广州"之间加"去",作谓语。

Usually，the two elements joined by "不是…就是" are the same or similar in category and structure. Here，the second clause also needs a verb as the first one. "去" should be used between "就是" and "广州" to function as the predicate.

例 463

误：这支歌叫名字"社会主义好"。

正：这支歌的名字叫"社会主义好"。

句子的主干应是"名字叫社会主义好"。除了把主语和谓语颠倒过来外，还应该在"这支歌"后加"的"，用来连接定语和中心语。改成"这支歌的名字"。

The main body of the sentence is "名字叫社会主义好". Besides transposing the subject and the predicate，"的" must also be placed after "这支歌" to join the attributive and the head word. The grammatical form is "这支歌的名字".

例 464

误：屈原投汨罗江自杀死了。

正：屈原投汨罗江了。

"投江""自杀"和"死"三个词部分意思重复，删去"自杀"和"死"。"投江"足以准确表达句子的意思。

"投江"，"自杀" and "死" all hold the same meaning of "die". The last two are unnecessarily used. "投江" is enough to express the precise meaning of the sentence.

例 465

误：今天上午我们有上课。

正：今天上午我们有课（或"上课"）。

"有课"与"上课"是两个含义不同的动宾词组。"有课"同"没有课"相对；"上课"是指教师讲课或学生听课，可以说"不上课"、"没上课"。或者去掉"上"，或者去掉"有"。

The two verb-object phrases "有课" and "上课" carry different implications. "有课" is the opposite of "没有课", "上课" means to lecture or to attend classes. The opposite is "不上课" or "没上课". "上" or "有" is to be deleted.

例 466

误:如果你去上海,可以给我买带来一个录音机吗?

正:如果你去上海,可以给我买(或"带")来一个录音机吗?

两个表示不同意义的动词"买"和"带"不能混在一起用。只能取其一。

As two verbs with distinct meanings, "买" and "带"can not be used in combination. A choice is required between them.

3. 宾语使用不当

Improper use of objects

例 467

误:我每天早上做很多东西,锻炼身体,去食堂吃早饭,去教室上课。

正:我每天早上做很多事儿,锻炼身体,去食堂吃早饭,去教室上课。

"东西"指各种具体的或抽象的事物。句中指的却是各种活动,"锻炼身体","吃早饭"和"上课",应改宾语"东西"为"事儿"或"事情"。

"东西" denotes things, concrete or abstract. In the present sentence, "锻炼身体", "吃早饭" and "上课" are activities. They should be indicated by "事儿" or "事情" rather than "东西".

例 468

误:早上我开开门一看,外边有很多雨。

正:早上我开开门一看,外边有很多雨水。

原句指外边有很多由于下雨而积存的水,而不是指从云层中

176

降下地面的水。改宾语"雨"为"雨水"。

What the speaker means is that there is a lot of water on the ground after the rain. He is not speaking of the rain that is falling. Thus "雨" should be replaced by "雨水".

例 469

误：如果不听父母，就要挨骂。

正：如果不听父母的话，就要挨骂。

谓语动词"听"后缺少宾语，根据上下文，应加"话"。"听话"是一个词组，表示听从长辈的话。

The predicate verb "听" in the sentence should carry an object. According to the context, we add "话". The phrase "听话" means to obey what an elder or superior says.

例 470

误：办公楼在学校医院。

正：办公楼在学校医院的东边。

这里要说某事物存在于某处，应在表示实体的"学校医院"后边加方位词，如"东边"等，表示处所。

This sentence is to tell that something exists somewhere. It requires a noun of locality after the entity "学校医院". One may use such a word as "东边" to denote location.

例 471

误：下雨了，我们别长城去了。

正：下雨了，我们别去长城了。

在汉语里，当叙述进行什么动作时，一般是谓语在前，宾语在后。这个句子却是宾语"长城"在谓语"去"前，应把顺序颠倒过来。

In Chinese, to narrate the carrying out of an activity, the predicate is normally required before the object. But this sentence is just the opposite with "长城" preceding "去". One should reverse the word order of "长城去".

例 **472**

误:您这是五块,找两毛二分钱您。

正:您这是五块,找您两毛二分钱。

动词"找"后边的两个宾语易位。指人的宾语"您"须移到指物宾语"两毛二分钱"的前头。

The two objects after the verb "找" are in reverse order. The object referring to person ("您") should be moved to the front of the object referring to something ("两毛二分钱").

例 **473**

误:这本小说的内容又丰富又生动,因为这是作者写自己的经历事儿。

正:这本小说的内容又丰富又生动,因为这是作者写自己的经历。(或"自己的事儿")

宾语"经历"指"亲身见过、做过或遭受过的事",在语义上与"事儿"重复。或者删掉"事儿",保留"经历",或者删掉"经历",保留"事儿"。

The object "经历" refers to events or activities that one has encountered, seen or done. It contains the meaning of "事儿". One should delete "事儿" and retain "经历" or vice versa.

例 **474**

误:这个问题我们一定要解决它。

正:这个问题我们一定要解决。

"它"是指代"这个问题"的。句子显得不简洁,应该删去"它"。

As a replacement for "这个问题", "它"is an additional unnecessary word here. It should be deleted.

例 **475**

误:你买了一本书词典吗?

178

正：你买了一本书（或"一本词典"）吗？

由于定语是"一"，所以中心语所指的只能是一种物件，或者是"书"，或者是"词典"。

Since the attributive is "一", the head word must be singular. It is either "书" or "词典".

例 476

误：我常常跟同学说中国汉语。

正：我常常跟同学说汉语（或"说中国话"）。

宾语用词重复。可以改成"说汉语"，也可以改成"说中国话"。"说汉语"指说汉族的语言，是中国的主要语言，现在汉语的标准语是普通话。"说中国话"指说中国人民的语言，特指汉语。

The error lies in the duplication of meaning in the object. One should simply say "说汉语" or "说中国话". "汉语" is the language of Han nationality and plays the leading role in China. Modern Chinese takes *putonghua* as its standard form. "中国话" literally means the languages spoken by Chinese people. It refers in particular to modern Chinese.

4. 定语使用不当

Improper use of attributive

例 477

误：打架的戏有意思。

正：武打的戏有意思。

定语"打架"用词不当。此句是指戏曲中用武术表演的搏斗，应改为"武打"。

The attributive "打架" dose not meet the meaning of the sentence. One should use "武打" to indicate the performance of martial arts in drama.

例 478

误:她是唱歌学院的学生。

正:她是音乐学院的学生。

专门培养声乐和器乐人才的高等学府称为音乐学院。应改定语"唱歌"为"音乐"。

Institutions where people are trained to specialize in vocal or instrumental music are called "音乐学院". "音乐" should be used instead of "唱歌" as the attributive.

例 479

误:广大部分的农民不认识字。

正:大部分的农民不认识字。

定语"广大"与中心语"部分"不搭配。"广大"指人数多,"部分"指整体中的局部,应改"广大"为"大"。"大部分"指超过一半以上的范围。

The attributive "广大" does not match the head word "部分". "广大" means "a vast number of", and "部分" refers to part of a whole. One should use "大" instead "广大". "大部分" indicates the scope that embraces more than half.

例 480

误:外国留学生的北京语言学院很多。

正:北京语言学院的外国留学生很多。

按照病句的说法,"北京语言学院"是主语,形容词"多"作谓语,显然与事理不符。应把"外国留学生"同"北京语言学院"的位置对调一下,"留学生"是主语,"北京语言学院"作定语。在汉语中,无论什么成分充任的定语,一律放在被修饰成分的前边。

In the present sentence, "北京语言学院" is the subject, and the adjective "多" is the predicate. Such a sequence makes no sense. One should exchange the positions of "外国留学生" and "北京语言学院" to make "留学生" the subject and "北京语言学院"

the attributive. In Chinese, attributives always precede the head word irrespective of their constituents.

例 481

误:他们在前边我们宿舍打网球。

正:他们在我们宿舍前边打网球。

介宾词组"在前边"表示处所。原意是说,在我们宿舍的前边,而不是其他建筑物的前边打网球。把表示实体的"(我们)宿舍"与合成方位词"前边"的顺序调换一下就可以了。

The prepositional phrase "在前边" denotes location. The sentence means they play tennis in front of "我们宿舍" rather than any other buildings. The order of the two constituents (the entity "我们宿舍" and the compound locality noun "前边") should be reversed.

例 482

误:第二天下起大雾漫天。

正:第二天下起漫天大雾。

"雾"下得非常大,布满天空时,常用"漫天"来形容。"漫天"应放在"大雾"的前边作定语。

"漫天" is often used to describe a heavy fog that blackens the sky. It should precede "大雾" as its attributive.

例 483

误:那个我们学院的操场很小。

正:我们学院的那个操场很小。

"那个"和"我们学院"是主语"操场"的修饰成分。虽然都放在中心语"操场"的前边,但是先后顺序不当。在汉语中,指量词"那个"要紧挨着中心语"操场",其次是名词性词组"我们学院"及结构助词"的"。

"那个" and "我们学院" serve as modifiers of the subject "操

181

场". They are both in front of the head word but in reverse order. In Chinese, a demonstrative measure word ("那个") stays close to the head word ("操场") and a noun phrase ("我们学院") with the structural particle "的" stands a little further.

例 484

误:这是一本书新。

正:这是一本新书。

句子的主干是"这是书"。"一"、"本"和"新"是"本"的修饰成分。这三个成分的排列顺序是:形容词"新"紧靠中心语"书",其次是量词"本",再其次是数词"一"。

"这是书" is the main body of the sentence. "一", "本" and "新" function as modifiers of "书". These three elements should be ordered like this: the adjective "新" stays closest to the head word "书", then the measure word "本", and lastly comes the numeral "一".

例 485

误:请给我二十只那快船。

正:请给我那二十只快船。

"二十"、"只"、"那"和"快"都是中心语"船"的定语。它们的排列次序一般是,具有描写性的形容词"快"靠近中心语"船",其次是量词"只",再其次是"二十",离中心语最远的是指示代词"那"。

"二十", "只", "那" and "快" are all attributives of the head word "船". They must be placed in this sequence: the modifying adjective "快" stands the closest to the head word "船", then comes the measure word "只" and next comes the numeral "二十", the demonstrative pronoun "那" is the farthest from the head word.

例 486

误:他是一位我们学校的好老师。

182

正：他是我们学校的一位好老师。

"一"、"位"、"我们学校"和"好"是"老师"的定语。在汉语中,这几个成分的先后位置是,形容词"好"挨着中心语"老师",其次是数量词"一位",再其次是名词性词组表示领属关系的"我们学校"和定语的标志结构助词"的"。

"一", "位", "我们学校" and "好" are attributives of "老师". They should follow this order: the adjective "好" is the closest to the head word "老师", then is the numeral measure-word phrase "一位", and the farthest is the noun phrase "我们学校" showing classification and with the structural particle "的" attached to it.

例 487

误：他们化他们的悲痛为力量。

正：他们化悲痛为力量。

定语"他们"与主语用词重复。应删去定语"他们"和结构助词"的",使句子简洁明白。

The attributive "他们" is an unnecessary repetition of the subject. It should be deleted together with the structural particle "的" for terseness.

5. **状语使用不当**

Improper use of adverbial adjuncts.

例 488

误：他们也亲切地照顾我。

正：他们也经常照顾我。

形容词"亲切"放在谓语动词"照顾"前,作状语,用词不当。"亲切"含有很熟悉而有盛情的意味,常说"亲切地告诉"、"亲切地谈心"、"亲切地说"、"亲切地问"。动词"照顾"则表示放在被爱护的位置上,给予优待和帮助,常受"非常、特别、很、经常、尽量、优惠"等词 的修饰。可以把"亲切"改成"经常"。用作状语的"经常"后不带状语标志"地"。

It is inappropriate for the adjective "亲切" to premodify the predicate verb "照顾". "亲切" implies "familiar" and "affectionate". It is common to say "亲切地告诉", "亲切地谈心", "亲切地说", "亲切地问". The verb "照顾" means to give care and help. It is often modified by such words as "非常，特别，很，经常，尽量，优惠". "经常"may be used in place of "亲切" to serve as an adverbial adjunct, but it can not be followed by the adverbial marker "地".

例 **489**

误:王进喜积极地下决心帮助国家解决困难,参加开采新油田的大会战。

正:王进喜下决心帮助国家解决困难,积极地参加开采新油田的大会战。

形容词"积极"表示"有热心",动宾词组"下决心"表示人的坚定不移的意志,语义上不搭配,"下决心"不能接受"积极"的修饰。"积极"却与"参加"配得拢,应把"积极"移到后一个分句谓语动词"参加"的前边。

The adjective "积极" indicates "enthusiastically". The verb-object phrase "下决心" expresses one's firm will. These two elements do not match semantically. "积极" can not modify "下决心", but it can be a modifier of "参加". Thus one may move "积极" to the front of the predicate verb "参加" which is in the second clause.

例 **490**

误:这本小说很有意思,我想看多几遍。

正:这本小说很有意思,我想多看几遍。

谓语动词"看"后有数量词组"几遍"作补语,句中又有表示泛

184

量的"多",一般地,"多"放在谓语动词"看"之前,作状语,有"超出原来限量"的意思。

In the present sentence, the predicate verb "看" is followed by the numeral measure-word phrase "几遍" serving as the complement and "多". "多" normally precedes the predicate verb ("看") as an adverbial adjunct, meaning "exceed the usual limit".

例 491

误:请你替问你的父母亲好。

正:请你替我问你的父母亲好。

介词"替"表示代替的意思。它的后边缺少动作的对象"我"。加上"我"以后,构成介词词组"替我",用来作谓语动词"问"的修饰成分。

The preposition "替" means "on behalf of". It should take the object "我" to form the prepositional phrase "替我" which premodifies the predicate verb "问".

例 492

误:甚至他不能回答这个问题。

正:甚至他也不能回答这个问题。

用"甚至"突出像"他"这样水平高的人都不能回答,言外之意,水平低的人更不能回答了。后边应加"也"(或"都"),与之配用,起强调的作用。

"甚至" is used to stress that such an able person like him can not answer the question, let alone ordinary people. "也" or "都" should be used to go with "甚至" for emphasis.

例 493

误:星期三和星期六我们每天在礼堂看电影。

正:星期三和星期六我们在礼堂看电影。

"星期三和星期六"指一周内的两天;"每天"指"天天",两者所

185

表示的时间范围不相等。根据实际情况只删去"每天"。

"星期三" and "星期六" are only two days in a week, but "每天" means "everyday". They imply different frequency of the activity. One should delete "每天" according to the context.

例 494

误：好像田地可能是很肥沃的。

正：好像田地是很肥沃的。

正：田地可能是很肥沃的。

副词"好像"是"有些像"的意思；能愿动词"可能"表示不能肯定，用词不妥。或者删去"可能"，或者删去"好像"，任选其一。

The adverb "好像" means "seem", and the auxiliary verb "可能" implies uncertainty. They can not be used together. One of them must be deleted.

例 495

误：我们好久时间不见了。

正：我们好久不见了。

用作状语的"好久"指"时间久"，与"时间"含义重复。删去"时间"。

"好久" which is used here as an adverbial adjunct indicates a long time. It already contains the notion of "时间". Thus "时间" is redundant.

例 496

误：丁力的妈妈工作很忙，她去工厂早上六点。

正：丁力的妈妈工作很忙，她早上六点去工厂。

正：丁力的妈妈工作很忙，早上六点她去工厂。

句中时间词后置是英语的表示法。汉语里时间词"早上六点"作状语，可以放在动词谓语"去"前，也可以放在主语"她"前。

The post-position of the time phrase as in the above sentence is the English way of expression. In Chinese, a time phrase like "早上六点" serving as an adverbial adjunct should be placed before the verb predicate ("去") or the subject ("她").

例 497

误:天安门很远离我们学校。

正:天安门离我们学校很远。

表示地点的状语后置是受英语说法的影响。在汉语里,由介词"离"及其宾语"我们学校"构成的介宾词组,只能放在谓语"远"的前边。

Influenced by the English language, the speaker misplaces the adverbial adjunct of place after the predicate. The prepositional phrase formed by the preposition "离" and its object "我们学校" must precede the predicate "远".

例 498

误:在家乡因为没有办法过日子,他就十八岁跑到北京来了。

正:在家乡因为没有办法过日子,他十八岁就跑到北京来了。

"就"强调"跑到北京来"的行为发生得早,要放在动词谓语"跑"前作修饰成分。

"就" emphasizes that "跑到北京来" is an early occurrence. It should be put before the verb predicate "跑" as its modifier.

例 499

误:在公园他昨天划船划了多长时间?

正:他昨天在公园划船划了多长时间?

"昨天"是时间词,"在公园"是表示处所的介宾词组,虽然它们都用在动词谓语"划"的前边,但是排列次序不当。通常表示处所的介宾词组"在公园"紧挨着动词谓语"划",其次是时间词"昨天"。

"昨天" is a time noun and "在公园" is a prepositional phrase denoting location. Although they both precede the verb predicate

187

"划", they are improperly ordered. One should place the time noun "昨天" before the prepositional phrase "在公园" which should stand closer to the verb predicate "划".

例 500

误:张老师热情地给我们非常介绍了学校的情况。

正:张老师非常热情地给我们介绍了学校的情况。

表示程度的副词"非常"与表示动作行为的动词"介绍"不搭配。应当把"非常"放在形容词用作状语的"热情"的前边,指明"热情"的程度。

The degree adverb "非常" does not match with the action verb "介绍". It should go before the adverbial "热情" to show its degree.

例 501

误:他们比我们今天早回来一个小时。

正:他们今天比我们早回来一个小时。

中心语"回"前边有三个状语:"今天"、"比我们"和"早"。在这个用介词"比"构成的比较句里,它们的排列顺序通常是:比较两上动作发生"早晚"的"早"靠近动词谓语"回",其次是表示比较成份的介宾词组"比我们",再其次是时间词"今天"。

The head word "回" is premodified by three adverbials adjuncts, i.e. "今天", "比我们" and "早". In this comparative sentence in which the preposition "比" is used, the order should be: "早" stays the closest to the verb predicate "回", then is the prepositional phrase "比我们" introducing the object against which the comparison is made, and last comes the time noun "今天".

例 502

误:他每天早上在教室都跟阿里一起听录音。

正:他每天早上都在教室跟阿里一起听录音。

188

用在动词"听"前的四个修饰成分错位。它们的排列次序是：最靠近中心语的是表示动作对象的"跟阿里一起"，其次是表示处所词语"在教室"，再其次是用来总指时间的副词"都"，离中心语最远的是时间词语"每天早上"。

The four premodifiers of the verb "听" are in a wrong order. The right order should be the closest one to the head word is "跟阿里一起" which introduces the partner, the second is "在教室" indicating place, the third is the time adverb "都", and the furthest one is the phrase "每天早上" denoting time.

例 503

误：请你给我们把你的学习方法介绍一下。

正：请你把你的学习方法给我们介绍一下。

在"把"字句中，还有表示动作对象的介宾词组"给我们"作状语。通常表示动作对象的"给我们"紧挨着动词谓语"介绍"，其次是由"把"构成的介宾词组"把你的学习方法"。

In this "把"-sentence, there is another adverbial adjunct which is expressed by the prepositional phrase "给我们" introducing the recipient of the action. One should put it after the prepositional phrase formed by "把" and before the verb predicate "介绍".

6. **补语使用不当**

Improper use of complements

（1）结果补语

the complement of result

例 504

误：刚才我听中文广播懂了。

正：刚才我听懂中文广播了。

由动词充当的结果补语"懂"与宾语"广播"错位。动词"听"后带有结果补语和宾语时，宾语要在动词和补语之后，即"广播"须在

"听懂"之后。是说"听"只是一种行为,"听懂"是听的结果。

The complement of result indicated by the verb "懂" and the object "广播" are in reverse order. When the verb "听" is followed by both a resultant complement and an object, the object stays behind. That is, "广播" follows "听懂". "听" is an action, and "听懂" is the result of the action.

例 505

误:中国医生接了他的手指,所以他绣了"友谊"两个字送给中国人民。

正:中国医生接上了他的手指,所以他绣了"友谊"两个字送给中国人民。

如果只说"接手指",看不出断指是否达到连接的目的。原句是要说,中国医生已经使他扎断的手指重新连在一起了,他才能用手绣了"友谊"两个字给中国人民。这就要在动词"接"后加动词"上",作结果补语,表示通过动作使某事物附着于某处的意思。

Only from "接手指", one can not see whether the bones are joined or not. This sentence means that the Chinese doctors set his broken fingers, therefore he embroidered the two characters "友谊" for Chinese people. "上" should be added after "接" as the resultant complement which indicates that something is fixed somewhere through an action.

例 506

误:星期天我吃早饭就去看朋友。

正:星期天我吃完早饭就去看朋友。

表示动作的完成或终结,可以在动词后加"完"作结果补语。此句表示完成一动作后紧接着进行另一个动作,应在动词"吃"的后边加表示完成的"完",即"吃完早饭就进城看朋友"。

To express completion of an action, "完" may be used as the

190

resultant complement after the verb. The present sentence shows
that an action will take place directly after another action finishes.
One should add "完" denoting completion after "吃" to indicate that
the speaker will go to see friends after he finishes breakfast.

例 507

误:我昨天一天没看他。

正:我昨天一天没看见他。

是要表示昨天一天没有见到他的面,以结构上说,应该在"看"
的后头加上必不可少的结果补语"见"。

The speaker means that he did not see him the whole day yesterday. The resultant complement "见" is obligatory after the verb
"看".

例 508

误:你告诉他,我来这儿看见他了。

正:你告诉他,我来这儿看他了。

是说"我"来这儿看望过"他",但访友不遇,没能和他见面。这
里强调的是曾来看望。不该用"见"。

The speaker means that he came here to visit him but did not
see him. Thus "见" should not be used.

例 509

误:正在坐前边的是丁老师,坐后边的是马老师。

正:坐在前边的是丁老师,坐在后边的是马老师。

表示通过动作使人或事物处在某个地方时,动词后应带"在"
作结果补语,后边要有处所宾语。此句不是表示丁老师和马老师
"坐"这一动作行为,而是老师们"坐"这一动作实现后所处的位置。
按照原句结构应改成"坐在前边的是丁老师,坐在后边的是马老
师","坐在"已表示处所的状态,这是一种静态描写,无需用表示态
的"正"。

To express that something or somebody settles somewhere through an action, the verb should carry "在" as the resultant complement which is followed by a place object. This sentence is not meant to express the action "坐", but to show the position of the two teachers after the action "坐" finished. The grammatical form should be "坐在前边的是丁老师,坐在后边的是马老师". "坐在" which is a static state can not be modified by the progressive "正".

例 510

误:我每天上课十二点(钟)。

正:我每天上课上到十二点(钟)。

动词带结果补语也可以表明动作持续到某一时间。此句要表明"学习"这一动作延续到"十二点(钟)",应加结果补语"到"。

A verb may take a resultant complement to indicate that an action lasts until a certain time. The present sentence means that the action "学习" lasts until twelve o'clock. One should use "到" as the resultant complement.

例 511

误:今天下午我给妈妈寄到了生日礼物。

正:今天下午我给妈妈寄去了生日礼物。

"去"作结果补语,可以表示动作使人或事物到达某处,动补后边要有表示处所的词语。此句要说的是"今天下午"仅作了一件事:"给妈妈寄生日礼物",至于礼物是否到达妈妈那里,这个句子没有谈及,动补后也没有到达某处的宾语,因此应去掉动词后的结果补语"到",改为趋向补语"去"。

"到"serving as a complement of result expresses that a person or thing reaches a certain place through an action. It is often followed by an object of place. The speaker means that he posted a birthday gift to his mother this afternoon, but he does not mention whether the gift has reached the destination or not. Additionally, the object is not one that indicates the place. Thus the verb "寄" should take the directional complement "去" instead of the resultant complement "到".

例 512

误:那辆自行车没让人走骑。

正:那辆自行车没让人骑走。

动词"骑"可以和"自行车"搭配,而动词"走"没有这种组词能力,只能作"骑"的结果补语,表示离开原来的地方。应把"走骑"改为"骑走"。

The verb "骑" matches "自行车", but the verb "走" does not. "走" can only be the resultant complement of "骑" to denote departure. "走骑" should be changed into "骑走".

例 513

误:请你把这张表填完清楚。

正:请你把这张表填清楚。

正:请你把这张表填完。

动词"填"后,有两个结果补语:一个是动词"完",一个是形容词"清楚",两个词的意思截然不同,不能混用。可以任取其一。

In this sentence, the verb "填" has two complements: one is the verb "完" and the other is the adjective "清楚". These two words are different and cannot be used together. One has to choose between them.

例 514

误:我听懂明白你的话了。

正:我听懂你的话了。

正:我听明白你的话了。

动词"听"后带两个结果补语:"懂"和"明白"的意思相同。任取一个。

The verb "听" should not take two complements of result. A choice must be made between "懂" and "明白" which are similar in meaning.

例 515

误：电影里的人说得很快，我不听懂。

正：电影里的人说得很快，我没听懂。

正：电影里的人说得很快，我听不懂。

动词带结果补语的否定式一般是在动词前加"没"，而不是"不"。这是因为动作有了结果，所以要用"没"来否定。如果强调没有能力达到某种结果也可以用可能补语的否定式"听不懂"。

A verb with a resultant complement is negated by adding before the verb "没" rather than "不". This is because, the action has already achieved a result. To emphasize inability to achieve a certain result, one may use the negation of the potential complement, i. e. "听不懂".

例 516

误：如果没学好汉语，那么学习专业就很困难。

正：如果不学好汉语，那么学习专业就很困难。

这是一个假设复句，说明动作的结果是没有实现的，动词前要用"不"，不能用"没"。

This is a hypothetical complex sentence, which implies that the action has not achieved a result. Therefore "不" rather than "没" should be used before the verb.

（2）程度补语

　　the complement of degree

例 517

误：丁力学习很努力，他英语说不错。

194

正：丁力学习很努力，他英语说得不错。

因为要表明丁力努力学习后，说英语的水平达到较高的程度。应该在动词"说"和补语"不错"之间加"得"。

To express that Ding Li's English has reached a high level, one should insert "得" between the verb "说" and the complement "不错".

例 518

误：他打篮球越来越好。

正：他打篮球打得越来越好。

是说打篮球的技术逐步达到好的程度，应当用程度补语表示。由于动词"打"的后边带有宾语"篮球"，"得"字只能加在重复的动词和补语"越来越好"之间。

To express that one becomes better and better in playing basketball, the degree complement should be used. Since the verb "打" has an object ("篮球") after it, "得" can only be placed between the reduplicated verb and the complement "越来越好".

例 519

误：由于考试的缘故，大家来了很早。

正：由于考试的缘故，大家来得很早。

是要说明大家来的时间早晚，不是说明动作是否完成，况且"来了"后不能带形容词词组。应把动词"来"后的"了"改为表示对动作评价判断的程度补语的标志"得"。

This sentence is not speaking of completion of the action "来", but is making judgement about how early the event occurred. Besides, "来了" can not be followed by an adjectival phrase. Thus "了" must be replaced with "得" which is the marker of a degree complement that expresses the judgement of the action.

例 520

误：我学得很忙。

正：我学习很忙。

句中动词"学习"与程度补语"很忙"，在语义上不搭配。"学习"这一动词能带的程度补语可以是表示学习成绩的优劣，或学习进度的快慢。如要说明他学习方面繁忙的情况，可用主谓谓语句"他学习很忙"。

"很忙" used as a degree complement does not match the verb "学" (or "学习") semantically. "学" (or "学习") can only take those complements that show achievements or rate of progress. To express "I am busily engaged in study", one may say "我学习很忙" which is a sentence with a subject predicate phrase as the predicate.

例 521

误：他排球打得很好极了。

正：他排球打得很好。

正：他排球打得好极了。

程度补语只能带一个附加成分。或者用表示程度的副词"很"作状语，或者用表示程度的"极了"作补语。

A degree complement can have only one adjunct. "好" should either be premodified by the degree adverb "很" or complemented by "极了" which also denotes degree.

例 522

误：他们法文不说得很慢。

正：他们法文说得不慢。

带"得"的程度补语的否定式是用"不"，否定由形容词"慢"充当的程度补语，而不是否定谓语动词"说"。

A degree complement with "得" is negated by adding "不" in front of the complement. Thus "不" should precede the adjective

"慢" rather than the predicate verb "说".

例 523

误:谢力汉字写不写得很快?

正:谢力汉字写得快不快?

带程度补语句子的提问,重点问程度如何。要是用正反疑问句,只能就得字后的形容词提问,即"写得快不快"。

In a question with a degree complement the semantic focus is on the degree. If it is an affirmative negative question with an adjective as the degree complement, it is the affirmative and negative forms of the adjective rather than the predicate verb that are to be placed together. One should say "写得快不快".

例 524

误:他来得怎么样?

正:他来得早不早?(他来得准时不准时?)

用"怎么样"提问程度补语句,多指动作行为的状态、技能、质量,而表示趋向的动词"来"不具有这种性质,它与时间的早晚,速度的快慢有关。应改特指问的"怎么样"为正反问"早不早"。

"怎么样" serving as the degree complement in a question, asks about the state, technique or quality of an action. The directional verb "来" has nothing to do with these aspects, but is related to time and speed. One should replace "怎么样" used in a special question with "早不早" which is an affirmative negative question.

(3) 简单趋向补语

the simple complement of direction

例 525

误:我送你们出来。

正:我送你们出去。

句中"我"与"你们"的动作方向一致,都是从所在处所里边往

197

外走,离处所的距离远。动词谓语"送"后的补语要改"来"为"去"。

"我" and "你们" move in the same direction. i. e. from inside towards outside, away from where the speaker is. Thus the verb predicate "送" should take "去" rather than "来" as the complement.

例 526

误:你们快上山去,这里的风景美极了。

正:你们快上山来,这里的风景美极了。

根据原句意,说话人在"这里"(指山上),对方("你们")是由低处向高处走,动作向着说话人进行。动词"上"后的补语不应用"去",要用"来"。

By using "这里", the speaker implies that he is on the mountain and "你们" should come up towards him. Thus the complement should be "来" instead of "去".

例 527

误:你常常到我这儿去帮助我,我很感激。

正:你常常到我这儿来帮助我,我很感激。

"你"的动作方向是朝着说话人"我"进行的,动词"到"后应当用补语"来",不能用"去"。

Here, "你" moves in the direction of the speaker "我". In this case, one should use "来" rather than "去" as the complement of the verb "到".

例 528

误:刚才我给妈妈寄来生日礼物了。

正:刚才我给妈妈寄去生日礼物了。

说话人"我"由一处往"妈妈"的住处"寄生日礼物","礼物"距离说话人越来越远。趋向补语"来"应改为"去"。

The speaker posted a birthday gift to his mother. The motion

of the gift is away from the speaker. Therefore，"来" should be replaced by "去".

例 529

误：他出书店去买书了。

正：他进书店去买书了。

"买书"必跨到书店里边去，动词谓语用"出"显然不妥，应改
"出去"为"进去"。

To buy books，one must go into the store. It is obviously
wrong to use "出". One should say "进书店去买书".

例 530

误：你在宿舍等我，我马上就进来。

正：你在宿舍等我，我马上就回来。

说话人（"我"）有事要先去别处，让对方（"你"）在宿舍等待，然
后再返到"宿舍"，谓语动词应当用"回"。

The speaker（"我"）is going out somewhere and asks the other
person（"你"）to wait in the room until he is back. "回" should be
used as the predicate verb.

例 531

误：安娜不在，她回去美国了。

正：安娜不在，她回美国去了。

"美国"是表示处所的宾语，不能用在动补词组"回去"立后，只
能紧跟在动词"回"的后头。

The object "美国" denotes place. It can not be put after the
verb-complement phrase "回去"，but must be inserted in between.

例 532

误：你们进去一个一个。

正：你们一个一个地进去。

数量词"一个"重叠后表示动作进行的方式，应当放在谓语动

词"进"前,作状语。状语与中心语之间应用"地"联系。

When the numeral measure-word phrase "一个" is reduplicated to indicate the manner of an action, it must precede the predicate verb ("进") as an adverbial adjunct, and "地" is required between the modifier and the head word.

例 533

误:明天我们到去参观。

正:明天我们到农村去参观。

动词"到"与简单趋向补语"去"之间须有表示处所的词语,用作动词"到"的宾语。此句应加上诸如"农村"一类的词。

Between the verb "到" and the directional complement "去", a place object should be used. For example, one may say "到农村去参观".

例 534

误:一个月之内,你一定寄来我那本新书。

正:一个月之内,你一定给我寄来那本新书。

"寄来"后只能带一个表示事物的宾语"那本新书"。要引出动作对象"我"时,须用介词"给",构成介宾词组"给我",放在"寄"之前,作状语。

"寄来"can only have objects referring to things. The receiver "我" must be introduced by the preposition "给", and the prepositional phrase "给我" should precede "寄" as its adverbial adjunct.

(4) 复合趋向补语

the compound complement of direction

例 535

误:同学们看见老师进来了,立刻站上来。

正:同学们看见老师进来了,立刻站起来。

动词"站"后的复合趋向补语"上来"使用不当,应改为"起来"。

200

表示通过行为动作"站"改变"同学们"原来"坐"的姿势,也有由低处到高处的意思。

Here, it is improper to use "上来" as the directional complement of the verb "站". The right word should be "起来" which indicates the change from a sitting posture to a standing posture, and it also implies "from a lower position to an upper position".

例 536

误:我朋友从医院里走过来了。

正:我朋友从医院里走出来了。

用作状语的"从医院里"指明"我的朋友"从里往外走,动作是向着在医院外边的"我"进行的。很明显,动词"走"后的补语应改为"出来"。

The adverbial adjunct "从医院里" shows that "我的朋友" is going out from inside, and that the motion is towards "我" who is outside the hospital. Clearly, the verb "走" should take "出来" as its complement.

例 537

误:刚才我看见丁力跑山下去了。

正:刚才我看见丁力跑下山去了。

例 538

误:上课了,我们走进去教室吧!

正:上课了,我们走进教室去吧!

(537)(538)谓语动词"跑"和"走"后分别带有复合趋向补语"下去"、"进去",还有表示处所名词"山"和"教室"作宾语。宾语"山"和"教室"须放在复合趋向补语"下去"和"进去"的中间。

In (537), (538), the predicate verbs "跑" and "走" have "下去" and "进去" as their respective complements of direction. The two place nouns "山"and "教室" serving as the objects must be inserted between the two constituents of "下去" and "进去".

例 **539**

误：我们刚走到校门口，就下雨起来了。

正：我们刚走到校门口，就下起雨来了。

谓语动词"下"后跟有复合趋向补语"起来"以及表示自然现象的名词"雨"充任的宾语。通常把"雨"放在复合趋向补语"起来"之间。

The predicate verb "下" is followed by the compound directional complement "起来" and the object "雨" which is a natural phenomenon. The usual way is to insert "雨" into the complement "起来".

例 **540**

误：我同屋从图书馆借一本中文书回来。

正：我同屋从图书馆借回一本中文书来。

正：我同屋从图书馆借回来一本中文书。

谓语动词"借"后有补语"回来"，和表示一般事物的名词"书"充当的宾语。但"书"不能直接跟在动词"借"的后面。这个句子的主语是"我同屋"。有两种改法，一是把"书"放在复合趋向补语"回来"的中间，二是把"书"放在复合趋向补语"回来"的后边。

The predicate verb "借" has a complement ("回来") and an object (expressed by the common noun "书"). "书" can not immediately follow the verb. It has two possible positions in this sentence：between "回" and "来"；after "回来".

例 **541**

误：我的自行车被朋友骑去城里到了。

正：我的自行车被朋友骑到城里去了。

"到……去"也可以放在别的动词后表示趋向。此句谓语动词"骑"后的复合趋向补语易位，把"去"和"到"的位置颠倒过来就可以了。

"到…去" may follow other verbs to show direction. In the present sentence, the two constituents ("去", "到") of the compound directional complement are misplaced and should be reversed.

例 542

误：解放军战士很快跑过马来了。

正：解放军战士很快向马跑过来了。

动词"跑"后的补语"过来"，表示通过行为动作（"跑"）改变位置，离"马"越来越近。"马"是非处所名词，不能跟在动词"跑"的后边，须要用表示动作的接受者的介词"向"，与"马"构成介宾词组放在谓语动词"跑"前，作状语，说明动作的方向。

The complement "过来" expresses a change in position through the action "跑", i.e. the soldier is approaching the horse. "马" is not a place noun; therefore, it cannot occur after the verb "跑"; and must be introduced by the preposition "向". The prepositional phrase "向马" should precede the predicate verb "跑" as an adverbial adjunct to indicate the direction of the action.

例 543

误：他跑过宿舍进去了。

正：他跑过宿舍去了。

正：他跑进宿舍去了。

"跑"后的复合趋向补语中的"过"和"进"代表不同的趋向，不能混在一起用。要么删去"进"保留"过"，表示通过"跑"，"他"经过"宿舍"跑向别处。要么删去"过"，保留"进"，同时把宾语"宿舍"移到复合趋向补语"进去"的中间。

"过" and "进" indicate different directions, and can not be used together. One may delete "进" and maintain "过" to express "He ran past the dorm", or delete "过" maintain "进" and insert the object ″宿舍″ into the compound directional complement ″进去″.

例 544

误:请你把画儿在墙上挂起来。

正:请你把画儿挂起来。

正:请你把画儿挂在墙上。

"在墙上"与"起来"用词有些累赘,要么删去"在墙上",保留"起来",要么删去"起来"把"在墙上"放在动词"挂"后,作补充成分。表示借助于钉子、钩子、绳子等使"画儿"附着于"墙上"的某一点。

This sentence is wordy, with both ″在墙上″ and ″起来″ present. One should delete ″在墙上″, or delete ″起来″ and place ″在墙上″ after the verb ″挂″ as the complement to express to fix the picture onto the wall with such things as nails, hooks or strings.

例 545

误:桌子上太乱了,你包上来这些东西吧!

正:桌子上太乱了,你包起来这些东西吧!

此句是建议对方把分散在桌子上的东西集中到一处,应改动词谓语"包"后的"上来"为"起来"。

The speaker is asking the other person to put together the things scattered on the table. ″起来″ rather than ″上来″ should follow the verb predicate ″包″ as the complement.

例 546

误:我听懂了,但是我写不来。

正:我听懂了,但是我写不出来。

谓语动词"写"后的复合趋向补语缺少"出",应改"来"为"出来",表示还不能通过"写"的动作显露听懂的内容。

One constituent is missing from the compound directional complement which is after the predicate verb ″写″. ″出″ should be added before "来" to express one's inability to write down what he heard.

例 547

误:老师让我把课文接着念。

正:老师让我把课文接着念下去。

根据"把"字句的结构特点,动词"念"不能是个光杆。从语义上说,原句有使"念"这个行为动作继续进行的意思,应该在动词"念"的后边加上补语"下去"。

According to the structural feature of the 把-sentence, the verb "念" here can not stand alone. Since the action "念" will be carried on, we add "下去" to be the complement of "念".

(5) 可能补语

the complement of potentiality

例 548

误:太晚了,咱们还爬山得了(liǎo)吗?

正:太晚了,咱们还爬得了(liǎo)山吗?

动词谓语"爬"后带有可能补语"了"和宾语"山",宾语不能紧跟着动词,要放在动补词组"爬得了"的后头,询问有没有爬山的可能。

The verb predicate "爬" is followed by the potential complement "了" and the object "山". "山" can not directly follow the verb, but should stay after the verb-complement phrase "爬得了". The speaker questions the chance of climbing the mountain.

例 549

误:请你大点儿声,我听不懂。

正:请你大点儿声,我听不清楚。

因说话时声音小,使人听起来很费劲,但是,不一定听不懂。改用"不清楚",更符合事理。

The low voice of the speaker causes difficulty for the hearer，but not necessarily non-understanding. Therefore ″不清楚″ is more reasonable than ″不懂″.

例 **550**

误：这台洗衣机又大又重，我们抱不动。

正：这台洗衣机又大又重，我们抬不动(或"搬不动")。

动词"抱"表示用手臂围住，可能补语"动"表示使"洗衣机"移动位置。怎么能抱动"洗衣机"呢?宜用动词"搬"或者"抬"。

The verb ″抱″ means ″hold in the arms″. The potential complement ″动″ expresses to move ″洗衣机″. It is unreasonable to say ″抱洗衣机″. One should use ″搬″ or ″抬″.

例 **551**

误：你说得不清楚，所以我不听懂。

正：你说得不清楚，所以我听不懂。

作为可能补语否定式标志的"不"，不能放到动词的前边，只能放在动词的后边，改为"听不懂"。

As the mark to negate a potential complement，″不″ must follow the verb rather than precede it. One should say ″听不懂″.

例 **552**

误：你想得起来不起来他叫什么名字?

正：你想得起来想不起来他叫什么名字?

可能补语的否定式前缺少动词，应在"不"前加"想"。

The negative form of the potential complement should have a verb in front of it. We add ″想″ before ″不″.

例 **553**

误：五道口剧场坐得下坐得不下一千人?

正：五道口剧场坐得下坐不下一千人?

这是并列动词及其可能补语的肯定式和否定式的正反问句。

其中否定式的动补词组中的补语是可能补语肯定式标志"得"与否定式标志"不"的杂糅，应去掉"得"。

In this affirmative-negative question where the affirmative and negative forms of the potential verb-complement phrase should be juxtaposed，the second verb-complement phrase is ungrammatical with both "得"(the marker of the affirmative form of the potential complement) and "不"(the marker of the negative form of the potential complement) present. "得" should not be used.

例 554

误：坐那么远，你能不能看得清楚？

正：坐那么远，你看得清楚吗？

正：坐那么远，你能不能看清楚？

此句是并列的能愿动词"能"的肯定、否定形式与可能补语的肯定形式的混用。或者删去"能不能"在句尾加"吗"，改成是非问；或者删去"得"，改可能补语为结果补语。

Here，the affirmative negative forms of the auxiliary verb "能" and the affirmative form of the potential complement are mixed in one sentence. One should delete "能不能" and add "吗" at the end to make the sentence a general question. One may also change the potential complement into a resultant complement by deleting "得".

例 555

误：我把那篇文章翻译得完。

正：我能把那篇文章翻译完。

用介词"把"构成的句子，动词后边的成分是表明怎样处置或处置的结果的，而可能补语"翻译得完"表示的只是一种可能，通常可能补语不用在"把"字句的动词后边，应改为结果补语"翻译完"。根据句意应在"把"前加能愿动词"能"，表示具备"翻译那篇文章"的能力。

In a 把-sentence, the element after the verb shows in what way the object of the action is affected or the result of the action. However, in the present sentence, "翻译得完" indicates a possibility and is a potential complement which does not normally occur after the verb of a 把-sentence. It should be changed into a resultant complement ("翻译完"). According to the sentence meaning, we add the auxiliary verb "能" before "把" to express that one has the ability to finish translating the article.

（6）时量补语

the complement of duration

例 556

误：我去图书馆看报了半个小时。

正：我去图书馆看报看了半个小时。

正：我去图书馆看了半小时报。

"看"后的时量补语"半个小时"和由名词"报"充当的宾语易位。由于动词"看"所表示的动作是能持续的，这个句子有两种改法：一、重复动词"看"，把宾语"报"放在重复的动词之前；把时量补语"半个小时"放在重复的动词之后。二、不必重复动词，只是把时量补语"半个小时"放在动词谓语"看"与宾语"报"之间。

The complement of "半个小时" and the object expressed by the noun "报" are in reverse order. "看" is a durable action, and we have two ways to correct the sentence. One way is to repeat the verb "看", then put the object "报" before and the complement of "半个小时" after the second "看". The other way is to place "半个小时候" between "看" and "报".

例 557

误：我在公园里等他了一个小时。

正：我在公园里等了他一个小时。

动词谓语"等"后带有时量补语"一个小时"和由人称代词"他"充当的宾语。在这种条件下,宾语"他"不能跟在动词"等"后,应放在时量补语"一个小时"前。

The verb predicate ″等″ have the complement of duration ″一个小时″ and the object ″他″ after it. In this case, ″他″ can not directly follow ″等″ but should precede ″一个小时″.

例 558

误:他来教室来了一刻钟。

正:他来教室一刻钟了。

"来"是趋向动词,所表示的动作是不能持续的。动词"来"不能重复。

″来″ is a directional verb which does not last. Therefore, it can not be reduplicated.

例 559

误:昨天上午的会一个小时开了。

正:昨天上午的会一个小时开完了。

表示时段的词语,也可以用作状语,说明在某一段时间内发生什么事。在这种句子里,谓语动词前后要有附加或补充的成分加以限制或补充。此句应在动词谓语"开"后加结果补语"完"。

Words denoting duration may serve as adverbial adjuncts to indicate the time during which something lasts or exists. In this case, the predicate verb must have adjuncts or complements for qualification. One should use the resultant complement ″完″ after the verb ″开″.

例 560

误:他没上课两天了。

正:他两天没上课了。

"没"是对"上课"的否定,自然谈不上"上课"占用的时间,应把表示时段的"两天"放在谓语动词"上"前,作状语。强调"两天"这段时间之内,出现了"他没上课"这样的事。

Already negated by ″没″, ″上课″ naturally can not carry a complement of duration to indicate how long it took. To express ″ He has not come to class for two days″, one should place ″两天″ before the predicate verb ″上″ as an adverbial adjunct.

(7) 动量补语

　　the complement of frequency

例 561

误:这个故事比较难,我听了八九次才听懂。

正:这个故事比较难,我听了八九遍才听懂。

因为要说明一个动作从开始到结束的整个过程,应该把"次"改成"遍",才符合句子的本意。

To stress the whole process of an action from beginning to end, ″遍″ should be used instead of ″次″.

例 562

误:我以前来过一遍上海。

正:我以前来过一趟上海。

误用动量词"遍"。这里指来往的次数,应改用"趟"。

The complement of frequency ″遍″ does not fit this sentence. ″趟″ is the proper word to indicate frequency of traveling.

例 563

误:刚才下了一次雨,凉快点儿了。

正:刚才下了一阵雨,凉快点儿了。

动量词"次"与"阵"混淆。这个句子是指"下雨"经过的段落,应改用"阵"。

The complements of frequency ″次″ and ″阵″ should not be confused. ″阵″ is often used to indicate a period (usually short)of

210

rain.

例 **564**

误:让他们来这里避雨一下儿。

正:让他们来这里避一下儿雨。

动词"避"后有宾语"雨"和动量补语"一下儿",动量补语须紧跟在动词"避"的后头,表示时间短暂。

The verb ″避″ is followed by the object ″雨″ and the complement of frequency ″一下儿″. ″一下儿″ should come immediately after the verb to denote temporariness.

例 **565**

误:我的朋友住院了,我一次去看了他。

正:我的朋友住院了,我去看了他一次。

是要说明行为动作"看"已进行的次数,"一次"应放在动词"看"后作动量补语。句中动词"看"后由人称代词"他"充当的宾语,要放在动量补语"一次"前。

″一次″ should come after the verb ″看″ as an complement to indicate frequency of the action. In the case of a verb with a pronoun object (″他″), the object must precede the complement of frequency (″一次″).

例 **566**

误:我送送你们一下。

正:我送送你们。(我送你们一下。)

"送送"是动词"送"的重叠形式,表示短暂的时间,"一下儿"表示动作的短暂。"送送"与"一下儿"重复。二者只能取其一。

As the reduplicative form of the verb ″送″, ″送送″ implies temporariness which is also indicated by ″一下儿″. To avoid repetition, one of them should be deleted.

例 **567**

误:这本小说很有意思,我想再看这本小说。

正:这本小说很有意思,我想再看一遍。

"再"表示重复的行为动作"看"还没有成为事实。"再"用在肯定句里,谓语动词"看"后应加上数量补语"一遍"与其配用。宾语"这本小说"可省去,避免与主语相重。

"再" indicates that the speaker's hope to read again has not been realized. An affirmative sentence with "再" requires a complement of quantity (e. g. "一遍") after the predicate verb ("看").

例 568

误:这些句子很容易,我能翻译一下儿。

正:这些句子很容易,我能翻译。

既然"这些句子很容易",自然"翻译这些句子"是不成问题的。而动量词"一下儿"有"试试"的意思,前后矛盾,应删去"一下儿"。

By saying "这些句子很容易", one implies that his ability to translate the sentences is beyond doubt. But the complement of frequency "一下" expresses "attempt or trial." It contradicts the meaning of the sentence and should be deleted.

三、单句的误用
Errors in the Use of Simple Sentences

1. 主谓句使用不当
Improper use of the subject-predicate sentences

（1）名词谓语句

sentences with a noun predicate

例 569

误:今天第一九八六年五月四日。

正：今天一九八六年五月四日。

原句"第一九八六年"表示年代，不该用"第"。

To express the time of the year, one should not use "第".

例 570

误：我和你哥哥都是我们学校的篮球队员，他今年几岁了？

正：我和你哥哥都是我们学校的篮球队员，他今年多大了（或
　　"二十几了"）？

"几岁"作谓语，只用于询问小孩儿的年龄。篮球队员都是十几
岁到二十几岁的年轻人，询问年龄时，要用"多大"或"十几"、"二十
几"。

"几岁" is used to inquire the age of small children. It does not
apply to people above ten. One should say "多大", or "十几" or
"二十几".

例 571

误：他美国的人。

正：他美国人。

用作定语的"美国"与中心语"人"粘合得很紧，形成稳固的词
组，表示国籍。不用"的"。

The attributive "美国" and the head word "人" must stick together to indicate nationality. They can not be separated by "的".

（2）形容词谓语句

　　　sentences with an adjectival predicate

例 572

误：这是很贵，有便宜的吗？

正：这（个）很贵，有便宜的吗？

这是 It is very expensive 的直译。在汉语里，一般的形容词谓
语句与英语同类句型的结构不同，即谓语的前边不能用"是"，须删
去多余的"是"。

"这是很贵" is the verbatim translation of "It is very expensive". In Chinese, a sentence with an adjectival predicate does not have "是" in front of the predicate. "是" should be deleted.

例 573

误：虽然他们住在一个富国，但是他们是很穷。

正：虽然他们住在一个富国，但是他们是很穷的。

这个句子有两种改法，一是删去"是"。二是在句尾加"的"，构成"是……的"格式，有说明、解释的意思。这样更符合原意。

There are two possible ways to correct the sentence. The first one is to delete "是". The second one is to use "的" at the end of the sentence to form the "是 … 的" pattern which has an explanatory function. The latter best suits the speaker's intention.

例 574

误：你看，这件衣服干净。

正：你看，这件衣服很干净。

形容词谓语句中，单个形容词作谓语表示比较，有"这件衣服干净，那件衣服不干净"的意味。根据病句原意，不含比较，应该在形容词前加"很"（这里"很"的意义弱化）。

A sentence with a single adjective as the predicate shows a contrast. In this sentence, the speaker implies, "That shirt is not clean, but this one is". If the speaker intends no contrast, he should use "很" before the adjective (here "很" does not express an obvious degree).

例 575

误：今天天气太好。

正：今天天气太好了。

谓语形容词"好"受程度副词"太"的修饰，句末应当加"了"，与之呼应。表示程度加重。

In a sentence where the predicate adjective "好" is modified by the degree adverb "太","了" must be present in the final position.

例 576

误:我认为他们夫妻生活不是幸福。

正:我认为他们夫妻生活不幸福。

形容词谓语句的否定形式同样不能用"是"字。如若强调否定语气,也可用"是……的"结构,"他们夫妻生活是不幸福的"。

Just as the affirmative form, the negative form of a sentence with an adjectival predicate can not use "是" either. To intensify the negation, one may use the structure "是…的", i.e. "他们夫妻生活是不幸福的".

例 577

误:你们屋子是大不大?

正:你们屋子大不大?

形容词谓语句的正反式是:形/"不"/形。句中的"是"使用不当,应删去。

The affirmative-negative form of a sentence with an adjectival predicate is: adjective / "不" / adjective. "是" should be deleted.

(3) 主谓谓语句

sentences with a subject-predicate phrase (S-P phrase) predicate

例 578

误:他考试成绩很好,因为他很努力地学习。

正:他考试成绩很好,因为他学习很努力。

前一分句是"他考试成绩很好",说话人想据此作出判断,说明"他"这个人学习怎么样,不是一般叙述"他怎样学习",因此用主谓谓语句"他学习很努力"代替"他努力地学习"更恰当。由此可见,主谓谓语句的作用是它的说明性,而不是叙述性。

On the basis of "他考试成绩很好", the speaker comments on his attitude towards study, not just makes a general statement of how he studies. Therefore, "他学习很努力" of which the predicate is a subject-predicate phrase is the proper structure to replace "他努力地学习". On this evidence, we may say the function of a sentence with an S-P phrase predicate lies in exposition rather than narration.

例 579

误：我最近非常忙学习。

正：我最近学习非常忙。

"忙"带有宾语时，不能受程度副词的修饰。这个句子可改为主谓谓语句，谓语是主谓词组"学习非常忙"。

With an object, "忙" can not be modified by a degree adverb. One may change the sentence into one with an S-P phrase predicate-"学习非常忙".

例 580

误：尽管他不学习努力，他的考试成绩还可以。

正：尽管他学习不努力，他的考试成绩还可以。

用在主谓谓语句中的否定词"不"错位，应当移到小主语"学习"之后，否定小谓语"努力"。

The negation word "不" is in the wrong position. It should go after the subject "学习" of the S-P phrase predicate to negate its predicate "努力".

例 581

误：谢力和丁力都身体很好。

正：谢力和丁力身体都很好。

用在主谓谓语句中的"都"位置不当。一般应该在小主谓"身体"的后边。

216

"都" is misplaced. One should put it after "身体", the subject of the S-P phrase predicate.

2. 非主谓句使用不当

Improper use of the non-subject-predicate (non-S-P) sentences

例 582

误：它下雨了，咱们快点儿走吧。

正：下雨了，咱们快点儿走吧。

这是 It is raining 的直译。英语用代词"它"来代表大自然，作主语。在汉语里叙述自然现象，无需说出主语。删去"它"。

"它下雨了" is the literal translation of "It is raining". In English, the pronoun "it" may serve as the subject to represent "Nature". But in Chinese, a sentence stating a natural phenomenon need not have a subject. "它" should be deleted.

例 583

误：无气刮大风了，把衣服收进来吧！

正：刮大风了，把衣服收进来吧！

在汉语里，需要说出主语的话，可以用"天"，但不能用"天气"或"它"。一般不用主语，这样还比较自然，别人也不会追问。

If one persists in having a subject, he may use "天", but not "天气" or "它". Usually this kind of sentence is subjectless, and it would sound unnatural with a subject imposed on it.

四、几种特殊动词谓语句的误用

Errors in the Use of Several Special Types of Sentences with a Verbal Predicate

1. "是"字句使用不当

Improper use of the 是-sentence

例 584

误：他是不英国人，他是法国人。

正：他不是英国人，他是法国人。

"是不"是受英语词序的影响。在汉语里，动词"是"的否定形式一定是把否定副词"不"放在"是"的前边。

"是不" results from the influence of the English word order. The negative form of "是" should be "不是" with "不" in the front.

例 585

误：谢力跑得最快的运动员。

正：谢力是跑得最快的运动员。

"谢力"是主语，"运动员"是宾语。从主语和宾语的关系看，二者是有条件搭配的。如果在"谢力"与"运动员"之间加上表示判断的动词"是"，就成了"是"字句。说明"谢力"就是跑得最快的运动员。

"谢力" is the subject and "运动员" the object. They should be connected by the verb "是" expressing judgement to show their identical relation.

例 586

误：今天不十二月二十七号。

正：今天不是十二月二十七号。

"今天"是主语，"十二月二十七号"是宾语，从充当主语和宾语的具体内容可以看出都是指时间的词语，只是两者之间缺少判断动词"是"。在"不"后补上"是"，就成了"是"字句的否定式。

The subject "今天" and the object "十二月二十七号" both refer to time. Verb "是" which is absent must be added after "不" to

218

make the negative form of a 是-sentence.

例 587

误：这支钢笔是弟弟。

正：这支钢笔是弟弟的。

"钢笔"是主语，"弟弟"是宾语。从字面上看，符合"是"字句的结构特点。从语义上说，"钢笔是弟弟"讲不通。因为"是"字两边的成分不同同类事物，也没有类属关系。在"弟弟"后加"的"，构成"的"字词组"弟弟的""弟弟的钢笔"。这样，就符合表示判断的"是"字句的要求了。

This sentence satisfies the structural requirements of a 是-sentence. But semantically, "钢笔" and "弟弟" belong to distinct categories and share nothing in common. It does not make sense to say "钢笔是弟弟". To satisfy the semantic requirements of the 是-sentence, "的" should be added after "弟弟" to form the "的" phrase "弟弟的" which means "弟弟的钢笔".

例 588

误：食堂是宿舍旁边。

正：宿舍旁边是食堂。

"是"也可以表示存在。表示存在的"是"作谓语时，基本格式是"表示处所的词语——'是'——表示事物的名词"。此句"是"前后的两个成分错位，应把表示处所的词语"宿舍旁边"移到句首；把表示事物的名词"食堂"挪到"是"的后面。

"是" also expresses existence. When "是" of such use serves as the predicate, the sentence should follow this order："Locality noun (or phrase)—'是'—noun (or phrase) of object". In the present sentence the two parts before and after "是" are reversed. "宿舍旁边" should be shifted to the initial position and "食堂" referring to object should go after "是".

2."有"字句使用不当

Improper use of the 有-sentence

例 589

误：他有没自行车。

正：他没有自行车。

由动词"有"充当谓语的否定形式，只能把否定词"没"放在"有"前，作状语，不能放在"有"的后边。此句"有"表示领有。

The negative form of the verb predicate "有" is "没有", with "没" premodifying "有" as an adverbial adjunct. "没" can not come after "有". In this sentence, "有" expresses possession.

例 590

误：对不起，我现在不有时间。

正：对不起，我现在没有时间。

动词"有"不能接受否定副词"不"的修饰，只能用副词"没"。

The verb "有" can not be negated by "不". "没" is the only possible word.

例 591

误：(A：你有电影票吗?)

　　B：我没有一张电影票。

正：(A：你有电影票吗?)

　　B：我没有电影票。

此句是 I have no one 的直译。但在汉语中既然对于"有电影票"一事已经否定，宾语"电影票"前无须再用表示数量的词。或者用格式"一……也……"，即"一张电影票也没有"强调根本没有票。

This sentence is a literal translation of "I have no one". According to Chinese grammar, before the object "电影票" there is no need to use words indicating the number, since "有电影票" is entirely negated by "没". However, one may apply the pattern "一…

也" to intensify the meaning of "none", i. e. "一张电影票也没有".

例 592

误：明天下午两点半我们有开会。

正：明天下午两点半我们有会。

正：明天下午两点半我们开会。

在汉语里，"有会"、"开会"是两个意义不同的动宾词组，不能混用于同一个句子之内。要么删去动词"开"，改成"有会"；要么删去动词"有"，改成"开会"。

"有会" and "开会" are two verb-object phrases different in meaning. There is no such form as "有开会". We simply say "有会" or "开会".

例 593

误：等你没有时间，我再来。

正：等你有时间，我再来。

正：等你没事儿，我再来。

在汉语里，"没有时间"与"有时间"相对，"没有事儿"与"有事儿"相对。此句不合事理。应改"没有时间"为"有时间"或"没事儿"。

In Chinese，"没有时间" is the opposite of "有时间" and "没有事儿" is the opposite of "有事儿". This sentence does not stand to reason. "没有时间" should be replaced by "有时间" or "没事儿".

例 594

误：这个问题对我们有十分重要。

正：这个问题对我们十分重要。

在语义上，动词"有"与形容词"重要"不搭配。应删去"有"，改成由"重要"充当谓语的形容词谓语句。

Semantically，the verb "有" and the adjective "重要" do not

match. By deleting "有", we make "重要" the predicate of the sentence.

例 595

误：那个班几乎有日本留学生。

正：那个班有日本留学生。

正：那个班几乎都是日本留学生。

句中"有"表示存在，旨在说明"那个班有一些日本留学生。而用作状语的"几乎"含有接近全部人数的意思。在语义上，这两个词相互矛盾，或者删去"几乎"，或者改动词"有"为与"几乎"顺意的、表示存在的动词"是"，然后再在"是"前加上表示总括的"都"，强调接近"那个班"的全部人数。

"有" expresses existence here to indicate that there are some Japanese students in that class. "几乎" serving as an adverbial adjunct means "nearly (all)". By using "有" or "几乎", the speaker means differently. To express "there are (some)", one should delete "几乎". To express "nearly all", one should delete "有" and add after "几乎" the verb "是" modified by "都"which is an adverb of scope meaning "all".

例 596

误：教学楼有图书馆北边。

正：图书馆北边有教学楼。

此句是说"在某一个空间里存在着什么东西"。它的基本格式是"表示处所的词语——'有'——表示事物的名词"。根据"格式"的要求，应把"有"前后的两个成分的位置对调一下，"图书馆北边"放到前边，"教学楼"移到后边。

To express that there is something existing somewhere, the basic pattern is :"Locality noun (or phrase)——'有'—— word (or phrase) of object". According to this pattern, one should exchange the positions of "图书馆北边" and "教学楼" in the sentence.

例 597

误:这个教室十张桌子和十把椅子。

正:这个教室有十张桌子和十把椅子。

"这个教室"是表示空间的词语,"十张桌子和十把椅子"是表示事物的词语。显而易见,句中缺少谓语,在这两个成分之间加上表示存在的动词"有",就成了"某一空间存在着某物"的"有"字句。

"这个教室" is a place and "十张桌子和十把椅子" are objects. The predicate is absent. "有" should serve as the predicate in between to express the notion that there is something existing somewhere.

例 598

误:你家有口人?

正:你家有几口人?

正:你家几口人?

动词"有"后,如果是数词"一",可省略不说。原句是个特指疑问句,通常要用询问数目的疑问代词"几",加在量词"口"前,询问家庭成员的数目。或者去掉"有","几口人"作谓语,改成名词谓语句。

If the numeral after "有" is "一", it can be omitted. This sentence is a special question asking about the number of people in a family. It requires the interrogative pronoun "几" to precede the measure word "口". "有" is optional. If it does not occur, the noun phrase "几口人" becomes the predicate.

3. 兼语句使用不当

Improper use of the pivotal sentence

例 599

误:玛丽,我们祝你好生日。

正:玛丽,我们祝你生日好。

兼语句的基本格式是:

宾语

主语——动词谓语—— 兼 ——兼语的谓语

主语

作"兼语谓语"的成分不符合兼语句的特点,"你"是兼语,"祝"是行为,兼语的谓语是陈述行为的对象,要用主谓词组充当。原兼语的谓语"好生日"却是偏正词组,应改为主谓词组"生日好"。这个句子是说庆贺的原因是什么。

The basic pattern of a pivotal sentence is:

object

subject—verb predicate— also —predicate to the pivot

subject

Here, the element serving as the predicate to the pivot does not conform to the feature of the pivotal sentence. Here, "你" is the pivot and "祝" indicates the action. The predicate of the pivot which is a statement about the object of the action should be an S-P (subject-predicate) phrase. "好生日" is an endocentric phrase and must be converted into an S-P phrase "生日好". This sentence explains the reason for congratulation.

例 **600**

误:马教授请我叫您去吃饭。

正:马教授叫我请您去吃饭。

句中谓语有两项兼语关系,"请我"和"我叫您去","我"和"您"都是兼语。其中动词"请"和"叫"词义混淆。从情理上讲,"请"的宾语是"我",宜改为表示自谦的动词"叫";"叫"的宾语是"您",宜改动词"叫"为敬辞"请"。此句是"马教授叫我请您干什么"。

This sentence contains two pivotal constructions. "我" and "您" are the two pivots. "请" is a polite word while "叫" is neu-

224

tral. The former should take "您" as its object to show respect, and the latter should take "我" as the object for modesty.

例 601

误:阿里让我那件事告诉你。

正:阿里让我告诉你那件事。

"我"是兼语。"告诉"是兼语的谓语动词,它的后边有两个宾语"你"和"那件事",这两个宾语都要跟有"告诉"的后边,不能一个在动词前,一个在动词后。

"我" is the pivot the predicate of which is the verb "告诉". "告诉" has two objects that must stay after it, not before it.

例 602

误:请明天晚上你来我这儿一趟。

正:明天晚上请你来我这儿一趟。

正:请你明天晚上来我这儿一趟。

动词谓语"请"与兼语"你"结合得很紧,中间不能插入与兼语无对待关系的状语"明天晚上",时间词语"明天晚上"可以放在谓语动词"请"前,也可以放在兼语的谓语动词"来"前。

The verb predicate "请" and the pivot "你" can not be separated. "明天晚上" serving as the adverbial adjunct of time should either precede "请" or precede the verb "来", the predicate of the pivot.

例 603

误:丁力让马上我去。

正:丁力让我马上去。

同(602)。副词"马上"只能放在兼语的谓语动词"去"前。

Similarly, adverb "马上" should come before "去", the verb predicate of the pivot.

例 604

误:老师让我通知去教室练习汉语节目。

正:教师让我通知你去教室练习汉语节目。

谓语是两项兼语关系又套有连动关系。"老师让我"、"我通知(?)"、"(?)去练习"。很明显,"我"是一项兼语,还缺少另一项兼语。根据全句需要,应加上遗漏的兼语"你"。

Here, we have two pivotal constructions including two verbal constructions in series. "老师让我", "我通知(?)"、"(?)去练习". Clear enough, one pivot is "我", but the other one is missing. We add "你" as the pivot to meet the meaning of the sentence.

例 605

误:今天的参观很高兴。

正:今天的参观使我们很高兴。

主语"参观"与谓语"高兴"不搭配,怎么能说"参观很高兴"呢?应当说"人"很高兴。这样,不妨在"参观"和"高兴"之间补上一个必须涉及人的动宾词组,如"使我们",于是,构成了兼语句。是说"参观使我们怎么样"。

The subject "参观" and the predicate "高兴" do not match. It is impossible to say "Visiting is glad". It should be a person that is glad. Thus, we insert between "参观" and "高兴" a V-O(verb-object)phrase to introduce a noun of person, e. g. "使我们". In this way, we make the sentence a pivotal sentence which tells what effects the visiting has on us.

例 606

误:叫智叟的一个人。

正:有一个人叫智叟。

"叫智叟的一个人"是个偏正词组,不成句。根据语句的实际情况,可以改成用表示存在的动词"有"引进无定的兼语"一个人"构成兼语句。句中动词"有"表示兼语"人"的存在;兼语的谓语部分

226

"叫智叟"是对兼语的陈述。

The endocentric phrase "叫智叟的一个人" does not make a sentence. One may use the verb "有" expressing existence to form a pivotal sentence where "一个人" is the pivot. "有" shows existence of the pivot the predicate section of which "叫智叟" is the statement about it.

例 607

误:谢力让我在操场不等他。

正:谢力不让我在操场等他。

兼语句中,表示否定的副词"不"通常放在谓语动词"让"前,不能放在兼语的谓语前边。

In a pivotal sentence, the negation word "不" normally precedes the verb predicate of the whole sentence, not the predicate of the pivot.

4. 连动句使用不当

Improper use of sentences with verbal constructions in series

例 608

误:我学习汉语来中国。

正:我来中国学习汉语。

连动句的基本格式是:主语——动词词组(1)——动词词组(2)。此句两个动词词组错位。根据客观的实际情况应先说"来中国",后说"学习汉语"。这是后一个动作补充说明前一个动作目的的连动句。

For this type of sentence, the basic pattern is: subject-verb phrase(1)-verb phrase(2). In the present sentence, the two verb phrases are in reverse order. According to the context, "学习汉语" should occur after "来中国". It is the second action that indicates the purpose of the first.

例 609

误:阿里出去了穿上衣服。

正:阿里穿上衣服出去了。

应当是先"穿上衣服",紧接后一个动作"出去",两个动作有时间先后的关系,次序不能颠倒。这是动作依次连续发生的连动句。

In this sentence, the two actions happened in succession, i. e. "阿里" first put on clothes and then went out. The two verb phrases must be arranged according to the sequence of the actions and can not be reversed. Thus "穿上衣服" should precede "出去".

例 610

误:现在他们可以会话用汉语了。

正:现在他们可以用汉语会话了。

由动词"用"构成的动宾词组有表明后一个动作("会话")的手段的作用,略含修饰的意味。在句中应放"会话"之前,不能放在"会话"之后。

A V-O (verb-object) phrase with the verb "用" often indicates the means of another action ("会话"), and it performs a modifying function. Therefore, "用汉语" should precede "会话" rather than follow it.

例 611

误:很多旅游者来这儿开着汽车。

正:很多旅游者开着汽车来这儿。

"开着汽车"是动词词组"来这儿"这个行为的伴随动作。前一个动词("开")后的"着",表示这个动作行为在后面的作行为进行的过程中一直持续着、伴随着。应把"开着汽车"移到"来这儿"的前边。

"开着汽车"is the concomitant action of "来这儿". "着" after the first verb ("开") shows that this action continues throughout the process of the other. "开着汽车" should be moved to the front of "来这儿".

例 612

误：丁力去火车站了送米希尔。

正：丁力去火车站送米希尔了。

在连动句里，动词"了"不能插在两个动宾词组之间，可以用在全句的末尾。

The particle "了" can not go between the two verbal constructions. It should occupy the final position of the sentence.

例 613

误：以后我们要别的大学学习五年专业。

正：以后我们要去(到)别的大学学习五年专业。

动词词组(1)缺少动词，应当在"别的大学"之前补上动词"去"或者动词"到"。

Verb phrase (1) needs a verb. Verb "去" or "到" may be used before "别的大学".

例 614

误：我同屋去商店了一件毛衣。

正：我同屋去商店买了一件毛衣。

动词词组(2)缺少动词，应在动态助词"了"前加上动词"买"。带有数量词的宾语"一件毛衣"应放在"了"后。

Verb phrase (2) needs a verb. One may add "买" before the aspect particle "了" which is followed by "一件毛衣".

例 615

误：每当见到朋友的时候，她总是有很多事告诉。

正：每当见到朋友的时候，她总是有很多事告诉他(他们)。

前一个动词是由"有"构成的动词词组，后一个动词"告诉"是对"有"的宾语加以说明。但是"告诉"后缺少动作的对象，句意不明。根据上下文的需要，必须补上"他"或"他们"，作宾语。

The first verb is "有" and the second verb is "告诉" which gives information about the object of "有". This sentence is incomplete without words denoting the receiver of "告诉". To meet the need of the sentence，"他" or "他们" may be used as the object.

例 616

误：祥子想买一辆新的拉车。

正：祥子想买一辆新的车拉。

在这个连动句里，后一个动作"拉"是以前一个动词"买"的宾语为对象，同时又表明前一个动作的目的。从语义上分析，"买"的宾语不是"一辆新的"，而是"车"，"拉"的对象也不是"一辆新的"，而是"车"，应把错位的"车"移到"一辆新的"后边作中心语。

In this sentence with two verbal constructions in series，the object of the first action "买" is also the recipient of the second action "拉"，and "拉" indicates the purpose of "买". Semantically，it is "车" rather than "一辆新的" that is the object of "买" and recipient of "拉". "车" is misplaced and should come after "一辆新的" as its head word.

5. "把"字句使用不当

Improper use of the 把-sentence

例 617

误：她在柜子里把衣服放。

正：她把衣服放在柜子里。

此句词序有误。"把"字句的基本格式是：主语——把＋宾语——谓语动词——其他成分。

处所词语"在衣柜里"误作状语，应移到谓语动词"放"后，用作"其他成分"。是说动词表示的动作行为"放"加到受事事物（"衣服"）上，并影响受事事物存在的处所。

The words are improperly ordered. The basic pattern of the 把

-sentence is: subject—把＋object—predicate verb—other elements. In the present sentence, the locality phrase "在衣柜里" is misused as an adverbial adjunct, and must be moved after the predicate verb "放" to occupy the position of "other elements". It shows where the recipient ("衣服") arrives as the result of the action.

例 618

误：阿里把带回来了录音机。

正：阿里把录音机带回来了。

"录音机"是动作（"带"）的受事，但不能放在动词后边，而应移到动词的前边，即凭借介词"把"的作用，组成介宾词组，用来限定动词"带"，作状语。

"录音机" is the patient of the action ("带"). But here it can not follow the verb; instead, it should precede the verb to serve as the object of the preposition "把". The prepositional phrase "把录音机" modifies the verb "带" as an adverbal adjunct.

例 619

误：把那棵小树大风刮倒了。

正：大风把那棵小树刮倒了。

"大风"是主语，是动作的施事者，应将易位的主语移到句首。

As the doer of the action, "大风" must occur initially as the subject.

例 620

误：黑板把阿里擦干净了。

正：阿里把黑板擦干净了。

介词"把"将处置的对象搞错了。"阿里"应当是动作行为的施事者，"黑板"是受处置的对象，即受事者，两者的位置调换一下就对了。

The preposition "把" carries the wrong object. "阿里" is the

231

agent and "黑板" is the recipient. Their positions in this sentence should be changed.

例 621

误:人们把粽子扔了在河里,好让鱼吃粽子,不吃屈原的尸体。

正:人们把粽子扔在了河里,好让鱼吃粽子,不吃屈原的尸体。

充当"其他成分"中的动态助词"了"与结果补语"在"易位。一般结果补语"在"要紧接着动词谓语,其次是"了"。

In the position of "other elements", the aspect particle "了" and the resultant complement "在" are in reverse order. Generally, "在" immediately follows the verb predicate and "了" comes after.

例 622

误:谢力昨天把那个照相机进城买来了。

正:谢力昨天进城把那个照相机买来了。

在这个"把"字句与连动词套用的句子中,介宾词组"把那个照相机"的位置不妥。前个动作"进"是表示趋向的动词,没有处置意味。后个动词"买"是表示行为动作的及物动词,有处置作用。因此"把那个照相机"应放在第二个动词"买"前,限定动词。

In this sentence where a "把" construction and two verbal constructions in series are used in combination, the prepositional phrase "把那个照相机" is in the wrong position. The first verb "进" indicates direction and carries no implication of "acting on" or "affecting". The second verb "买" is a transitive verb and does imply "affecting". Therefore, "把那个照相机" can only occur before "买" to define the action.

例 623

误:玛丽把安娜给自己的自行车了。

正:玛丽把自己的自行车给安娜了。

宾语"安娜"与"其他成分""自己的自行车"易位。在"给"作动词谓语的"把"字句里,宾语应是指事物的名词("自行车"),"其他成分"应由指人的名词("安娜")充任。

"安娜" and "自己的自行车" are in reverse order. In a 把-sentence where "给" is the verb predicate, the object of "把" should be a noun denoting to ("自行车"), and the position of "other elements" should be occupied by nouns referring to person ("安娜").

例 **624**

误:我同屋把收音机没弄坏。

正:我同屋没把收音机弄坏。

例 **625**

误:他把练习不作完,不休息。

正:他不把练习作完,不休息。

(624)、(625)中否定词"没"和"不"的位置失当,都应提到"把"字前边。

The negation words "没" and "不" are misplaced in (624), (625). Both should precede "把".

例 **626**

误:我把新课在宿舍里预习好了。

正:我在宿舍里把新课预习好了。

说明动作行为对受事事物加以处置的处所状语("在宿舍里")不能放在"把"后,而应提到"把"字之前。

The adverbial adjunct "在宿舍里" here shows the place where the action is applied to something. It must precede "把" rather than follow it.

例 **627**

误:从书包里谢力把票拿出来了。

正:谢力从书包里把票拿出来了。

说明受事事物所从来的地方（"从书包里"）的位置不当。或者放在"把"字之前，或者放在动词之前。

"从书包里" indicates where the recipient of the action came from. It is in the wrong position. One should place it either before "把" or before the verb 拿.

例 **628**

误：每天上课的时候，我们都本子拿出来听写。

正：每天上课的时候，我们都把本子拿出来听写。

"把"字句的标志是句中有介词"把"，此句缺少"把"字，必须在受事事物（"本子"）前加上这个必不可少的成分。

The preposition "把" which is the marker of the "把" sentence is absent here. One should add it before the recipient （"本子"）.

例 **629**

误：那位先生把提包在座位上。

正：那位先生把提包放在座位上。

"把"字句中缺少对受事成分加以处置的动词，应在"其他成分"（"在座位上"）前，补上这个必不可少的动词"放"。

This "把"-sentence lacks a verb that can govern or influence the object of "把". Such a verb as "放" is needed before the "other elements"（"在座位上"）.

例 **630**

误：孩子们把门前的堆成一个雪人。

正：孩子们把门前的雪堆成一个雪人。

由"把"字构成的介宾词组中缺宾语，根据句子的实际情况，应在"把门前的"后边补上能够受动作处置的受事事物"雪"，作中语。

The object of "把" is missing here. To fit the context, we add "雪" (the recipient of the action "堆") after "门前的" as the head word.

例 631

误：我上午要把这篇文章翻译。

正：我上午要把这篇文章翻译完。

缺"其他成分"。"把"字句中的动词一般不能是一个单个动词，它的后边总要有"其他成分"。在动词"翻译"后加上补语"完"，是说"翻译"表示的动作，施加到受事事物"文章"上，并能明显地影响"文章"的变化。

The verb of a "把"-sentence can not go alone. It is always followed by "other elements". One may use "完" as the complement of "翻译" to show the change brought about by the action that is applied to the recipient "文章".

例 632

误：放假以后，我们打算去把上海旅行。

正：放假以后，我们打算去上海旅行。

动词"旅行"是一个不能带受动宾语的动词，此句不能用"把"字句。可改为"去上海旅行"。

The verb "旅行" is an intransitive verb; thus, it can not serve as the predicate of a 把-sentence which is improper to be used here. One should say "去上海旅行".

例 633

误：他把那件不愉快的事知道了。

正：他知道那件不愉快的事了。

"知道"是行为心理动词，不含处置意义，即"知道"表示的动作所为，只能施加到受事事物（"事"）上，并产生影响。这个句子不能用"把"字句，应改成一般的主谓宾句式。

"知道" is an intellectual verb and does not imply "affecting", i.e. the action "知道" can not act upon or influence a person or thing ("事"). Thus, this sentence can not use "把" and should be changed into an ordinary subject-predicate sentence with an object.

例 **634**

误：希望你们把这个地方喜欢。

正：希望你们喜欢这个地方。

"喜欢"是状态心理动词，没有处置作用，不能用"把"字句。可改为主谓宾句式。

"喜欢" is a verb expressing mental state. It has no function of influence and may not be used with "把". This sentence may take the pattern：subject-predicate-object.

例 **635**

误：大家都把《基础汉语课本》有了。

正：大家都有《基础汉语课本》了。

句中"有"是一个表示有无的动词，没有处置作用，不能用"把"字句，改为一般的主谓宾句式。

"有" which indicates existence can not produce influence upon people or things and never serves as the predicate of a 把-sentence. One may simply use a subject-predicate-object sentence.

例 **636**

误：我们把排球打了半个小时。

正：我们打了半个小时排球。

时间词语"半个小时"说明动作（"打球"）持续的时间，并不是动作行为对受事事物（"排球"）处置后的结果。这个句子不宜用"把"字句，可改为"打了半个小时排球"。

Instead of being the result of the action applied to the recipient ("排球"), the time phrase "半个小时" expresses the duration of "打". It is improper to use "把" here. One should say "打了半个小时排球".

例 **637**

误:我也把北京烤鸭吃过。

正:我也吃过北京烤鸭。

用在动词("吃")后的动态助词"过",表示过去有过某种经验,并非动作行为对受事事物处置后产生的影响。此句不能用介词"把",应改为主谓宾句式。

The aspect particle "过" after the verb "吃" shows a past experience. It does not indicate the influence produced by an action. Thus, "把" can not be applied here. We simply adopt the pattern: subject-predicate-object.

例 638

误:阿里挂这张地图在那张世界地图旁边了。

正:阿里把这张地图挂在那张世界地图旁边了。

充当"其他成分"的是由"在"构成的处所词语("在……旁边"),表示动作行为处置受事事物("这张地图")后,影响受事事物的存在处所。所以就按照格式"把……(动词)+……(表示处所的名词)"改正原句,即"把这张地图挂在那张世界地图旁边"。

The "other elements", realized by "在" taking an object ("…旁边") to indicate locality, shows where the recipient ("这张地图") is as the result of the action. The sentence should follow the pattern "'把'…(verb)+'在'…(locality noun), i. e. "把这张地图挂在那张世界地图旁边".

例 639

误:你扔果皮进垃圾箱里(边)。

正:你把果皮扔进垃圾箱里(边)。

"进"含有"到里面"的意思,用来充当"其他成分"("进……里边"),表示动作行为处置受事事物("垃圾")后,使其处于某处,这样的句子应该用"把"字句。按照"把……(动词)+'进'……(表示处所的名词)"格式,将原句改成"把果皮扔进垃圾箱里(边)"。

237

"进" means "into". It often takes an object to form "进…里边" which occupies the position of "other elements" showing where the person or thing has arrived as the result of the action. A 把-sentence is required on such occasion. According to the pattern "'把'…(verb)＋'进'…(locality noun)", one should change the sentence into "把果皮扔进垃圾箱里(边)".

例 640

误：我写"太"成"大"了。

正：我把"太"写成"大"了。

充任"其他成分"的是结果补语"成"，表示动作行为处置受事事物("太")后，使之变为另一种事物，这个句子要用"把"字句。依照"'把'……(动词)＋'成'……"格式，将原句改成"把'太'写成'大'了"。

In the position of "other elements" is the resultant complement "成" which shows that the thing ("太"), affected by the action, has changed into one of another kind. Such a sentence should use "把". According to the pattern "'把'…(verb)＋'成'…", the right form should be "把'太'写成'大'了".

例 641

误：我们要搬到外边这些椅子。

正：我们要把这些椅子搬到外边。

充任"其他成分"的是结果补语"到"，表示动作行为处置受事事物("这些椅子")后变更的位置。这样的句子要用"把"字句。应当按格式"'把'……(动词)＋'到'……(表示处所的名词)"将原句改为"把这些椅子搬到外边。"

The 把-sentence must be used here, since the "other elements" realized by the resultant complement "到" indicates that the objects ("这些椅子") have arrived at a new position through the action.

238

Based on the pattern "'把'…(verb)＋'到'…(locality noun)", the sentence should be changed into "把这些椅子搬到外边".

例 **642**

误：人们都叫做她孟姜女。

正：人们都把她叫做孟姜女。

用来作"其他成分"的是结果补语"做"，表示对受事者（"她"）称呼什么，这样的句子要用"把"字句。按格式"'把'……叫做……"将原句改为"把她叫做孟姜女"。

The 把-construction should be used when the verb "做" serves as the resultant complement to indicate the way to address a person. The right pattern is "'把'…叫做…". Thus one should say "把她叫做孟姜女".

例 **643**

误：我想把美元换了人民币。

正：我想把美元换成人民币。

误用"其他成分"。此句是要将受事事物（"美元"）变换为另一种事物（"人民币"），谓语动词"换"后不能用动态助词"了"，应改用"成"，即格式"'把'……换成……"。

The error lies in the "other elements". To express to change something into something else, the predicate verb "换" should take "成" as its complement in place of the aspect particle "了". One should use the pattern "'把'…换成…".

例 **644**

误：他把箱子送给我这儿了。

正：他把箱子送到我这儿了。

"这儿"是说明受事事物（"箱子"）运去的处所。谓语动词"送"后误用的结果补语"给"，应改为"到"。即"把……（送）到……"格式。

"这儿"indicates the place that the object ("箱子") has reached. The predicate verb "送" should take "到" instead of "给" as the complement of result, i. e. "把…(送)到…".

例 645

误:她把花儿摆上桌子上了。

正:她把花儿摆在桌子上了。

"桌子上"指受事事物"花儿"存在的处所,应改补语"上"为"在",即"把……(摆)在……"格式。

"桌子上"shows the location of the object "花". The complement "上" should be replaced with "在", i. e. one should use the pattern "把…(摆)在…".

例 646

误:我已经把本子上写上我的名字了。

正:我已经在本子上写上我的名字了。

介词和"本子上"是修饰动词"写"的,表示"写"的范围,不能用"把",应改用表示处所的"在"。

Here, with "本子上", the prepositional phrase premodifying the verb "写" to indicate the scope of the action should be formed by "在" rather than "把".

例 647

误:你把一本书放在什么地方了?

正:你把那本书放在什么地方了?

"把"字后边的宾语一般是有定的,此句却误用为无定的。须把无定的"一本书"改为有定的"那本书",即指交际双方共知的书,并不是随便的哪一本书。

The object of "把" is normally definite. But "一本书" in the present sentence is indefinite. It should be changed into "那本书" which instead of referring to any other book refers in particular to

240

the one known to both sides of the conversation.

6. 意义被动句使用不当

Improper use of notionally passive sentences

例 648

误:我的作业被作完了。

正:我的作业作完了。

例 649

误:那件衣服已经被洗过了。

正:那件衣服已经洗过了。

(648)(649)的主语都是受事事物("作业","那件衣服"),动词都含处置义("作"和"洗"),动词后边还有表示完结义的补语("完"和"过")。具有这种特点的句子不能用"被"字,应当用意义上的被动句,表明某事物受动作影响产生了预期完成的结果。

In both (648)and (649),the subject is the recipient of the action ("作业", "那件衣服"); the predicate verb ("作", "洗") carries the implication of "affecting" and is followed by a complement denoting completion ("完", "过"). In a sentence with such characteristics, "被" should not be used. The notionally passive sentence is the proper construction to express that something affected by an action, has achieved a certain result.

例 650

误:我的钱包被丢了

正:我的钱包丢了

例 651

误:这月房租还没被交呢

正:这月房租还没交呢

(650)(651)的主语("钱包"、"房租")分别是动作的受事,动词("丢"、"交")都是表示消失意义的单音节词,句尾有"了"。这样的

句子应该用意义被动词,删去"被"字,说明受事主语受动作影响而
消失。

In (650) and (651), the subject ("钱包", "房租") is the recipient of the action, the verb ("丢", "交") is monosyllabic with a
sense of "disappearing", and "了"（呢）comes at the end. Such
sentences that express disappearance of something with the influence of an action are notionally passive and don't have "被".

例 652
误:北京1949年被解放了。
正:北京是1949年解放的。

例 653
误:困难已经被克服了。
正:困难已经克服了。

(652)(653)的动词("解放"、"克服")本身都是有完结义的双
音节词,这样的句子不宜用"被"字,要用意义上的被动句,说明受
事主语受动作影响产生了预期完成的结果。

"被" does not occur in such sentences as (652) and (653) with
disyllabic verbs carrying the implication of accomplishment. The
notionally passive sentence should be used to express that a person
or thing (the subject) is subject to a certain result with the influence
of the action.

例 654
误:房子是怎么被卖掉的?
正:房子是怎么卖掉的?

例 655
误:大家的意见正在被研究中。
正:大家的意见正在研究中。

汉语里,受事主语句用在"是……的"或"在……中"格式中时,
242

都可以表示被动意义,不能用"被"字。

Sentences with the recipient of an action as the subject in the construction of "是···的" or "在···中" are notionally passive. They do not need "被".

例 656

误:课文已经能被念熟了。

正:课文已经能念熟了。

例 657

误:这些旧习惯早该被改了。

正:这些旧习惯早该改了。

受事主语句中,动词前有能愿动词"能"、"该"、"应该"、"可以"、"要"等,不能用"被"字句。

In a sentence where the recipient of an action is the subject, "被" is not used if the main verb is preceded by an auxiliary verb, such as "能","该","应该","可以","要" etc.

例 658

误:衬衣被洗得很干净。

正:衬衣洗得很干净。

主语是受事事物("衬衣"),动词("洗")后又带程度补语,这样的句子要用意义上的被动句,不能用"被"字。说明受事主语受动作影响,呈现出某种状态。

In this sentence with the recipient of the action ("衬衣") as the subject, the verb ("洗") is followed by a degree complement. Here "被" may not be used, since such a sentence is notionally passive, showing that something is under certain condition brought about by the influence of the action.

例 659

误:汽车被开得太快了。

正:汽车开得太快了。

是说受事主语("汽车")承受某种动作行为后达到的程度。宜用意义被动句,不能用"被"字句。

This sentence expresses that the subject ("汽车"), affected by an action, has attained a certain degree. It is notionally passive and should do without "被".

例 660

误:你的衣服被送到宿舍里去了。

正:你的衣服送到宿舍里去了。

动词("送")后带补语"到",说明受事主语("衣服")通过动作达到某个地方。要用意义被动句,不宜用"被"字句。

When the predicate verb is followed by the complement "到" to express that the subject ("衣服") has reached somewhere as the result of the action, the notionally passive sentence rather than the "被"-sentence is used.

例 661

误:他的书被放在桌子上了。

正:他的书放在桌子上了。

动词后带补语"在",说明受事主语("书")承受某种动作行为后存在于某个位置,要用意义被动句,不能用"被"字句。

"被" does not occur in a notionally passive sentence where the predicate verb is followed by the complement "在" to indicate that the subject ("书"), affected by the action, has arrived at a certain position.

例 662

误:那些画报被还给图书馆了。

正:那些画报还给图书馆了。

动词谓语后边带有补语"给","给"的后边又是给予的对象(人

244

或者地方)表示受事的主语通过动作("还")交给某一对象,必用意义被动句,不能用"被"字。

In this sentence, the verb predicate is followed by the complement "给" and after "给" is the object indicating the recipient of the action. To express that the subject which is passive reaches where another person or thing is through the action ("还"), one should use a notionally passive sentence without "被".

例 663

误:这个电影两个小时被演得完演不完?

正:这个电影两个小时演得完演不完?

例 664

误:书架里边的书被看不到。

正:书架里边的书看不到。

动词后带可能补语是要说明受事主语受动作影响能否达到某种结果,一律要用意义被动句。

The notionally passive sentence must be used when the verb is followed by a potential complement showing whether the subject affected by the action, has attained a certain result.

7. "被"字句使用不当
Improper use of the 被-sentence

例 665

误:这样好的茶杯偏偏他打碎了。

正:这样好的茶杯偏偏被他打碎了。

"被"字句的基本格式是:主语——"被"——宾语——谓语动词其他成分。句中有"偏偏"表示不满意的修饰语,又有"打碎"这样的动补词语,全句被动义和不如意色彩很鲜明,须在用作状语的"偏偏"后加上"被"字,以引出施事者("他")。

The basic pattern of the 被-sentence is: subject—"被"—object—predicate verb—other elements. With the verb-complement phrase ″打碎″ and the modifier ″偏偏″ which shows discontent, the present sentence carries a strong overtone of passivity and dissatisfaction. ″被″ should be added after the adverbial ″偏偏″ to introduce the agent ″他″.

例 666

误：我被收音机醒了。

正：我被收音机吵醒了。

″被″字句中的动词必须是动作行为动词,而且能够支配受事主语,″醒″是不及物动词,应改为″吵醒″。

The predicate of a ″被″-sentence must be an action verb that can govern the subject indicating the patient. In the present sentence, the predicate ″醒″ is intransitive and should be replaced with ″吵醒″.

例 667

误：他被人骗。

正：他被人骗了。

主要动词一般要带″其他成分″,不能是单个动词,这个句子是说用虚伪的言语或行动使人上当已成事实。应当在″骗″的后头加″了″,作″其他成分″。

The predicate verb can not stand alone and must be followed by some other elements. This sentence expresses that somebody has been fooled. ″了″ may be used after ″骗″ to function as ″other elements″.

例 668

误：那张画儿让刮掉了。

正：那张画儿让风刮掉了。

例 669

误:那两条鱼叫吃光了。

正:那两条鱼叫猫吃光了。

(668)、(669)缺施事者。根据句意分别在介词"让"和"叫"的后边补上"风"和"猫"。

In (668) and (669), the agent is absent. To fit the context we add "风" and "猫" respectively after "让" and "叫".

例 670

误:一辆自行车被小王搬到外边去了。

正:那辆自行车被小王搬到外边去了。

受事主语应是有定的,此句"一辆自行车"却是无定的,须改"一辆"为交谈双方共知的"那辆"。

The subject indicating the patient is usually definite. "一辆自行车" is indefinite. One should use "那辆" referring to the one which is known to both sides of the conversation.

例 671

误:那件事被我忘了。

正:那件事我忘了。

"被"字句的主语不像主动句那样随便,决定是否能用"被"字句的关键是动词,能用于"被"字句的动词一般都是要有处置性,这种动作对另一事物有影响,动词"忘"是表示人的主观感觉动词,不含处置义,不能用"被"字句。

The subject of a 被-sentence which is passive is much more bound than that of an ordinary active sentence. What determines the need for a 被-sentence is the verb which in such construction must be transitive and can govern or affect people or things. The verb "忘" in the present sentence denotes a state of mind. It does not meet the mentioned requirements and hence can not be used in a 被-sentence.

例 672

误：外国客人们被工人们热烈欢迎。

正：外国客人们受到工人们热烈欢迎。

动词"欢迎"是表示高高兴兴迎接某人，一般不能构成"被"字句，只能说"受欢迎"。此句应改为"受到欢迎"，到表示动作有结果。

The verb "欢迎" meaning "welcome", does not go with "被", but is normally used with "受". The proper way is to say "受到⋯欢迎". "到" indicates that the action has attained a result.

例 673

误：他被人非常热情。

正：他对人非常热情。

这是形容词"热情"作谓语的句子，应用介词"对"引进对象"人"。说明"他"对待人的态度。此句不能用"被"字句。

The adjective "热情" may not serve as the predicate of a 被-sentence. To express "his" attitude towards other people, one should use the preposition "对" instead of "被" to introduce the object "人".

例 674

误：家长是重要的人，每件重要的事情被他负责解决。

正：家长是重要的人，每件重要的事情由他负责解决。

汉语中若要指出进行某事的责任属于什么人，而丝毫不涉及受到什么动作行为的影响时，不用"被"字句，要用介词"由"代替。此句说明解决重要事情的责任属于"他"，因为"他"是家长。

When one points out that something is somebody's responsibility, he is not concerned with the influence of an action. On such occasion, he should use the preposition "由" instead of "被". This sentence means that the patriarch is responsible for solving all the important family affairs.

例 **675**

误:这件事能被他知道吗?

正:这件事能让他知道吗?

"被"字句绝大部分是叙述已完成的事实,而且多是肯定句,很少用于疑问句。此句改用"让"("叫"),是表示"允许"的意思。

In most cases, the 被-sentence states accomplished facts. It is often affirmative and seldom used for a question. One should replace ″被″ with ″让″ or ″叫″.

例 **676**

误:那些画被他都卖了。

正:那些画都被他卖了。

例 **677**

误:自行车被丁力没骑走。

正:自行车没被丁力骑走。

"被"字句中,修饰成分一般都放在"被"字前,而不是动词前。(676)(677)中,已经错位的"都"和"没"应提到"被"字前边。

In the 被-sentence, adverbial normally precedes the verb rather than ″被″. ″都″and ″没″ which are misplaced must be moved to the front of ″被″.

例 **678**

误:我的自行车被朋友骑去城里到了。

正:我的自行车被朋友骑到城里去了。

动词"骑"后充当"其他成分"的"去"和"到"易位,应调换过来,成为"到……去"。

In the position of ″other elements″ after the verb ″骑″, ″去″ and ″到″ are in the wrong place. To produce the right form ″到…去″, one should exchange their positions.

例 **679**

误：信被寄走了。

正：信已经寄走了。

此句应用意义被动句。虽然含被动意义，但不含不满意感情，一般不用"被"字句。（详见意义被动句）。

This sentence should be notionally passive without "被". The reason is that although it is passive in meaning, it has no emotional colouring of dissatisfaction. (For more, refer to "The notionally passive sentence")

例 680

误：屈原被鱼拉回尸体。

正：屈原的尸体被鱼拉回。

在此"被"字句中，动词（"拉"）后的"其他成分"不能用名词"尸体"，应把"尸体"移到前边，充当受事成分，改为"屈原的尸体"。动词"回"是受事事物承受动作"拉"后的结果。

Here, the noun "尸体" wrongly occupies the position of "other elements" after the verb ("拉"). As the patient of the action, it should be moved to the front to function as the subject, i. e. "屈原的尸体". The verb "回" shows the result of the action "拉" which is applied to the patient.

8. 存在句使用不当

Improper use of the existential sentences

例 681

误：在桌子上放着很多书。

正：桌子上放着很多书。

是要说明某处存在什么事物，应该用存在句表示。存在句的基本格式是：处所词——动词（"着"）——存在的人或事物，所以"在桌子上"应当改为"桌子上"。

To express that there is something existing somewhere one

should use the existential sentence, of which the basic pattern is: locality noun (or noun phrase)——verb ("着")——person or thing that exists. Hence, "在桌子上" should be changed into "桌子上".

例 682

误：操场上站着运动员，等着比赛。

正：操场上站着一些(许多)运动员，等着比赛。

在存在句中，动词后边的名词往往用表示数量的词语作修饰成分，"运动员"的前边可以加"一些"或"许多"。

In the existential sentence, the noun after the verb is usually modified by a numeral-measure word phrase. "一些" or "许多" may be added before "运动员".

例 683

误：座位上放那位同学的衣服。

正：座位上放着那位同学的衣服。

动词后必须加"着"，这里"着"不表示动作进行，而是表示动作的状态。

The verb "放" must be followed by "着" which does not indicate here that the action is in progress but shows the state of the action.

例 684

误：椅子上放在那个同学的书。

正：椅子上放着那个同学的书。

要表示某处存在某一事物，动词("放")的后边一定要加"着"。如果要强调某一事物通过动作存在于某处，此句也可改为"那个同学的书放在椅子上"。这两个句子的语义重点不同。

To express that there is something somewhere one should attach "着" to the verb ("放"). However, to emphasize that something exists somewhere as the result of an action, one may say "那个同学的书放在椅子上". These two different constructions have different semantic focus.

例 685

误:巴里亚的箱子里放着了一些衣服。

正:巴里亚的箱子里放着一些衣服。

正:巴里亚的箱子里放了一些衣服。

一个动词的后边不能同时存在两种状态,所以"着"和表示完成的动态助词"了"不宜连用。此句是说某处存在某事物,用"着"更合适,删去"了"。或者用"了",删去"着"。

A verb can not be followed by two different aspect particles, hence "着" and "了" denoting completion may not be used together. "着" best suits this sentence which means that there is something somewhere. However, one may also delete "着" and retain "了".

五、几种比较句的误用
Errors in the Use of Several
Types of Comparative Sentences

1. 用"更"比较的句子使用不当
Improper use of sentences with "更"to express comparison

例 686

误:他连最简单的汉字也写不好,复杂的汉字写不好。

正:他连最简单的汉字也写不好,复杂的汉字更写不好。

这是就同一主体("他")的两种属性进行比较,但在形式上,比较级的"写不好"与原级的"写不好"没有区别。这是因为在比较级的谓语的动词"写"前遗漏了表示程度又进一层的副词"更","更"应当加在第二个动词"写"的前边。

Here，the comparison is made between two aspects related to the same person ("他")．With the absence of the adverb "更" as the modifier to denote a further degree，"写不好" in the comparative sense shows no difference in form from the base．"更" is required before the second verb "写"．

例 **687**

误：前两天太热了，这两天更热。

正：前两天热，这两天更热。

这是要比较两种事物的同一属性。由于原级谓语形容词"热"前用了副词"太"，肯定"热"已经达到极端的程度，自然谈不上同另一种事物进行比较。这个句子或者改成"这两天跟前两天一样热"，或者删去"太"和"了"，"这两天更热"就用得上了。

This sentence compares two things with regard to the same respect．But the speaker blocks the way to comparison by using the adverb "太" before the first predicate adjective "热" to denote an extreme degree．One should change the sentence into "这两天跟前两天一样热"，or delete "太" and "了"and simply say "前两天热，这两天更热"．

例 **688**

误：虽然课文简单，但是他更看不懂。

正：虽然课文简单，但是他看不懂。

这是表示转折关系的复句，全句不具备表示比较的任何条件，删去"更"。

This is a complex sentence expressing an adversative relation．It has no comparative sense，hence "更" must be deleted．

2. 用"更加"比较的句子使用不当

Improper use of sentences with ″更加″ to express comparison

例 689

误:这个城市建设得更加美了。

正:这个城市建设得更加美丽了。

正:这个城市建设得更美了。

"更加"与"更"的用法基本相同。但是"更加"只用于双音节词前,而谓语形容词"美"是单音节词。此句有两种改法,或者改"美"为双音节"美丽",或者用单音节"更"替代双音节"更加"。

″更加″ is the same with ″更″ in basic usage. The difference is ″更加″ can only be applied to disyllables. However, the predicate adjective ″美″ here is a monosyllable. The sentence may be corrected in two possible ways. One is to replace ″美″ with ″美丽″; the other is to use ″更″ instead of ″更加″.

例 690

误:这个商店的商品越来越更加丰富了。

正:这个商店的商品越来越丰富了。

正:这个商店的商品更加丰富了。

两个含有比较意味的"更加"和"越来越"用词重复。要么删去"更加",保留"越来越",表示商品丰富的程度随着时间而发展。要么删去"越来越",保留"更加",表示商品丰富的程度又深了一层。

The error lies in the repetition of a comparative sense manifested through both ″更加″ and ″越来越″. To express that the abundance of goods is increasing as time continues, only ″越来越″ should remain. On the other hand, to mean that abundance of goods has increased, ″更加″ remains.

3. 用"最"比较的句子使用不当

Improper use of sentences with ″最″ to express comparison

例 691

254

误：阿里汉语说得好，杜朗说得最好。

正：阿里汉语说得好，巴里亚说得更好，杜朗说得最好。

正：杜朗汉语说得最好。

正：阿里汉语说得好，杜朗说得更好。

"最"是比较的最高级，是对两个以上的人的同一属性进行比较。而句中只是比较"阿里"和"杜朗"两个人在汉语表达能力方面的高低程度。这个句子有三种改法：一、在原级"说得好"和最高级"说得最好"之间加上个比较级"更"，即"巴里亚说得更好"。二、删去原级"阿里汉语说得好"，改成"杜朗汉语说得最好"，言外之间，"杜朗"汉语的表达能力超过同类的人。三、改"最"为"更"。

"最" is the superlative degree. It is used when comparison is made on one aspect among at least three people. In the present sentence, the comparison is only between two people, "阿里" and "杜朗", regarding their speaking ability of Chinese. There are three possible ways of rectification: 1) insert a comparative "更" between the absolute degree "说得好" and the superlative degree "说得最好"; 2) delete "阿里汉语说得好", and say "杜朗汉语说得最好" to imply that in speaking Chinese, "杜朗" excels others of his kind; 3) replace "最" with "更".

例 692

误：他家养的花都不错，特别是水仙花美丽。

正：他家养的花都不错，特别是水仙花最美丽。

副词"都"意在"他家养的花"包含一定的数量。"特别"是说"水仙花"同其他种花相比，与众不同。因此，须要在谓语形容词"美丽"的前边加上表示最高级比较形式的副词"最"。

The adverb "都" implies that the flowers have reached a generous quantity. "特别" stresses the outstanding beauty of "水仙花" compared with other kinds of flowers, thus "最" which is the adverb of the superlative degree should be placed before the predicate adjective "美丽".

例 693

误：这个地方最安静极了。

正：这个地方最安静。

正：这个地方安静极了。

"最"和"极"都表示程度高，"最"含有比较意义；"极"不含比较意，这两个词不能作同一个词的连带成分，可以任择其一。

"最" and "极" both indicate a high degree, but "最" contains a comparative sense while "极" does not. They may not occur together as the adjuncts of the same word, only one should remain.

4. 用"比"比较的句子使用不当

Improper use of sentences with "比" to express comparison

例 694

误：这些年人们的生活比以前非常好。

正：这些年人们的生活比以前更好了。

例 695

误：我觉得武戏比文戏很有意思。

正：我觉得武戏比文戏还有意思。

（694）和（695）都是比较两种事物差别的，不能用高程度的"非常"、"很"，应改用表示进一层的"更"、"更加"和"还"。

（694）and（695）are meant to indicate the difference between two things. Hence, such words as "更"、"更加" and "还", which denote a further degree, should be used instead of "非常" and "很" showing a high degree.

例 696

误：我们学了生词比他们学了生词多。

正：我们学的生词比他们学的生词多。

在比较句中,强调表示相比较的事物在一个特定时间的相对差异,这种比较是静态的。此句是"学的生词"多少的比较,不能是动作完成与否的比较。所以,动词后不能带"了",而要改用"的",成为两种事物的比较。

Comparative sentences that show the relative difference at a particular time between objects are static. In the present sentence, the comparison is made with respect to the number of words learnt, not the completion of the action. Thus, the verb can not be followed by "了". One should use "的" in place of "了".

例 697

误:他小时候比你淘气了。

正:他小时候比你淘气。

两个比较项有相同的确指某个时间的词语"小时候",句子末尾不能用表示变化的"了"。

"小时候", specifying a particular time, is related to both sides of comparison, "他" and "你". "了"denoting change may not occur at the end of the sentence.

例 698

误:风比刚才小多。

正:风比刚才小多了。

因为要表示同一事物(风)从一个时点(刚才)到另一时点(说话人说话的时间)风力的变化("多"表示变化差异量大),这是一种动态的比较,要在句末加表示变化的"了"。

Comparative sentences implying a change of state are dynamic. The present sentence shows the change of wind force between one and another point of time (just now and the moment of utterance). "多" indicates that the difference is great. In such kind of sentence, "了" denoting change is required at the end of the sentence.

例 699

误：他比我多有五块钱。

正：他比我多五块钱。

要以确切的数字表示具体差别时，通常用含有比较义的形容词"多"或"少"作谓语，数量词（"五块钱"）直接跟在谓语后，作补语，无需用动词"有"。

In showing a concrete difference with a definite numeral, adjectives "多" and "少" with a comparative sense normally serve as the predicate, followed by a numeral-measure word phrase ("五块钱") as the complement. Verb "有" is unnecessary.

例 700

误：丁力比我来了早教室。

正：丁力来教室的时间比我早。

比较两个动作发生时间的差别时，应当用"早"或"晚"作谓语。此句不符合"A-'比'-B-比较的结果"的结构特点，不能相比。需要重新调整结构，改成"时间"相互比较，即"丁力来教室的时间"和"我来教室的时间"。

To compare two actions concerning their time of occurrence, "早" or "晚" should be used as the predicate. This sentence does not fit in with the comparative construction："A-'比'-B-result of comparison". It has to undergo some change to take "时间" as the objects of comparison, i. e. "丁力来教室的时间" and "我来教室的时间".

例 701

误：我比他来得早一天。

正：我比他早来一天。

这是要比较两个动作发生的时间，并要显示具体差别。通常将"早"提到谓语动词（"来"）前，作状语。表示具体差别的（"一天"）紧

258

跟在动词谓语"来"的后边,不能用结构助词"得"。

This sentence makes comparison on the time of occurrence between two actions and shows the concrete difference. "早" should precede the predicate verb ("来") as an adverbial adjunct, and words indicating the concrete difference ("一天") should immediately follow the verb as the structural particle "得" can not be used.

例 702

误:她跳得比那个运动员高九厘米。

正:她跳得比那个运动员高一点儿。

正:她比那个运动员跳得高得多。

正:她比那个运动员跳得高,高九厘米。

这里是要比较两个动作产生的结果。动词"跳"后已带有由形容词"高"充当的程度补语,若程度补语后还要有其他补充成分时,大多用"一点"、"一些"、"得多"等词语,大略地指出差别程度,而不能接表示具体差别的数量词"九厘米"。用"比"的介词词组,可用于动词"跳"前,也可用于补语"高"前。如要说明具体差别,这个句子宜一分为二。

Here, the comparison is between the results of two actions. The verb "跳" has the adjective "高" as the degree complement. On this occasion, other complement elements following the degree complement, if there are any, must be words which show a rough estimate of the degree of difference, like "一点"、"一些"、"得多"; they can not be numeral-measure word phrases indicating concrete difference, such as "九厘米". Prepositional phrases using "比" may come before the verb "跳" or before the complement "高". To express a concrete difference, the sentence has to be separated into two.

例 703

误：弟弟学中文比他的学习好。

正：弟弟中文学得比他学得好。

正：弟弟中文比他学得好。

在比较句中,两个相比项目的类别(语义)与语法关系(词类和句法结构)应是一致的。在这个句子里,学中文(动宾词组)和"他的学习"(偏正词组)在语法上不一致,造成语义不清,逻辑不通。应当改成在学中文方面的程度之间的比较。

In a comparative sentence, the objects compared must be the same in semantic category and grammatical relation (referring to parts of speech and syntactic structure). This sentence is senseless and illogical, since "学中文" (a verb-object phrase) and "他的学习" (an endocentric phrase) are grammatically different. The comparison should be made on the same aspect, here "学中文".

例 704

误：我参加工作比他不晚。

正：我参加工作不比他晚。

否定词"不"的位置失当。句中的否定词"不"应提到介词"比"前,否定"比"。是说我参加工作的时间跟他参加工作的时间差不多。

The negation word "不" is in the wrong position. It should be placed before the preposition "比" as its qualifier to express that "I" started working no later than him.

例 705

误：我的意见比他的完全不同。

正：我的意见比他的好。

正：我的意见跟("同"、"和")他的不同。

两种比较句杂糅。句子前边的介词"比"用来比较两种事物的差别,后边的"不同"是比较两种事物的异同。这个句子有两种改

260

法,或者保留"比",改"不同"为"好",或者用"跟"("同"、"和")代替介词"比",保留"不同"。

Here we have a blend of two types of comparative constructions. The preposition "比" is used for indicating the difference between two objects；"不同" exactly means "different". There are two ways to correct this sentence：1) retain "比" and replace "不同" with "好"；2) use "跟" (or "同"，"和") in replace of "比" and retain "不同".

例 706

误：一天比一天学的语法多。

正：学的语法一天比一天多。

"一天比一天"用作状语。应将误放在句首的"一天比一天"移到形容词谓语"多"前,表示随时间的推移所学的语法日益增多。

"一天比一天" serves as an adverbial adjunct. It can not occur in the initial position before the subject，but should stay after the subject before the adjective predicate "多"，to express that one learns more and more grammatical points each day.

例 707

误：他一天比一天学习有很大的进步。

正：他学习一天比一天有进步。

理由同(706),"一天比一天"应移到由主谓词组充当谓语的谓语动词"有"前,是说随着时间的推移,在学习方面不断提高。

For the same reason with (706)，"一天比一天" must be moved backwards after the subject "学习" and before the predicate verb "有" of the subject-predicate phrase serving as the predicate of the entire sentence，meaning to make more progress each day in study.

5. **用"没有"比较的句子使用不当**

Improper use of sentences with "没有" to express comparison

例 708

误:这篇作品比那篇没有好。

正:这篇作品没有那篇好。

这种比较句的基本格式是:A-"没有"-B-比较的结果。这是用"比"和"没有"两种比较句的杂糅。根据句子的实际情况,删去"比",然后把"没有"放在原来"比"所在的位置上。是说那篇文章比这篇好。

This type of comparative sentence follows the basic pattern of "A-'没有'-B-result of comparison". Here, two types of comparative constructions using "比" and "没有" respectively are improperly blended into one sentence. To meet the original meaning of the speaker, i.e. this article is not as good as that one, we delete "比" and put "没有" in its position.

例 709

误:我的词典没有你那么好。

正:我的词典没有你的(词典)那么好。

由于比较项结构不完整,造成两种比较的内容不相当而无法比较的毛病。应在"你"的后边加上"的"字或"的词典",就可以相互比较了。

Comparison is impossible between objects of different types, like "词典" and "你". One should add "的" or "的词典" in order to make the comparison possible.

例 710

误:我哥哥的身体没有你哥哥那么高。

正:我哥哥的身体没有你哥哥那么好。(或"健康")

谓语用词不当。形容词"高"与比较双方的中心语"身体"不搭配。删去"高",改用"好"或"健康"。是说你哥哥的身体比我哥哥的

262

身体好(健康)。

The adjective "高" is an improper predicate here, in that it is not a usual match for the head word "身体". To express "your brother is healthier than my brother", one should use "好" or "健康" instead of "高".

例 711

误：这棵树没有那棵树这么粗。

正：这棵树没有那棵树那么粗。

"那棵树"是比较的标准。"那"是远指,应当用与"那"顺意的"那么"作状语,删去近指的"这么"。

"那棵树" is the standard of comparison. "那" refers to something in the distance. "那么" is the proper adverbial to go with it. "这么" which is of close reference should be deleted.

例 712

误：他们没有我们来这么早。

正：他们没有我们来得这么早。

这个句子是要比较两个已发生的动作时间的差别,在结构上,应当用程度补语加以补充说明,但是,句中缺少补语的标志,应在动词谓语后补上结构助词"得"。

This sentence compares two actions as to which one happened earlier. Structurally it requires a degree complement for supplement. Hence the structural particle "得" should be attached to the verb predicate to mark the complement.

6. 用"不如"比较的句子使用不当
Improper use of sentences with "不如" to express comparison

例 713

误：吃的饭不如在家,但是还行。

正：在这里吃的不如在家吃的，但是还行。

"不如"是动词，本身可以构成一个完整的句子，A-"不如"-B，意思是"A 不如 B 好"。句中两个比较成分内容类别、语法结构不同，不能相比。应改成内容相当、结构相一致的比较成分"在这里吃的"和"在家里吃的"。意思是在这儿吃的比不上在家吃的。

The verb ″不如″ is used to form the pattern：A-″不如″-B, meaning ″A can not compare favourably with B″. A and B must belong to the same semantic and grammatical class；otherwise，they can not be compared. Hence，for the present sentence，we use ″在这里吃的″ and ″在家里吃的″ as A and B，to indicate that the food here is not as good as that at home.

例 714

误：她翻译句子不如你翻译的句子准确。

正：她翻译的句子不如你翻译的句子准确。

由于被比较项"她翻译句子"遗漏了结构助词"的"，造成两个比较成分的内容不相当的毛病，"的"字应加在"她翻译"的后边，这样就可以进行比较了。意思是她翻译的句子的准确程度比不上你。

With the absence of the structural particle ″的″，″她翻译句子″ can not be compared with ″你翻译的句子″，since they are not of the same type. ″的″ should follow ″她翻译″ to express that the accuracy of her translation can not compare with that of yours.

例 715

误：那个公园不如这个公园那么安静。

正：那个公园不如这个公园这么安静。

比较项"这个公园"的"这"是近指，用来修饰谓语"安静"的却是远指的"那么"，先后不一致，就改"那么"为近指的"这么"。是说那个公园的安静程度比不上这个公园，也可以说这个公园比那个公园安静。

This sentence means "That park is not as quiet as this one", in other words, "This park is quieter than that one". "这" in "这个公园" is of close reference while "那么" modifying the predicate "安静" is of distant reference, hence they do not accord. The latter should be replaced by "这么".

例 716

误：小王不如小马安排作息时间。

正：小王不如小马会安排作息时间。

表示行为动作的动词不宜用作这类比较句的谓语，应在"安排"前加上含有程度意味的能愿动词"会"。

Action verbs are improper to be the predicate of this kind of comparative sentences. The auxiliary verb "会" which carries an implication of "degree" is needed before "安排".

例 717

误：谢力不如巴里亚说法语。

正：谢力不如巴里亚说法语说得流利。

正：谢力不如巴里亚法语说得流利。

理由同（716），在谓语动词"说"后应补上由形容词"流利"充当的程度补语以及补语的标志"得"。

For the same reason with (716), the predicate verb "说" must take a degree complement, which here may be indicated by the adjective "流利" with the complement marker "得".

例 718

误：我写的汉字不如他写的好看得多。

正：我写的汉字不如他写的好看。

在用"不如"比较的句子里，谓语后不能带任何表示差别的词语，应删去"得多"。

In a comparative sentence with "不如", the predicate can not

be followed by any words denoting difference. ″得多″ must be deleted.

例 719

误:上海冷不如北京的冬天。

正:上海不如北京的冬天冷。

词序易位。应将比较成分"不如北京的冬天"与谓语"冷"的顺序颠倒过来。意思是上海的冬天没有北京的冬天那么冷。

This sentence is disordered. One should reverse the order of ″不如北京的冬天″ and the predicate ″冷″ to express that the winter in Shanghai is not as cold as in Beijing.

7. 用"跟……一样"比较的句子使用不当

Improper use of sentences with ″跟…一样″to express comparison

例 720

误:这件衣服的颜色跟那件的是一样。

正:这件衣服的颜色跟那件(的)一样。

这个句子是要比较两种事物的异同。这类比较句的基本格式是 A-"跟"-B-"一样"。"一样"是形容词,作谓语,表示经过比较以后而得出的结论。形容词谓语前的"是"是受英语说法影响,应去掉。

For comparative sentences expressing the meaning of ″same″ or ″different″, the basic pattern is A-″跟″-B-(不)″一样″. ″一样″ is an adjective. It serves as the predicate here to indicate the result of comparison. Influenced by the sentence structure in English, the speaker unnecessarily put ″是″ before the adjective predicate.

例 721

误:他买了一本书跟我买了一本书不一样。

正:他买的书跟我买的书不一样。

句子的原意是就两种事物加以比较。因此,必须把句中表示动作完成的"了"改成定语标志"的",形成以"书"为中心语的词组。同时,删去指无定的"一本",变为有定的"我买的书"和"他买的书"。这样,才能进行比较。

Here, the comparison is between two objects. Instead of "了" indicating completion of action, one should use the attributive marker "的" to form a noun phrase with "书" as the head word. Meanwhile, "一本" which is indefinite should be deleted.

例 **722**

误:他借的小说跟我一样好。

正:他借的小说跟我借的(小说)一样好。

两个比较成分的内容和语法关系不一致,无法比较。在"我"后加上"借的",成为"我借的"=我借的小说。只有这样,才能够同"他借的小说"相互比较。由于中心语相同,比较项的"小说"可以省略不说。

Here, the two objects being compared are of different semantic and grammatical categories, thus should not be compared. "借的" must be added after "我" to form "我借的"=我借的小说. Only in this way can the comparison be made possible. Since the two head words (小说) are the same, the second one may be left out.

例 **723**

误:我也希望你跟白求恩大夫对技术一样精益求精。

正:我也希望你跟白求恩大夫一样,对技术精益求精。

动词谓语"希望"的宾语是一个用"跟……一样"构成的主谓词组。在这个宾语中,"你"和"白求恩大夫对技术"不能相比。把比较项的"对技术"移到"精益求精"前,单独成句,"你"就可以作为求比的方面。

The object of the verb predicate "希望" is an S-P (subject

predicate) phrase in the pattern of "跟…一样". But "你" may not be compared with "白求恩大夫对技术". To make the comparison possible, "一样" must be moved to the front of "对技术" and consequently, "精益求精" with "对技术" immediately preceding it may function as a separate sentence.

例 724

误：我要买一件毛衣跟他的那件颜色一样。

正：我要买一件跟他的那件颜色一样的毛衣。

句子的主干是"我买毛衣"，"跟……一样"是修饰中心语"毛衣"的，应将误放在中心语后的"跟……一样"提到中心语前，同时在"跟……一样"与中心语"毛衣"之间补上结构助词"的"。

The main part of the sentence is 我买毛衣. As the modifier of the head word "毛衣", "跟…一样" must precede it rather than follow it. Additionally, the structural particle "的" is required in between.

例 725

误：他跑得快极了，跑跟飞一样。

正：他跑得快极了，跑得跟飞一样。

先行句用"快极了"作程度补语，说明"跑"的速度之"快"。后续句则应该用"跟飞一样"作"跑"的补语，描述"跑"的情态。在谓语动词"跑"与补语之间还须补上"得"字。

The anticipatory sentence here uses "快极了" as the degree complement to show the high speed of "跑". Accordingly in the follow-up sentence, "跟飞一样" should also serve as the complement of "跑" to illustrate the manner of the action, "得" the marker of complements must be present.

例 726

误：那个国家的人口比我们国家的人口一样多。

正：那个国家的人口比我们国家的(人口)多。

正：那个国家的人口跟我们国家的(人口)一样多。

两种比较句混用在一起。这个句子有两种改法，要么删去用作状语的形容词"一样"，保留"比"；要么改介词"比"为"跟"。两句话所表示的意义不同，前者说明差别，后者说明同异。

The present sentence is a mixture of two types of comparative constructions. It may be corrected in two ways: 1) delete the adjective "一样" which here serves as the adverbial adjunct. 2) replace the preposition "比" with "跟". These two ways result in two distinct sentences, with the former showing difference, and the latter similarity.

8. 用"有"比较的句子使用不当

Improper use of sentences with "有" to express comparison

例 727

误：天坛有大同那么有名。

正：天坛像云岗石窟那么有名。

"天坛"是北京市的名胜古迹之一。"大同"是中国有名的城市之一。比较的双方不属于同一类别，应改"大同"为大同市的名胜古迹"云岗石窟"。此外，还应把表示估量或比较的"有"改成具有共同点的"像"，更符合实际。

"天坛" is a famous park in Beijing, whereas "大同" is a famous city of China. They are of two distinct classes, hence may not be compared. "大同" should be replaced with "云岗石窟" which is the famous relic in the city. Besides, "像" meaning "as" or "like" is more suitable here than "有" expressing estimate or comparison.

例 728

误：玛丽有我高一点儿

正：玛丽有我这么高。

在这种比较句里,作为比较结果的谓语("高")后不能带有粗略差别的数量词"一点儿"。谓语前却可以用近指的"这么"作状语,表示程度。应删去"一点儿",再在"高"前加上"这么"。

In this kind of comparative sentence, the predicate indicating the result of comparison ("高") can not be followed by the numeral-measure word phrase "一点儿" to show a slight difference. However, it may be premodified by "这么" as an adverbial adjunct showing degree. Delete "一点儿" and add "这么" before "高".

例 729

误:这个班的学生有那个班的学生多十个人。

正:这个班的学生有那个班的学生那么多。

句中的谓语"多"后不能带具体差别的数量词"十个人"。谓语前可以用表示远指的"那么"作状语。是说这个班的学生和那个班学生人数相当。

Here, the predicate "多" may not be followed by a numeral-measure word phrase ("十个人") showing a concrete difference. To express that students in this class are no lesser than students in that class, "那么" of distant reference should precede the predicate as an adverbial adjunct.

例 730

误:这个游泳池有那么大。

正:这个游泳池有那个(游泳池)那么大。

句中缺少比较项"那个游泳池"。应加在动词"有"后。由于两个比较成分的中心语相同,比较项可省说成"那个"。

This sentence lacks a standard of comparison which probably is "那个游泳池". Since the second head word is the same as the first one, one may omit it and just add "那个" after "有".

例 731

270

误：今年大米的产量有去年的(产量)一样多。

正：今年大米的产量有去年的那么多。

正：今年大米的产量跟去年的一样多。

这是"有……那么"和"跟……一样"两种比较句的混用。要么删去"一样"，改用"那么"；有达到去年产量标准的意思。要么删去"有"，改用"跟"，表示相同。只能选用其中的一种。

Here the comparative construction using ″有…那么″ is mixed with the one using ″跟…一样″. One should either replace ″一样″ with ″那么″ to imply that the output this year has reached the same level of last year, or replace ″有″ with ″跟″ to express the meaning of ″same″. Only one of the two possible ways may by used.

例 **732**

误：这间屋子有那间屋子很大。

正：这间屋子有那间屋子那么大。

在用"有"的比较句里，谓语前经常用"那么"(或"这么")与之呼应，作程度状语。而不能用肯定程度之高的"很"一类副词。

In a comparative sentence using ″有″, the predicate is normally preceded by ″那么″ or ″这么″ as an adverbial adjunct showing degree. It can not be modified by such degree adverbs as ″很″.

9. 用"像"比较的句子使用不当

Improper use of sentences with ″像″ to express comparison

例 **733**

误：安娜很像她妈妈那么漂亮。

正：安娜像她妈妈那么漂亮。

在用"像……那么……"表示比较的句子里，谓语"漂亮"的前边已经带有表明程度的"那么"，"像"的前边就不能再用"很"之类含程度意义的词语了。应当删去"很"。

In comparative sentence using ″像…那么…″, with ″那么″

preceding the adjective predicate ("漂亮") to show degree，"像" can not be modified by such words implying degree as "很". "很" must be deleted.

例 734

误：他的发音那么像小王的发音清楚。

正：他的发音像小王的发音那么清楚。

"那么"的位置不妥。应把误 用在"像"前的"那么"，移到谓语"清楚"前，表示程度。

"那么" is misplaced. It should stay immediately before the predicate "清楚" to indicate degree.

例 735

误：阿里没像谢力那么喜欢踢足球。

正：阿里不像谢力那么喜欢踢足球。

"像"的否定式不能用否定词"没"，应当用"不"，改"没像"为"不像"。

The negative form of "像" is "不像", rather than "没像". Hence we use "不" to replace "没".

例 736

误：妹妹像弟弟那么不爱玩儿。

正：妹妹不像弟弟那么爱玩儿。

在这种比较句里，否定词"不"不能放在谓语动词前。否定动词表示的行为动作，同用"比"、"跟 "构成的比较句的否定形式相同，否定词"不"只能放在"像"的前边。

To negate the resemblance, the negation word "不" should not precede the predicate verb, which in such case negates the action. As in the negative forms of comparative sentences using "比" and "跟", it only comes before "像".

例 737

272

误:你买的自行车不像我这么结实。

正:你买的自行车不像我买的(自行车)这么结实。

求比的事物与比较项不相当。按照句子的意思,应把比较项"我"改成"我买的自行车"。这样,比较双方的事物类别和语法关系就一致了。比较双方的中心语相同,比较项可以省说中心语。

"你买的自行车"and "我" are of two distinct types and can not be compared. According to the context, the standard of comparison should be "我买的自行车" rather than "我"; however the head word may be omitted since it is the same as the one in "你买的自行车".

10. 用"越来越"比较的句子使用不当
Improper use of sentences with "越来越" to express comparison

例 738

误:我们越来越比较习惯这里的生活了。

正:我们越来越习惯这里的生活了。

正:我们比较习惯这里的生活了。

"越来越""比较"两个表示程度的词语混杂在一起,使得句意不清。要么去掉"比较",保留"越来越",表示随着时间的推移逐步提高习惯这里生活的程度。要么去掉"越来越",保留"比较",表示在一定程度上适应这里的生活习惯了。

The meaning here is obscure in that "越来越" and "比较" both indicating degree but different in meaning are mixed up. To express that one becomes more and more accustomed to the life there, "比较" should be dropped from the sentence, and "越来越" should be kept. To express that one becomes accustomed to some extent, "越来越" should be deleted and "比较" should be kept.

例 739

误：越来越学习汉语的人多了。

正：学习汉语的人越来越多了。

"越来越"的主要用途是作状语。应把误用在主语"学习汉语的人"前的"越来越"移到谓语形容词"多"的前边。

"越来越" is mainly used as an adverbial adjunct. It can not occur before the subject ("学习汉语的"), but should be moved backwards to precede the predicate adjective "多".

例 740

误：车越来越开得快了。

正：车开得越来越快了。

程度补语"快"很重要，它前面的动词"开"好像是一个话题，因此表示程度差别的"越来越"不能用在动词之前，要用在补语之前。

The degree complement "快" is an important element here to give information about the verb "开" which may be considered a topic. Hence, "越来越" showing degree difference must precede the complement "快" rather than the verb "开".

例 741

误：雨越来越下了。

正：雨越来越大了。

正：雨下得越来越大了。

表示趋向的动词"下"不宜用在含有比较意味的句子里。这个句子有两种改法。一、动词"下"改为形容词"大"。二、动词"下"后用"得"及"越来越大"作程度补语，说明雨下的程度。

The directional verb "下" is improper to be used in a sentence expressing comparison. To correct the sentence, one may either replace verb "下" with the adjective "大", or use "得越来越大" after "下" as its degree complement to indicate degree.

六. 几种表示强调的句子的误用
Errors in the Use of Emphatic Sentences

1. 反诘句使用不当

Improper use of rhetorical questions

例 742

误：你把这些东西不是称一称吗？

正：你不是要把这些东西称一称吗？

这是"把"字句和反诘句"不是……吗"套用在一起的句子。这个句子有两处失当。一、谓语动词"称"重叠以后中间加"一"，表明行为动作尚未发生，在这种情况下，可以加能愿动词"要"，表示希望作某事的意志。"要"应加在"把"字前边。二、将错位的"不是"提到主语的后边。"不是……吗"为否定形式，但表示肯定的意思，是说"要把这些东西称一称"。

This sentence is a combination of the 把-construction and the rhetorical pattern "不是…吗". The reduplicative form "称一称" implies that the action has not yet taken place. On this occasion, the auxiliary verb "要" may be used to express one's desire to do so. One should put it before "把". Furthermore, "不是" which is misplaced should immediately follow the subject "你". Though as a negative form, "不是…吗" is affirmative in meaning, i.e. "要把这些东西称一称".

例 743

误：站在东门口的那个人就不是阿里吗？

正：站在东门口的那个人不就是阿里吗？

副词"就"错位。"就"应放在谓语动词"是"前，作状语，强调确实性。句中的"不……吗"为反诘句。副词"不"要放在主语之后。意

275

思是"站在东门口的那个人就是阿里"。

The adverb "就" is misplaced. It should precede the predicate verb "是" as an adverbial adjunct for stress of affirmation. "不" should be placed directly after the subject. This is a rhetorical sentence meaning "站在东门口的那个人就是阿里".

例 744

误：我怎么能找到他的家了？

正：我怎么能找到他的家呢？

"怎么能"与语气助词"了"不搭配。"怎么"表示反诘，句尾经常用语气缓和、含有需要思考意味的语气助词"呢"与之呼应。"怎么能……呢"是肯定形式，表示否定的意思，是说"我不能找到他的家"。

"怎么能" does not go with the interjection "了". "怎么" expressing retort, often occurs with the interjection "呢" which carries a moderate tone and an implication of requiring a further consideration. "怎么能…呢", though in affirmative form, expresses the negative, meaning "我不能找到他的家".

例 745

误：你没告诉我，我哪儿知道这件事了？

正：你没告诉我，我哪儿知道这件事啊？

"哪儿"与语气助词"了"不搭配。"哪儿"用来反问时，句尾常常用引人注意，使人信服的语气助词"啊"。有"我不知道这件事"的意思。

"哪儿" and the interjection "了" do not match here. In a rhetorical question using "哪儿" to express retort, the interjection "啊" normally occurs at the end for conviction and arousing people's attention.

例 746

276

误：谁都不赞成呢？

正：谁都不赞成。

正：谁能不赞成呢？

这个句子有两种改法，一是去掉语气助词"呢"。"谁"是指任何人，"都"总括"谁"包括的每一"个体"。表示"任何人都不赞成"的意思。二是改"都"为"能""能不"，与语气助词"呢"形成反诘句。表示肯定的意思，是说"任何人都赞成"。

There are two ways of correction：1）delete the interjection "呢". "谁" has no specific reference. "都" includes all indicated by "谁"，expressing that every one disagrees. 2）replace "都" with "能". "能不" forms a rhetorical question in affirmative sense with the interjection "呢"，meaning that everyone agrees.

2. "是……的"使用不当

Improper use of "是…的"

例 747

误：他们是坐火车去上海了。

正：他们是坐火车去上海的。

"去上海"实际上是已经完成的动作，"坐火车"是动作的方式。当强调这个已经完成的动作进行的方式时，应当用"是……的"格式。"的"字加在句尾。删去误用的"了"。

Here，"去上海" is a completed action and "坐火车" illustrates its manner. To emphasize the manner in which an action was carried out，"是…的" pattern is used. Hence we replace "了" with "的".

例 748

误：我是在路上碰到了老朋友的。

正：我(是)在路上碰到老朋友的。

"碰到老朋友"是已经完成的动作，"在路上"是动作发生的处所。要强调已经完成的动作发生的地点时,须用格式"是……的",在这种情况下,句中不能再用表示动作完成的动态助词"了"。在表示肯定意义的句子里,可省说"是"。

"碰到老朋友" is a completed event and "在路上" indicates where it occurred. To emphasize the locale of a completed action,"是…的" pattern should be used. Under such circumstance,aspect particle "了" denoting completion of an action can not occur. "是" may be left out since the sentence is used in affirmative sense.

例 749

误:你是什么时候来中国?

正:你是什么时候来中国的?

"来中国"是已经完成的动作,"什么时候"是询问动作发生的时间,强调已经完成的动作发生的时间时,也要用格式"是……的"。这个句子里缺少"的",应在句尾补上这个必不可少的成分。

To emphasize particularly the time of a completed action,"是…的" is also used. The present sentence inquires about the time of the completed action "来中国".

Hence "的" which is obligatory must be added at the end of the sentence to form the "是…的" pattern.

例 750

误:是昨天上午欢迎代表团的大会举行的。

正:欢迎代表团的大会是昨天上午举行的。

句中词序有误。应将表示时点的"昨天上午",连同"是"字,一并移到主语"大会"之后,强调已经完成动作发生的时间。

This sentence is disordered. "昨天上午" together with "是" before it should be moved backwards after the subject "大会" to emphasize the time of the completed action.

例 751

误：阿里不跟他的朋友一起去日本的。

正：阿里不是跟他的朋友一起去日本的。

这个句子应当用"是……的"的否定式，但格式不完整，应在"不"后补上"是"，即"不是……的"。有强调已经完成的（"去日本"）活动不是通过某种方式（"跟他的朋友一起"）进行的意思。

This sentence should occur in the negative form of the "是…的" pattern which requires "是" after "不" to emphasize that the completed action ("去日本") was not carried out in the mentioned manner ("跟他的朋友一起").

例 752

误：是他们去年夏天在颐和园照的相。

正：他们是去年夏天在颐和园照的相。

既强调已经完成的动作发生的时间（"去年夏天"），又强调已经完成的动作发生的地点（"在颐和园"），"是"字一般放在这两个成分之前，应把错位的"是"移到主语（"他们"）之后。"的"字也可以放在宾语（"相"）的前边。

"是" occupies the wrong position. It should follow the subject ("他们") and precede the elements indicating the time ("去年夏天") and locale ("在颐和园")that are to be emphasized. "的" may occur before the object ("相").

3. "连……也……"使用不当

Improper use of "连…也…"

例 753

误：我连想也没有用，就回答出来了。

正：我连想也没想，就回答出来了。

这里是要用"连……也……"强调动词谓语句谓语的主要成分"想"。被强调的"想"应放在"连"和"也"之间，并且还必须重复动词"想"（重复的"想"放在"也"后），而不能用其它动词，这样，才能起到突出和强调的作用。应当用动词"想"替代动词"用"。

"连…也…" is used here to emphasize the main element "想" of the verb predicate. "想" that is emphasized must be inserted between "连" and "也" with its negative form following "也". Any other word like "用" is impossible. One should replace the verb "用" with "想".

例 754

误:甚至连他不能回答这个问题。

正:甚至连他也不能回答这个问题。

"连……也……"是常用格式。句中缺少"也"与"连"呼应。没有"也","连"就失去了强调主语"他"的意义,应在主语"他"后,谓语动词"回答"前加"也"。

"连…也…" is a fixed pattern frequently used. In the present sentence,"也" is missing. Without "也","连" loses its function of emphasizing the subject "他". Hence we add "也" after "他" and before the predicate verb "回答".

例 755

误:他连有急事,也没吃午饭就走了。

正:他有急事,连午饭也没吃就走了。

"连"字错位。此句强调的应是后续句中的宾语"午饭"。因宾语是强调的重点,"连……也……"和"午饭"必须提到谓语前边。改为"连午饭也没吃"。表示"急事"的紧迫。

"连" is misplaced. The element to be emphasized here is the object "午饭" in the follow-up sentence. Therefore,"连…也…" with "午饭" inserted in between must be shifted to the front of the predicate,i. e. "连午饭也没吃". Here it implies urgency of the event.

例 756

误:冬天到了,树上连一片叶子也没。

正:冬天到了,树上连一片叶子也没有。

动词"没"不能用在一个句子的末尾,"没"应改用动词"没有"。

The verb "没" never occurs at the end of a sentence. It should be replaced by "没有".

4. "一……也(不、没)……"使用不当

   Improper use of "一…也(不、没)…"

例 757

误:医生作了六个钟头的手术,一分钟也没休息了。

正:医生作了六个钟头的手术,一分钟也没休息。

数词"一"和"也"前后呼应构成否定格式,表示对过去某种动作行为作极端的否定。此句强调医生在作手术的六个小时的过程中,根本没有休息。而动词"休息"后肯定手术过程中已经"休息"的"了",与句意不符,应删去。

The numeral "一" is used with "也" to make a negative pattern expressing an absolute negation of a past activity. This sentence emphasizes that the doctors did not rest at all during the six hours of operation. But "了" after "休息" implies that they have rested. It contradicts the thought of the whole sentence and should be deleted.

例 758

误:这儿一点也一切没变,都跟从前一样。

正:这儿一点也没变,都跟从前一样。

"一点也没变"是说根本没有变化。"一切没变"是指全部没有变化,用词重复,删去"一切"。

"一点也没变" implies no change at all. "一切没变" means "nothing has changed". "一切" is unnecessary.

例 759

误：他没有钱，甚至一分钱找不到。

正：他没有钱，一分钱也找不到。

句中缺少与"一"相呼应的"也"，失去了完全否定的意思。"也"应加在"找不到"前，强调根本找不到钱。

With the absence of ″也″, the sentence can not express an absolute negation. ″也″ should be used before ″找不到″ to emphasize the impossibility of finding money.

5. 二次否定使用不当

Improper use of double-negation

例 760

误：没有人努力学习，所以我们班的同学汉语都学得不错。

正：没有人不努力学习，所以我们班的同学汉语都学得不错。

既然不努力学习，怎么能学得不错？应在"努力"前再加上一个表示否定的副词"不"，改成"没有人不努力学习"。"没有"和"不"两个否定副词互相抵消，取得肯定意思，是说"我们班的每一个同学都努力学习"。

It is illogical to attribute one's success in study to not working hard. ″不″ should be used in front of ″努力″ i. e. ″没有人不努力学习″. Two negative adverbs (″没有″ and ″不″) used in correlation express the affirmative. Here it means that everyone in the class works hard.

例 761

误：因为她明天就要回法国去了，我今天不能去看她。

正：因为她明天就要回法国去了，我今天不能不去看她。

这是因果关系的复句，由于后一个分句该用两次否定，却用了一次"不"，使得句子意思不清。应在"不能"后加上另一个否定词"不"，组成比较固定的词组"不能不"，表示由于某种需要一定要这样做。是说我今天一定要去看她。

This is a complex sentence of causative relation. But with only one negation word ″不″, it is not quite coherent. To express that he must go to see her, the speaker should use one more ″不″ to form the set phrase of double negation—″不能不″ which means ″must″.

例 762

误：没有钱，不能上大学。

正：没有钱，就不能上大学。

两个表示否定的词"没"和"不"分别用在两个分句里，但是两个分句之间缺少联接的副词"就"，应在后个分句首加"就"，表示从某种条件推出的结论。全句的意思是"只要有钱，就能上大学"。

The two negation words ″没″ and ″不″ occur respectively in the two clauses which should be joined by the correlative adverb ″就″ indicating inference. Place ″就″ at the beginning of the second clause. The whole sentence means ″One is able to go to college if he has money″.

例 763

误：我们不克服缺点，就我们不能进步。

正：我们不克服缺点，我们就不能进步。

副词"就"的位置失当，应移到主语"我们"之后，作状语。含有在上文所说的充分条件下，肯定可产生这种结果的语气。

Adverb ″就″ is misplaced. It must go after the subject ″我们″ to serve as an adverbial adjunct. ″就″ carries the implication that a certain result will surely come into being under certain conditions.

6. 疑问代词活用的句子使用不当

Improper use of interrogative pronouns in extended meanings

例 764

误：谁在学习上有困难，谁老师就帮助。

正：谁在学习上有困难，老师就帮助谁。

两个相同的疑问代词"谁"用在前后两个分句里，相互照应。它们的用途不同，前个句子里的"谁"作主语；后个分句里的"谁"本该放在谓语动词"帮助"后，作宾语。应将错位的"谁"调整到宾语的位置上。这个"谁"是指在学习上有困难的人。

Both clauses use an interrogative pronoun "谁". The two "谁" are identical in reference but different in function. The one in the first clause serves as the subject, while the other one wrongly positioned should stay after the predicate verb "帮助" as the object referring to people who have difficulty in study.

例 765

误：哪个问题没讨论完，咱们就讨论什么问题。

正：哪个问题（什么问题）没讨论完，咱们就讨论哪个问题（什么问题）。

前后照应的两个疑问代词不一致。前个分句里用"哪"，后个分句里用"什么"。或者都改成"哪个问题"，或者都改成"什么问题"，不论采取哪一种表达方式，都是指"没有讨论完的问题"。

The two pronouns "哪" and "什么" used respectively in the two clauses do not accord. They must reach an agreement, to be either "哪个问题" or "什么问题", either one of which refers to problems unsolved.

例 766

误：你什么时候方便，什么时候我就来看你。

正：你什么时候方便，我就什么时候来看你。

这两个句子中的"什么时候"是指"适宜的时间"。通常放在谓语之前，作状语。后个分句的"什么时候"与主语"我"易位，应该颠倒过来。

Here，"什么时候" refers to any time suitable. It normally precedes the predicate as an adverbial adjunct. In the second clause，"什么时候" and the subject "我" are disordered and must be reversed.

例 767

误：你念怎么，我就念怎么。

正：你怎么念，我就怎么念。

句中"怎么"的位置不当，应将已经错位的"怎么"提到动词谓语"念"前，作修饰语。这种用于前后两个分句，互相照应的"怎么"有模仿对方做法的意思。

"怎么" occupies the wrong position. It should be placed before the predicate verb "念" to be an adverbial modifier. Two "怎么" used in correlation in two related clauses express the idea of "follow the example of".

例 768

误：哪儿有意思，就我们去哪儿玩。

正：哪儿有意思，我们就去哪儿玩。

在用两个疑问代词相互照应的分句之间，通常用副词"就"联系。"就"不能放在后个分句主语"我们"的前头，只能放在主语的后头。

The adverb "就" is often used to join two clauses in which two interrogative pronouns occur in correlation. Its position is after the subject rather than before the subject as in the present sentence.

七、复句的误用
Errors in the Use of Complex Sentences

1. 并列关系复句使用不当

Improper use of co-ordinate complex sentences

不是……而是……

not…but…

例 769

误:这件毛衣的样子不是不好看,而是颜色不好。

正:这件毛衣不是样子不好看,而是颜色不好。

从字面上看,被说明的是"样子",其实指的是"毛衣"。关联词"不是"应当移到小主语"样子"的前边,删去"的"字,说明同一事物的肯定与否定两个方面的对比情况。

The subject of the whole statement is actually "毛衣" rather than "样子". Hence the correlative word "不是" must be moved to the front of "样子" which should serve as the subject of the S-P (subject-predicate) phrase functioning as the predicate of the first clause, "的" should be deleted. Here an affirmative statement and a negative one are made on the same object in regard to different respects.

例 770

误:她不是是北京大学的学生,而是是清华大学的学生。

正:她不是北京大学的学生,而是清华大学的学生。

"不是……而是……"连接的成分是由动词"是"组成的动宾词组,其中关联词"不是"、"而是"中的"是"与动词"是"在音节上显得重复,通常合二为一,只说一个"是"就可以了。

In this sentence, the elements joined by "不是…而是…" are two verb-object phrases formed by the verb "是". The succession of two "是" sounds redundant. Only one "是" should remain.

既……也……

as well as …; …neither…

286

例 771

误:他既跳远也跳高都不会,你教教他吧。

正:他既不会跳远,也不会跳高,你教教他吧。

用"既……也……"直接连接表示动作的动词("跳远"、"跳高"),并且把这个并列成分当作复加结构提到"不会"之前,用"都"突出它,不论从语义上还是结构上都说不通,应当改成表示并列关系的复句,删去多余的"都",表明"不会跳远"、"不会跳高"这两种情况同时存在。

With a construction of two action verbs connected by "既…也…" preceding "都不会", the present sentence is structurally as well as semantically not grammatical. One should delete "都" and change it into a complex sentence of coordinate relation, to express the existence of both facts—"不会跳远" and "不会跳高".

例 772

误:既阿里不喜欢唱歌,也不喜欢跳舞,别请他了。

正:阿里既不喜欢唱歌,也不喜欢跳舞,别请他了。

两个分句同属于一个主语"阿里","既"不能放在主语之前,应移到主语"阿里"之后。

The two clauses share the same subject "阿里". "既" may not precede the subject. One should put it after "阿里".

例 773

误:在月球上,既有水和空气,生物也不能生存下去。

正:在月球上,即使有水和空气,生物也不能生存下去。

"既"表示的是一种既成的事实,实际上,月球上没有水和空气,应改"既"为表示假设关系的关联词"即使"。

"既" is only applied to facts. There is no water and air on the moon. Hence, "既" should be replaced by the correlative word "即使" which expresses supposition.

例 774

误：圆柱形的容器既使用方便,比较美观。

正：圆柱形的容器既使用方便,也比较美观。

"既"后面常常用"也"与其呼应,后个分句缺"也"。在"比较"前加"也",表示另一方面的情况同样存在。

"既" is normally used in correlation with "也". "也" is absent from the second clause and must be added before "比较" to imply the existence of another fact.

也……也……

…as well as…

例 775

误：巴里亚汉字写得也快也好。

正：巴里亚汉字写得又快又好。

动词谓语"写"后的程度补语不宜用"也……也……",通常用"又……又……",表示同一事物的两种情况并存。

"也…也" can not be applied to the degree complement of the verb predicate ("写"). To indicate the existence of two facts about one thing "又…又…" is usually used.

例 776

误：也小王是你的朋友,也是我的朋友。

正：小王是你的朋友,也是我的朋友。

句中用"也……也……"反而累赘,删去第一个错位的"也",保留第二个表示同样的"也",可以表达原句意。

It is too wordy to use "也…也…" here. Delete the misplaced "也" in the first clause and keep the second one which is enough to express the original meaning.

边……边……

…as…; …while…

例 777

误:上课的时候,我们边儿听边儿说。

正:上课的时候,我们边听边说。

"边……边……"表示同一主语同时发出两种或两种以上不同的 动作行为。"边"不能儿化,应删去"边儿……边儿……"中的 "儿"。

″边…边…″expresses that the subject is carrying out two or more than two activities at the same time. ″边″ can not carry the retroflex suffix ″儿″. ″儿″must be deleted.

一边……一边……

…as…; …while…

例 778

误:他俩一边走了路,一边谈了话。

正:他俩一边走路,一边谈话。

"一边……一边……"侧重表示两个或两个以上不同动作行为 同时进行。在这种句子里,谓语动词后不能再用表示动作完成的动 态助词"了",或者"走"、"谈"后改"了"为"着"。

″一边…一边…″ emphasizes that two or more than two actions are going on simultaneously. In this type of sentence the predicate verb can not be followed by the aspect particle ″了″. However, ″着″ may be used instead.

例 779

误:听到这个消息,老人一边悲痛,一边气愤地离开了那里到 别的地方去找工作。

正:听到这个消息,老人又悲痛又气愤地离开了那里到别的地 方去找工作。

"一边……一边……"所连接的是动词或动词词组,不能连接 形容词"悲痛"和"气愤",改"一边……一边……"为"又……又……"。

"一边……一边……" is only used to join verbs or verbal phrases. "悲痛" and "气愤" are adjectives which should be joined by "又……又……" rather than "一边……一边……".

例 780

误：小朋友们一边作什么，一边作什么欢迎来参观的人？

正：小朋友们怎样（怎么样）欢迎来参观的人？

因要表示询问"欢迎"的方式，用复句"一边……一边"不妥。应该用"怎么样"替代"一边……一边"，作状语。单句简洁贴切。

The complex sentence "一边……一边" is improper to inquire the manner of "welcome". One should use a simple sentence with "怎么样" as the adverbial adjunct to replace "一边……一边".

例 781

误：一边儿我听录音，一边儿写汉字。

正：我一边儿听录音，一边儿写汉字。

"一边"是副词，不能用在主语前，只能移在谓语动词"听"的前边。

"一边" is an adverb and may not come before the subject. Its only possible position is before the predicate verb ("听").

一方面……一方面……

on the one hand … on the other (hand)

例 782

误：他一方面抓紧时间学习，一方面记生词。

正：他一方面抓紧时间学习，一方面考虑学习方法。

"一方面……一方面……"表示同一事物的两个方面。"抓紧时间学习"包括"记生词"这一环节。两者不是同一事物并存的两个方面，应把"记生词"改成"考虑学习方法"。

"一方面……一方面……" expresses two aspects of one thing.

290

Memorizing words is one part of study. They are not two co-ordinate aspects. One may replace "记生词" by "考虑学习方法".

例 783

误：老师一方面指出我们学习上的一些问题，一方面肯定我们的成绩。

正：老师一方面肯定我们的成绩，一方面指出我们学习上的一些问题。

这是以褒贬两个方面说明问题的并列复句。通常把表示褒义的分句放在前面，表示贬义的分句放在后面。应将并列的两个方面的顺序颠倒过来。

This is a co-ordinate complex sentence in which commendation and admonition are juxtaposed. Normally, the clause expressing commendation precedes the one expressing admonition. Hence the order of the two clauses here should be reversed.

例 784

误：他喜欢一方面吃饭，一方面看报。

正：他喜欢一边吃饭，一边看报。

"一方面……一方面"往往只连接表示抽象意义的并列分句。"吃饭"、"看报"是同时进行的两个动作，应改"一方面……一方面"为"一边……一边……"。

Most often, "一方面…一方面" connects co-ordinate clauses that express abstract meanings. "吃饭" and "看报" are concrete actions and can not be joined by "一方面…一方面". "一边…一边…" is the right pattern here.

例 785

误：在中国的五年里，一方面我要学好汉语，一方面要学好专业，一方面了解中国的建设情况。

正：在中国的五年里，我一方面要学好汉语，一方面要学好专业。

句中有两处失误。一、分句的主语相同,"一方面"应移到主语"我"的后边,谓语部分"要"前。二、一方面"一般只能两项叠用,不能增减。可以删去与学习生活直接关系不大的第三分句。

The speaker has committed two errors 1)With an identical subject,"一方面" must be placed after the subject "我" and before the predicate section. 2) Generally speaking,"一方面" is only applied to two co-ordinate clauses no more and no less. Hence, the third clause which is not closely related to the topic of the first two clauses should be deleted.

又……又……

··· not only ···, but also ···

例 786

误:这辆自行车又很好又很便宜。

正:这辆自行车又好又便宜。

用"又……又……"连接的形容词("好"、"便宜")前,不能再用肯定程度相当高的词语,应当删去"很",表示两种性质并存。

Adjectives ("好"、"便宜") connected by "又···又···" may not be modified by words denoting a high degree. One should not use "很". The sentence indicates the simultaneous existence of two properties.

例 787

误:风又刮又大。

正:风越刮越大。

"又……又……"与"越……越……"两组关联词混用。此句着眼于后个分句表示的结果随着前面条件的变化而变化,应改用"越……越……"。

Here, "又···又···" is confused with "越来越". To express

292

that the degree of the state indicated by the second predicate changes proportionally to the changes of condition indicated by the first predicate，"越…越…" is the proper pattern.

例 788

误：愚公决定搬走两座山，又高又大。

正：愚公决定搬走两座又高又大的山。

前一个分句的主语是"愚公"，后一个分句转换成主语"两座山"。"两座山"在前一个分句中是宾语，不能被后一个分句承为主语。显然，由于暗中更换主语而造成丢失主语的毛病。应改变一下句子结构，把"又高又大"移到"山"前，作定语，并在由并列成分充当的定语与中心语之间加"的"。这样表达才合理。

The subject of the first clause is "愚公" and the one of the second clause should be "两座山" which is the object of the first clause. The error lies in the absence of subject resulting from the misunderstanding that the object of the first clause may simultaneously function as the subject of the second clause. To correct the sentence，we place "又高又大" before "山" as its attributive and insert "的" in between.

2. 承接关系复句使用不当

Improper use of complex sentences of successive relation

先……再……

first…then…

例 789

误：先我坐汽车去天安门，再坐车去天坛。

正：我先坐汽车去天安门，再坐车去天坛。

副词"先"和"再"构成"先……再……"，表示两种动作前后相继发生。"先"不能放在主语"我"的前边，应放在谓语动词"坐"前。

Adverbs "先" and "再" are used in co-ordination to form "先

…再…" which indicates successive occurrence of two actions. "先" may not come before the subject ("我"), but must be put in front of the predicate verb ("坐").

例 790

误:我先念课文,就作练习。

正:我先念课文,再作练习。

"先……再……"与"一……就……"两组关联词混淆。"先"与"就"不能搭配,改"就"为"再"。

"先…再…" and "一…就…" are two distinct pairs of correlative words and should not be mixed up. "就" does not match with "先" and must be replaced by "再".

例 791

误:早上我先去友谊商店,中午我再要去友谊商店。

正:早上我去友谊商店,中午我还要去友谊商店。

原来句子意思要表示末然动作行为的重复,而不是说明前后两个动作一个跟着一个发生。应删去前一个分句的"先",改后一个分句的"再"为"还"。

The speaker originally means to express the repetition of a future action, not the successive occurrence of two events. Hence, one should delete "先" and use "还" in replace of "再".

一……就……

… as soon as …

例 792

误:我和我同屋学校一放假,就去中国的南方旅行。

正:学校一放假,我和我的同屋就去中国的南方旅行。

前后两个分句应当分属于两个不同的主语"学校"和"我和我的同屋",必须把误用在前个分句里的"我和我的同屋"移到后个分句句首,表示"学校放假"的情况才出现,紧接着发生另一种情况即

"我和我的同屋去中国的南方旅行"。

The two clauses should take two different subjects—"学校" and "我和我的同屋" respectively. "我和我的同屋" which improperly occupies the initial position of the first clause must be moved backwards to the beginning of the second clause. This sentence expresses that "学校放假" is closely followed by another event，"我和我的同屋去中国的南方旅行".

例 793

误:大脑的工作一停止,生命结束了。

正:大脑的工作一停止,生命就结束了。

"一"后常常用副词"就"与之呼应。后个分句却缺少"就",应在谓语动词"结束"前加上这个不能缺少的成分。

"一" is often used in correlation with "就". "就" which is absent from the second clause must be added before the predicate verb "结束".

例 794

误:一我作完练习,就去找你打球。

正:我一作完练习,就去找你打球。

"一"是副词,应移到主语"我"后,动词谓语"作"前,作修饰成分。

"一" here is an adverb. It must follow the subject "我" and precede the predicate "作" to serve as an adverbial modifier.

例 795

误:我一吃过晚饭以后,咱们就一起散步。

正:我一吃过晚饭,咱们就一起散步。

正:我吃过晚饭以后,咱们一起散步。

"一……就……"和"以后"是一对时间概念不相同的词语,不能混在一起用。这个句子有两种改法:一是去掉"以后",保留"一

295

……就……",表示"吃完晚饭,紧接着去散步"。二是去掉"一……就……",保留"以后",指比吃过晚饭要晚的时间去散步。

"一…就…" and "以后" are of different temporal concepts, thus may not be mixed up together. There are two ways to correct the present sentence. One way is to delete "以后" and keep "一…就…" to express that one is going to take a walk as soon as supper finishes. The other way is to delete "一…就…" and keep "以后" to indicate that walking is arranged after supper.

3. 递进关系复句使用不当

Improper use of complex sentences of progressive relation

不但……而且……

not only … but also …

例 796

误:阿里在这次比赛中,不但给我们拿到名次,而且自己取得好成绩。

正:阿里在这次比赛中,不但自己取得好成绩,而且给我们班拿到名次。

"给我们班拿到名次"应该是比"自己取得好成绩"更进一层的意思,应把"不但"和"而且"后边的成分调换一下。

"给我们班拿到名次" goes further in meaning, compared with "自己取得好成绩". Thus, the elements after "不但" and "而且" should exchange positions.

例 797

误:他不但会说汉语,而且认识很多中国朋友。

正:他不但会说汉语,而且会说英语。

正:他不但认识很多英国朋友,而且认识很多中国朋友。

"认识很多中国朋友"和"会说汉语"分属于不同类别,不宜用"不但……而且……"表示后项比前项进一层。应改成类别相同或

296

近似的内容。如会说汉语、会说英语，或认识很多英国朋友、认识很多中国朋友。

"认识很多中国朋友" and "会说汉语" are of different types, thus should not be connected by "不但…而且…" indicating that the second clause is further in meaning than the first one. The two clauses must belong to the same or similar categories in content. For instance, one may say "他不但会说汉语，而且会说英语" or "他不但认识很多英国朋友，而且认识很多中国朋友".

例 798

误：不但北京的冬天很冷，而且还常常刮风。

正：北京的冬天不但很冷，而且还常常刮风。

前后两个分句同属于一个主语"冬天"，"不但"不能放在主语前，而应放在主语后。

The two clauses share the identical subject "冬天". In this case, "不但" must follow the subject rather than precede it.

例 799

误：谢力不但爱打乒乓球，而且巴里亚也爱打乒乓球。

正：不但谢力爱打乒乓球，而且巴里亚也爱打乒乓球。

前后两个分句分属于两个主语"谢力"和"巴里亚"，"不但"不能放在主语后，应当放在主语"谢力"前。

The two clauses have different subjects—"谢力" and "巴里亚" respectively. On such occasion, "不但" should come before the subject rather than after it.

例 800

误：马老师不但教我们汉语，教玛丽她们汉语。

正：马老师不但教我们汉语，而且教玛丽她们汉语。

"不但"后面缺少与之搭配的关联词"而且"，使人有语意未尽的感觉。在后个分句谓语动词前加上"而且"。

With no such correlative word as ″而且″ to go in concert with ″不但″, the sentence sounds incomplete. One may add ″而且″ in front of the predicate verb of the second clause.

例 801

误:金属不但导电好,而且也导热好。

正:金属不但导电好,而且导热也好。

在由主谓词组"导热好"作谓语的句子里,副词"也"通常放在小谓语"好"的前头。

In a sentence with an S-P (subject-predicate) phrase (″导热好″) as the predicate, adverb ″也″ usually precedes the predicate of the S-P phrase (″好″).

不但……反而……

… on the contrary …

例 802

误:现在是春天了,天气不但不暖和,反而不冷。

正:现在是春天了,天气不但不暖和,反而很冷。

"不但"后带有否定词"不",是从否定方面说起("不暖和");用在后一个分句前的"反而"也是从否定方面引出否定意思的"不冷",全句讲不通。应改最后一个"不"为"很",引出肯定方面的意思,把意思推进一层,表示出乎意料。

This sentence makes no sense. The negation word ″不″ which is used after ″不但″ to form a negative construction (″不暖和″) should not occur in the second clause after ″反而″ to form another negative construction (″不冷″). We replace ″不″ with ″很″ in order to produce an affirmative form (″很冷″) which is further in meaning than the negative form (″不暖和″). In the first clause ″反而…″ meaning ″on the contrary…″ implies that a certain fact is beyond one's expectation.

298

例 803

误：水变成冰时，不但体积不收缩，反而膨胀。

正：水变成冰时，体积不但不收缩，反而膨胀。

在"不但……反而……"中，前后两个分句主语（"体积"）相同，"不但"不能放在主语之前，要放在主语之后。

In the construction of "不但…反而…", the two clauses share the same subject. Under such a circumstance, "不但" must follow the subject rather than precede it.

不仅……而且……

not only … but also …

例 804

误：我不仅能吃中国饭、菜，而且要喝中国酒。

正：我不仅能（要）吃中国饭、菜，而且能（要）喝中国酒。

"不仅"相当于"不但"，"而且"承接上文表示更进一层的意思。句子中的"能"表示一种能力，指现状。"要"表示一种意志，指欲望。两者的角度不同，不宜用"不仅……而且……"。要么把"能"改成"要"；要么把"要"改成"能"。

"不仅" is a synonym of "不但". "而且" shows that the second clause goes further in meaning. "能" indicates ability and "要" expresses will or desire. As two different aspects, they can not be connected by "不仅…而且…". To correct the sentence, one should replace "能" with "要" or vice versa.

例 805

误：那本书不仅你没看过，而是我也没看过。

正：那本书不仅你没看过，而且我也没看过。

关联词"不仅"与"而是"不能搭配，改"而是"成"而且"，表示进一层的意思。

"不仅" does not go in concert with "而是". To indicate a step

further "而且" should be used instead of "而是".

例 806

误：不仅他从星期一到星期六工作，而且星期天也工作。

正：他不仅从星期一到星期六工作，而且星期天也工作。

前后两个分句的主语都是"他"，"不仅"不该放在主语"他"前，应移到谓语部分"从"前。

As the subject，"他" is applied to both clauses. "不仅" can not precede it，but should be moved backwards to the front of the predicate section.

例 807

误：肺不仅能吸入氧气，能呼出二氧化碳。

正：肺不仅能吸入氧气，而且能呼出二氧化碳。

前个分句用了"不仅"，后个分句缺少与其相照应的关联词"而且"，分句之间的关系不清。应在后个分句"能"的前边加上"而且"。

Here，the relation between the two clauses is unclear，since the second clause lacks a corresponding correlative word to go with "不仅" in the first clause. "而且" should be used before "能呼出二氧化碳".

除了……以外，……还（都）

in addition to …；apart from …

例 808

误：除了外国留学生以外，北京语言学院有中国学生。

正：除了外国留学生以外，北京语言学院还有中国学生。

"除了……以外"后往往用"还"与之呼应，后一个分句缺少表示所说的之外还有补充的副词"还"。应把"还"加在谓语动词"有"的前边。意思是"北京语言学院又有外国留学生，又有中国学生"。

"除了…以外" is often used in concert with "还". "还" is absent from the second clause. It should be added before the predicate verb "有" to express that apart from foreign students, there are also Chinese students in Beijing Language Institute.

例 809

误：除了你们班去长城以外，我们班还去。

正：除了你们班去长城以外，我们班也去。

后一个分句用"还"不妥，改用"也"，表示行为动作相同。是说"我们班跟你们班一样，去长城游览"。

"还" is improper here. One should use "也" instead to express the idea of doing the same thing. The sentence means that "our class will also go to the Great Wall as your class will".

例 810

误：除了她俩学习中国历史以外，别的同学学习中国文学。

正：除了她俩学习中国历史以外，别的同学都学习中国文学。

后一个分句遗漏了表示范围的副词"都"，应加在动词谓语"学习"前，是说"别的同学学习中国文学，只有她俩学习中国历史"的意思。

The second clause has lost the adverb "都" indicating scope. One should add it before the verb predicate "学习". This sentence means that all the students study Chinese literature except they two who study Chinese history.

4. **假设关系复句使用不当**

Improper use of complex sentences of suppositional relation

即使……还（也）

… even if …

例 811

误：即使昨天晚上七点你去看他，他还没有从大使馆回来呢。

正：如果昨天晚上七点你去看他，他还没有从大使馆回来呢。

从形式上看，这是表示让步假设的复句，但是从内容上看，并不表示让步假设。因连词"即使"使用不妥,应改成"如果",表示假设的情况。

The correlative "即使" expressing concessive supposition is improper to be used here, since the present sentence carries no implication of concession. "如果" should take its place to indicate simple supposition.

例 812

误:你今天即使不来这儿,我也要你那儿去。

正:你今天即使不来这儿,我也要到你那儿去。

后一分句缺少谓语动词"到",补上后,与"去"构成"到……去"。还可以改成"我也要去你那儿",由"去"充当谓语动词。

The predicate verb is missing from the second clause. One should add "到" to form "到…去". One may also say "我也要去你那儿", using "去" as the predicate verb.

例 813

误:即使明天下雨,我们要去参观。

正:即使明天下雨,我们也要去参观。

前个分句用"即使",而后个分句缺少相应的词与之呼应,通常在"我们"的后边加"也",表示假设关系。

The second clause has no corresponding word to go with "即使", expressing suppositional relation. "也" is required after "我们".

假如……那么……

if …

例 814

误:假如接不到你的电话,我那么不到你那儿去。

正:假如接不到你的电话,那么,我就不到你那儿去。

"假如"相当于"如果",多用于书面;"那么"承接上文的假设,得出后边的结论。"那么"是连接前后两个分句的连词,只能放在两

302

个分句中间用来连接前后两个分句，应移到后一分句的主语"我"之前。"那么"后加逗号。后一分句还可在主语"我"后加上"就"，与"假如"相呼应，强调前边的假设条件实现的话，自然产生这样的结果。

〝假如〞is a synonym of 〝如果〞but mostly occurs in writing. 〝那么〞indicates the conclusion drawn from the previous supposition. As a conjunction to connect two clauses, it always goes between the two clauses. As a result, 〝那么〞in the present sentence must be shifted to the front of the subject 〝我〞and separated from the second clause by a comma. 〝就〞may be used after 〝我〞in concert with 〝假如〞to imply that the result is certain if the supposed condition comes true.

如果……就……

if

例 815

误：如果你看过那本书，就你给大家介绍一下。

正：如果你看过那本书，你就给大家介绍一下。

作为关联词的副词"就"，不能用在后个分句主语"你"的前边，只能移到主语的后边。

The correlative adverb 〝就〞may not precede the subject 〝你〞of the second clause. It should go after the subject.

例 816

误：如果大脑停止工作，生命结束了。

正：如果大脑停止工作，生命就结束了。

"如果"是提出假设情况的连词，后面往往用"就"与其呼应，推出结论。此句缺少关联词"就"，应加在主语"生命"之后。

〝如果〞expressing supposition is generally used in concert with 〝就〞indicating the conclusion drawn from the supposition. 〝就〞

which is absent should be added after the subject "生命".

要是……就……

if

例 **817**

误:要是明天刮大风,就没打篮球。

正:要是明天刮大风,就不打篮球。

"要是……就……"表示假设关系,否定假设的情况时,要用否定词"不"代替"没"。

"要是…就…" expresses a suppositional relation, the negation of which is indicated by "不" rather than "没".

例 **818**

误:你要是用词典,再到我这儿来借了。

正:你要是用词典,再到我这儿来借。

在此表示假设关系的复句里,有动作将在另一动作结束后出现的"再",句尾不宜用表示动作完成的"了"应删去。

In this complex sentence of a suppositional relationship "再" is used to show that an action will take place after the completion of another. In this case, "了" denoting completion of an action may not be used at the end of the sentence.

例 **819**

误:要是你不去,就你告诉我一声。

正:要是你不去,(你)就告诉我一声。

副词"就"与主语"你"易位,应调换两者先后顺序。由于两个分句同属一个主语"你",后个分句的主语"你"可省略。

Adverb "就" and the subject "你" are in reverse order. They should exchange positions. Since the subjects of the two clauses are identical, the second clause may be omitted.

例 **820**

304

误:要是明天下不下雨,我就不去参观。

正:要是明天下雨,我就不去参观。

"要是"后面不能用意义相对的并列词组"下不下雨"。"要是"引出的条件应是确指的。根据句意,去掉"不下(雨)",只留下"下雨",说明因下雨不便参观。

"要是" can not be followed by a co-ordinate phrase with elements opposite in meaning like "下不下雨" in the present sentence. The condition put forward by "要是" should be definite. According to the context, we drop "不下(雨)" and keep "下雨" to express the meaning that one will not go if it rains.

5. **条件关系复句使用不当**

Improper use of complex sentences of conditional relation

不管……都……

no matter (however, whatever)

例 821

误:不管学习上有什么困难,但是我们应该努力克服。

正:不管学习上有什么困难,我们都应该努力克服。

"不管"用于条件句,"但是"用于转折句,从语义上说前后不连贯。根据原句意,应该删去"但是",在主语"我们"后加"都",与"不管"配用,是说无论条件如何,结果都相同。

"不管" is applied to conditional sentences whereas "但是" adversative sentences. With both of these two words present, the sentence is incoherent. To meet the original meaning, we delete "但是" and add "都" after the subject "我们" to concert with "不管", indicating that the result will remain the same whatever the condition is.

例 822

误:不管天气不好,她都要去颐和园。

正:不管天气好不好,她都要去颐和园。

正:不管天气怎么样,她都要去颐和园。

"不管"同后边成分"不好"不相适应。这个句子有两种改法:一是把否定的"不好"改成肯定和否定相叠的句式"好不好"。二是改"不好"为任指性的疑问代词"怎么样",表示任何条件都加以排除。"不管"多用于口语。

"不管" and "不好" do not go together. There are two ways to correct the sentence. One is to change the negative "不好" into the affirmative negative form "好不好". The other is to replace "不好" with "怎么样" which is an interrogative pronoun of unspecific reference, to indicate the exclusion of all conditions. "不管" is mostly used in speaking.

例 823

误:冬天不管怎么冷,小王都坚持锻炼。

正:不管冬天怎么冷,小王都坚持锻炼。

"不管"放在了"冬天"后边。"冬天"是主语,在语义上与后一个分句联系不上。"不管"应放在"冬天"之前,表示不受任何条件限制。

"冬天" is the subject of the first clause. "不管" must be placed before it to express "despite the constraint of any condition".

例 824

误:不管今天怎么再忙,我都要把这个材料看完。

正:不管今天怎么忙,我都要把这个材料看完。

"再"用在形容词"忙"之前,有"无论怎么忙"的意思,与"不管怎么忙"的意思重复。应删去副词"再"。

"再忙" carries the meaning of however busy which is expressed by "不管怎么忙". "再" is an unnecessary repetition and should be deleted.

例 **825**

误:不管明天下雨不下雨,咱们都去游泳了。

正:不管明天下雨不下雨,咱们都去游泳。

在这个表示无条件的复句里,"明天"已明确指出行为动作"去游泳"尚未发生,句尾不能再用表示事情完成的语气助词"了"。

In this complex sentence expressing under no circumstances，"明天" definitely shows that the action "去游泳" has not yet taken place. Therefore，the interjection "了" denoting completion of an action may not occur at the end of the sentence.

不论……都……

no matter (what, who, how); whether … or …

例 **826**

误:不论每天没有时间,我们都要看报。

正:不论每天有没有时间,我们都要看报。

连词"不论"与其后边的成分不搭配。"不论"后不能只用否定的或肯定的任何一项,应改"没有时间"为肯定和否定相叠的"有没有时间"。意思是在任何条件下,结果完全一样。"不论"多用于书面语。

The conjunction "不论" does not match with its following element. It can not be followed by only a negative or an affirmative form，"没有时间" should be changed into the affirmative-negative form ("有没有时间"). This type of sentence expresses the idea that under no circumstances will the result change. "不论" usually occurs in writing.

例 **827**

误:不论明天你来,我们都去参观。

正:不论明天你来还是不来,我们都去参观。

应改"你来"为带有选择性的并列词组"来还是不来",方能与后面"都"相呼应。

To match with "都", one should replace "你来" with "来还是不来" which is a co-ordinate phrase in alternative form.

例 828

误：不论这个问题十分难，我们都要解决。

正：不论这个问题怎么难，我们都要解决。

应改只表示肯定一项的"十分难"为任指性的疑问代词"怎么"。

The affirmative "十分难" should be replaced by the interrogative pronoun "怎么" with no specific reference.

例 829

误：不论你们去哪儿，我们也去。

正：不论你们去哪儿，我们也都去。

在肯定形式的后一个分句里，缺少与"不论"前后照应的副词"都"，应加在动词"去"的前边。

The adverb "都" which is often used in concert with "不论" is absent from the second clause in affirmative form. It should be added after the verb "去".

只要……就……

provided; if … will …

例 830

误：同学们只要努力，就一定学好汉语。

正：同学们只要努力，就一定能学好汉语。

后个分句的成分残缺，推理的根据不够充分，"努力"不是"一定学好汉语"的条件，"努力"使"学好汉语"成为可能。在"学好汉语"前加"能"。

With some element missing from the second clause, the present sentence is a deduction without much ground. Rather than the condition of "一定学好汉语"，"努力" affords possibility of "学好汉语". Thus，"能" is needed before "学好汉语".

例 **831**

误：只要学好汉语，就要有决心。

正：只要有决心，就能学好汉语。

条件和结果弄颠倒了。"学好汉语"是"有决心"的结果，"有决心"才是"学好汉语"的条件。

The condition and the result have been confused. "学好汉语" is the result of "有决心" and "有决心" is the condition of "学好汉语".

例 **832**

误：只要什么生物，就离不开空气和水。

正：只要是生物，就离不开空气和水。

"只要"后面不能用表示任指的"什么"。"只要"引出的成分应是确指的条件，改为"是生物"就相应了。

"只要" may not take after it "什么" which is of unspecific reference. Its following element should indicate a definite condition. "是生物" is the proper form to replace "什么生物".

例 **833**

误：我们只要一起想办法，这件事才能办好。

正：我们只要一起想办法，这件事就能办好。

关联词"只要"与"才"不能相互呼应，应改"才"为"就"。"就"含有在前个分句所说的条件下肯定产生后边的结果的语气。

"只要" and "才" are not a matching pair of correlatives. "才" must be replaced by "就" which carries the overtone that the result will surely be attained under the condition indicated by the first clause.

例 **834**

误:只要学好汉语,就学专业不难了。

正:只要学好汉语,学专业就不难了。

副词"就"不能修饰该分句主语"学专业",应放在主语后,谓语部分前。

The adverb "就" can not premodify the subject "学专业", but should follow it to modify the predicate.

只有……才……

only

例 835

误:只有坐飞机去,今天晚上才到上海。

正:只有坐飞机去,今天晚上才能到上海。

后个分句缺少能愿动词"能"。"能"应加在"才"的后边,表示可能性。

The second clause has left out the auxiliary verb "能" which should be used after "才" to express potentiality.

例 836

误:只有努力学习,学习好中文。

正:只有努力学习,才能学习好中文。

前个分句用关联词"只有"引出唯一的、必要的条件;后个分句往往在谓语前用"才"与之呼应,引了结果"学好中文"。"才"的后边常常与"能"连用。

With the correlative "只有" occurring in the first clause to introduce the only necessary condition, the second clause generally uses "才" before the predicate to elicit the result ("学好中文"). On such occasion, "能" is often used in combination with "才".

例 837

误:只有七千美元,我才能买汽车。

正:只有准备好七千美元,我才能买汽车。

"只有七千美元"中的"只有"容易被误解成副词"只"和动词"有"组成的动词词组,表示数量少。这样,与原意不相符合,与后面的"才"也不相适应。在前个分句中应当加上动补词组"准备好"或"凑齐"。

"只有" in "只有七千美元" is likely to be misunderstood as a verbal phrase formed by adverb "只" and verb "有" to imply that the quantity is small. This does not accord with the original meaning of the sentence, neither does it concert with "才". To make the sentence grammatical, one may add the verb-complement phrase "准备好" or "凑齐"in the first clause.

例 838

误:什么事只有下功夫去做,就能成功。

正:什么事只有下功夫去做,才能成功。

正:什么事,只要下功夫去做,就能成功。

关联词"只有"与"就"不能配对使用。应当把"就"改为"才",或者把"只有"改成"只要"。

Correlative "只有" and "就" are not a usual match. Replace "就" by "才" or change "只有" into "只要".

越……越……

… the more … the more

例 839

误:雨越下越很大。

正:雨越下越大。

"越……越……"表示随着时间不断地延续,某种特性在程度上不断地加强。"很"表示程度相当高。这两个含有程度意味、但概念差异很大、用法不同的词语不能混同在同一个句子中。删去"很"。

"越…越…" shows that the degree of a certain property intensifies as time continues. "很" denotes a high degree. These two words both carry a sense of degree, but have different meanings and usages, hence can not be used in co-ordination in one sentence. "很" should be deleted.

例 840

误:你学习越刻苦,学习得好。

正:你学习越刻苦,越学习得好。

正:你学习越刻苦,学习得越好。

"越……越……"总是重叠合用的。后一个分句中的"越"不能少,或者加在谓语动词"学习"前,或者加在程度补语"好"前。

"越…" always occurs in co-ordination with another "越…". There is no "越" in the second clause. We add one before the predicate verb "学习"; however, it may also precede the degree complement "好".

例 841

误:越我们讨论,越问题清楚。

正:我们越讨论,问题越清楚。

"越"是副词,只能用谓语前,作状语。"越……越……"应分别加在前后两个分句谓语动词"讨论"和谓语形容词"清楚"的前边。

"越" is an adverb and normally precedes the predicate as an adverbial adjunct. One should put it before the predicate verb "讨论" and the predicate adjective "清楚" of the two respective clauses.

例 842

误:今天的生词越多越难。

正:今天的生词又多又难。

"今天的生词"怎么能用"越……越……"?不合事理。这个句子着眼于两种性状并存,应换用"又……又……"。

It does not stand to reason to apply "越…越…" to "今天的生

312

词". The speaker means to express the co-existence of two proper-ties. He should use "又…又…" in stead.

例 843

误:这个故事很有意思,我越听越好。

正:这个故事很有意思,我越听越爱听。

用于"越……越……"之间的"好",用词不当。看不出随着"听"的时间的不断延续,在"听"的程度上有什么变化,应改"好"为"爱听"或"喜欢听"。

"好" is an improper word here. It does not express one's inter-est in listening. One should say "爱听" or "喜欢听" instead of "好".

6. 选择关系复句使用不当

Improper use of complex sentences of alternative relation

不是……就是……

…or …

例 844

误:我不是想她来,就是她姐姐来。

正:我想不是她来,就是她姐姐来。

"想"是全句的谓语动词。"不是"应移到"想"后,与"就是"构成"不是……就是……"表示非此即彼的选择关系的复句,用作谓语动词"想"的宾语。

"想" is the predicate verb of the whole sentence. "不是" should be placed after "想" to form the construction "不是…就是…" which is an alternative complex sentence meaning it must be one or the other. "不是…就是…" serves as the object of "想" in the present sentence.

例 845

误:明天上午我们不是去图书馆,就是去阅览室了。

正：明天上午我们不是去图书馆，就是去阅览室。

"不是……就是……"可供选择的是指未来的情况，句末不宜用表示完成的语气助词"了"。

The two alternatives here are related to the future, hence interjection "了" denoting completion may not occur at the end of the sentence.

例 846

误：他告诉我他不是星期六来，就是星期日。

正：他告诉我他不是星期三来，就是星期日来。

"不是……就是……"后边的成分性质往往是同类型的、对称的。后一个分句缺少谓语，句意不清，应在句尾加动词"来"。

The elements joined by "不是…就是…" are normally of the same type. With no predicate verb in the second clause, the sentence meaning is obscure. Verb "来" should also be used in the final position of the second clause.

例 847

误：下一次旅游，不是我去桂林，就是去昆明。

正：下一次旅游，我不是去桂林，就是去昆明。

"不是……就是……"两个分句应同属于一个主语"我"，"不是"不能放在主语"我"的前边。应移到主语的后边。

The clauses joined by "不是…就是…" share the same subject "我". "不是" must follow the subject rather than precede it.

例 848

误：我们班的教室不是大，就是他们班的教室大。

正：不是我们班的教室大，就是他们班的教室大。

两个分句分属于两个主语"我们班的教室"、"他们班的教室"，"不是"要放在主语"我们班的教室"的前边。

Each clause has a different subject, i. e. "我们班的教室" and

314

"他们班的教室" respectively. In this case, "不是" must precede the subject "我们班的教室".

与其……不如……

better…than…

例 849

误：我想与其《红楼梦》，不如《水浒传》。

正：我想与其看《红楼梦》，不如看《水浒传》。

"与其……不如……"表示舍前取后的有定的选择关系，经常连接由动词构成的并列词组。此句连接的是名词《红楼梦》、《水浒传》。根据上下文的意思，应在"与其"、"不如"后分别加上动词"看"。意思是经过判断，还是认为看《水浒传》比较好。

"与其…不如…"indicates preference of the second thing to the first. It usually connects two co-ordinate verb phrases. But here, the elements joined by "与其…不如…" are nouns,《红楼梦》and 《水浒传》. According to the context, verb "看" should be added after "与其" and "不如". The speaker considers it better to read《水浒传》after making a judgement.

7. 因果关系复句使用不当

Improper use of complex sentences of causative relation.

既然……就……

since …; now that …

例 850

误：既然你去过长城，就你给我们介绍一下长城的情况。

正：既然你去过长城，你就给我们介绍一下长城的情况。

"既然……就……"用于推理性因果复句，"既然"提出理由，"就"引出由此推出的结果。关联词"就"是副词，不能用在主语"您"前，应移在主语后边。

"既然…就…" is applied to causative complex sentences making inference. "既然" puts forth the premise and "就" introduces the conclusion drawn from the premise. The correlative "就" is an adverb. It can not come before the subject "您" but should go after it.

例 851

误:既然我家里不想我,我不回国。

正:既然我家里不想我,我就不回国。

后一分句缺少"就"字。"就"用来跟前一分句已经证实的事相承接,引出由此推得的结果。"就"应加在主语"我"后。

"就" is absent from the second clause. It must be used to introduce the conclusion that is drawn from the fact confirmed in the first clause. We add "就" after the subject "我".

例 852

误:既然他的身体不太好,不可以来上班。

正:既然他的身体不太好,可以不来上班。

"既然"用于推理性因果复句的前面分句,应该把后面分句的否定词"不"移到动词"来"的前边,表示根据叙述的已经证实的"他的身体不好"这一事实,得出"允许他不来上班"这样的结果。

In this causative complex sentence with "既然" used in the first clause, the negation word "不" in the second clause should be moved to the front of the verb "来" to indicate that the confirmed fact "他的身体不好" leads to the conclusion "允许他不来上班".

例 853

误:既然你病了就不想去旅行。

正:既然你病了就不要去旅行。

"不想"是主观上不愿意,"不要"是客观地劝止。改成"不要"才符合原意。

"不想" shows one's reluctance to do something. It does not

316

meet the meaning of the sentence and should be replaced by "不要" which denotes discussion.

例 854

误：既然这些是学过的生词，所以我记住了。

正：既然这些是学过的生词，我们就应该记住。

后个分句引出由上文推出的结果。推理的根据不充分，不能推出"学过的生词，我都记住了。"事实上，总是要遗忘一些。"既然"句重点在后面的推断，含主观性，可以改后个分句为"我们就应该记住"。在主语"我们"后加"就"，与"既然"相呼应。

The second clause introduces the conclusion drawn from the preceding one. Here, the deduction has not much ground in that "我都记住了" can not be deduced from "是学过的生词". The fact is that forgetting is always possible. A sentence using "既然" lays emphasis on the conclusion which is subjective. The second clause may be changed into "我们就应该记住" with "就" following the subject "我们" to concert with "既然".

既然……那么……

now that … since

例 855

误：既然你请我，然而我一定去。

正：既然你请我，那么我一定去。

这是推论性的因果复句，后分句却用了表示转折的连词"然而"，"然而"不能用来连接有推论因果关系的两个分句。应改成"那么"，承接上文、引出结果，与前一分句的"既然"配合使用。

This is a causative complex sentence making an implication. But the second clause uses an adversative conjunction "然而" which does not join causative clauses. Rather than "然而", "那么" should be used in combination with "既然" to introduce the conclusion.

所以……是为了……

the reason … is …

例 856

误:人们所以把粽子扔到江中喂鱼,不让鱼吃屈原的身体。

正:人们所以把粽子扔到江中喂鱼,是为了不让鱼吃屈原的身体。

关联词"所以"用在前面分句的主语"人们"之后,谓语部分之前,是讲手段或措施,后个分句是对"把粽子扔到江中喂鱼"达到某种目的的判断。应在后个分句句首补上"是为了"。"所以……是为了……"格式表示目的和手段的关系。

In the first clause, the correlative "所以" occurs after the subject "人们" and before the predicate to show means or measure. The second clause is a judgement of the purpose that "把粽子扔到江中喂鱼" was intended for. It should start with "是为了…". "所以…是为了…" is a construction expressing the relation of purpose and means.

因为……所以……

例 857

误:因为冬天就要到了,他所以要进城买棉大衣。

正:因为冬天就要到了,所以他要进城买棉大衣。

"所以"在后个分句中的位置失当,应移到主语"他"之前。

"所以" in the second clause is misplaced. It must precede the subject "他".

例 858

误:因为报纸重要消息很多,他都看了。

正:因为这些报纸重要消息很多,所以他都看了。

这是因果复句,后面的句子缺少与其相照应的关联词。应在"他"的前边加上"所以"。

318

This is a complex sentence of causative relation, in which the second clause lacks a corresponding correlative to match "因为" in the first clause. "所以" should be added before "他".

例 859

误：因为天坛公园里的回音壁以奇妙的声音现象，所以吸引了很多游人。

正：因为天坛公园里的回音壁能够传递声音，所以吸引了很多游人。

介宾词组"以奇妙的声音现象"怎么样，语意不清。可以改为动宾词组"能够传递声音"，句子就完整了。

The prepositional phrase "以奇妙的声音现象" does not express a complete meaning. To produce a complete sentence, one should replace it by the verb-object phrase "能够传递声音".

例 860

误：因为由于他每天锻炼，所以他的身体不错。

正：因为他每天锻炼，所以他的身体不错。

"因为"和"由于"都表示原因，用词重复，删去"由于"。

Both "因为" and "由于" indicate reasons. It is unnecessary to use both. "由于" may be deleted.

例 861

误：因为我考试不及格，因此我不能毕业。

正：因为我考试不及格，所以我不能毕业。

前面的分句用"因为"，后面的分句又用"因此"，造成用词重复，可以改用"所以"。但用"由于"的分句后边，可用带"因此"的分句。

The sentence is repetitious in having "因为" in the first clause and "因此" in the second. "所以" should take the place of "因此" to match "因为". If "因此" is to be kept, "由于" should be used in

319

the first clause.

由于……因此……

due to … so

例 862

误：因此这儿不能游泳，由于水太深。

正：由于这儿水太深，因此不能游泳。

连词"由于"表示原因，不能用在第二分句中。若用"由于"，可把原因分句放在前面。

The conjunction "由于" indicates reasons. It may not occur in the second clause. The clause using "由于" to express the reason should be placed in the front.

例 863

误：由于他对这儿比较熟，但是还走了一个小时。

正：虽然他对这儿比较熟，但是还走了一个小时。

正：由于他对这儿比较熟，因此只走了一个小时。

前个分句用"由于"，表示原因，后个分句却用了表示转折关系的"但是"，关联词不搭配，可以改"由于"为"虽然"。副词"还"含有埋怨的意味，是说认识路，居然走了这么长时间。或者改"但是"为表示因果的"因此"，同时删去"还"，表示路上用的时间不算多。

"由于" and "但是" are not a matching pair of correlatives. This sentence is incoherent in using "由于" in the first clause to indicate reason, and "但是" in the second one to show adversity. "虽然" is the proper word to replace "由于". The adverb "还" here carries an emotional colouring of complaint, i. e., the person was too slow. The sentence is also grammatical if "因此" denoting causative relation is used to replace "但是" and "只" replaces "还" to imply a short time.

8. 转折关系复句使用不当

320

Improper use of complex sentences of adversative relation

尽管……但是……

although

例 864

误:尽管他每天来上课,但是身体不好。

正:尽管他身体不好,但是每天都来上课。

按理说,"尽管"应当表示姑且承认"身体不好"这一事实,然后用"但是"引出与前文相反的结果"每天都来上课"才合事理。显而易见"尽管"与"但是"弄颠倒了,须调整过来。

Normally "尽管" is used first to admit a certain fact ("身体不好") and "但是" comes in the second clause to introduce a result notwithstanding the fact. In the present sentence, "尽管" and "但是" occupy the position where the other one should be; thus, they must undergo an exchange of positions.

例 865

误:尽管月球上有水,但是在温度很高时,水就会变成气体。

正:即使月球上有水,但是白天温度很高时,水也会变成气体。

"尽管"和"即使"的用法混淆。"尽管"后面说的是确认的事实。月球上是没有水的,不能说"尽管月球上有水"。"即使"后面所说的情况成立与否都可以,此句应当用"即使"。同时,改后面的"就"为"也",与"即使"呼应。

Here, "尽管" is confused with "即使". What "尽管" introduces must be a truth. One can not say "尽管月球上有水", since there is actually no water on the moon. However, "即使" may be applied to supposition. Hence, "即使" should be used instead. Meanwhile, "也" should replace "就" to go with "即使".

尽管……还是……

…though; in spite…

例 866

误:尽管这个工作很困难,他完成了这个工作。

正:尽管这个工作很困难,他还是完成了。

后一个分句缺少与"尽管"相互照应的关联词,应在"完成"的前边加"还是"。"还是"表示所说的动作不因"困难"而改变。

The second clause should have a corresponding correlative to concert with "尽管". We add "还是" before "完成" to express the idea of "notwithstanding" or "in spite of".

例 867

误:尽管学习怎么忙,他每天还是坚持看报。

正:不管学习怎么忙,他每天都坚持看报。

"尽管"与"不管"混淆。"尽管"后面不能用诸如"怎么"一类的疑问代词。改"尽管……还是……"为"不管……都……"。

"尽管"is confused with "不管". "尽管" does not occur with such interrogative pronouns as "怎么". One should use "不管…都…" instead of "尽管…还是…".

例 868

误:尽管他家很难找,我就找到了。

正:尽管他家很难找,我还是找到了。

副词"就"与前面的"尽管"不搭配,须改成有转折意义的副词"还是"。

The adverb "就" does not match with "尽管" and should be replaced by adverb "还是" denoting adversity.

例 869

误:尽管他每天锻炼身体,他跑得很慢。

正:尽管他每天练习短跑,他还是跑得很慢。

"锻炼身体"包含多种运动项目,且对不同人有不同意义,和跑的速度没有必然的联系。"短跑"是锻炼速度的,和跑的快慢才能保

322

持意义上的一致。根据句意,后分句应加副词"还是",表示跑的速度跟以往一样"慢"。"还是"可以加在谓语动词"跑"前,也可以加在程度补语"慢"前。

"锻炼身体" includes many different items, and its effect varies from individual to individual. It has no direct influence on running speed. "短跑" helps to improve one's speed; thus, it is the kind of exercise that suits the context here. According to the meaning of the sentence, the adverb "还是" should be used in the second clause to indicate that the speed was as slow as before. It may precede the predicate verb "跑" or the degree complement "慢".

虽然……但是……

though

例 870

误:虽然简单,这是一个很好的办法。

正:虽然简单,但这是一个很好的办法。

这是表示转折关系的复句。前面用了关联词"虽然",后面却没有相应的关联词。后分句句首前加"但(是)"。

This is a complex sentence expressing adversity. The first clause has used the correlative "虽然", but there is no corresponding word in the second one. "但(是)" should be added at the beginning of the second clause.

例 871

误:天气虽然好了,但是注意身体。

正:天气虽然好了,但是仍要注意身体。

原意是:"注意身体"这件事不因天气变好而放松,后个分句中只用"但是"还不足以表达这层意思。"注意身体"前应加副词"还是"、"仍要"或"也要"等。

The speaker means one should not reduce attention on health

323

problems although the weather becomes better. "虽然···但是···" is not sufficient to express such meaning. The second clause requires the adverb "还是" or "仍要" or "也要" to be used before "注意身体".

例 872

误:但是他没来过中国,虽然他对中国的情况还是很了解的。

正:虽然他没来过中国,但是他对中国的情况还是很了解的。

"虽然"的分句应在先,带"但是"的分句应在后,"虽然"和"但是"搞颠倒了,应调整过来。

The clause with "虽然" always precedes the one with "但是". The two correlatives are reversed here and should exchange their positions.

第四章　标点符号方面常见的错误
CHAPTER FOUR　COMMON ERRORS IN PUNCTUATION

一、点号的误用
Errors in the Use of Dots

1. 句号使用不当
Improper use of the full stop

例 873

误：我们都是加拿大留学生.

正：我们都是加拿大留学生。

这是受英语句号书写方式的影响。在用汉字写完一句话以后，总是习惯地在句终点上一个小黑点儿"."，表示一句话完了以停顿。汉语的句号是个小圆圈儿"。"，应改"."为"。"号。

In English, the full stop is a dot ".". In Chinese, it is a tiny ring "。". "." should be changed into"。".

例 874

误：我的朋友在北京语言学院学习汉语

正：我的朋友在北京语言学院学习汉语。

陈述句句尾丢掉了句号。只有加上这个不可缺少的符号，才有可能表示陈述语气。

This statement has no full stop which is obligatory here to indicate the declarative tone.

例 875

误：这里的天气你现在习惯不习惯。

正：这里的天气你现在习惯不习惯？

在正反疑问句句尾不能用表示陈述语气的句号，要改用表示疑问语气的问号（"？"）。

As affirmative-negative question can not end with a full stop which indicates a declarative tone. Instead，a question mark ″?″ should be used to express the interrogative tone.

例 876

误：长城多么雄伟啊。

正：长城多么雄伟啊！

抒发感情的感叹句句尾误用了句号，应改用感叹号。表示感情强烈的句子完了之后的停顿。

This is an exclamatory sentence. Thus, the exclamation mark rather than the full stop should be used.

例 877

误：开会了，别说话了。

正：开会了，别说话了！

句终不宜用句号，通常用本身带有表示感情强烈的感叹号。

The full stop is improper here. One should use the exclamation mark which carries a strong emotional colouring.

例 878

误：那个地方好极了，咱们怎么能不去呢。

正：那个地方好极了，咱们怎么能不去呢！

带有强烈感情色彩的反诘句末尾一般不用句号，可以用感叹号。

The full stop is improper for a rhetorical question with a strong emotional colouring. One may use the exclamation mark instead.

例 **879**

误:你们喜欢不喜欢这种颜色。

正:你们喜欢不喜欢这种颜色?

这是正反式疑问句,应当在句尾加表示疑问语气的问号。

This is an affirmative-negative question which should end up with a question mark carrying an interrogative tone.

例 **880**

误:以前你看过京剧吗。

正:以前你看过京剧吗?

用"吗"构成的是非问句后误用句号,应改成问号。

This is a general question formed by ″吗″. A question mark should be used instead of a full stop.

例 **881**

误:那位先生是法国人,还是德国人。

正:那位先生是法国人,还是德国人?

由"……还是……"构成的选择式问句后,不能用句号。要改句号为问号。

This is an alternative question using ″…还是…″. The full stop should be replaced by the question mark.

例 **882**

误:你爸爸在哪儿工作。

正:你爸爸在哪儿工作?

由疑问代词构成的特指问句后,句尾要用问号,不能用句号。

A special question using the interrogative pronoun should end up with a question mark rather than a full stop.

2. 问号使用不当

Improper use of the question mark

例 **883**

误:你去大使馆呢?还是去国际俱乐部呢?

正:你去大使馆呢,还是去国际俱乐部呢?

选择式的疑问复句,问号通常用在全句未尾,前个分句的问号
应改为逗号。

This is an interrogative complex sentence of alternative relation. Normally the question mark occurs at the end of the sentence.
One should change the first question mark into a comma.

例 **884**

误:丁力最喜欢足球,他怎么能不来呢。

正:丁力最喜欢足球,他怎么能不来呢?

"怎么能不……呢"是反诘句,这类句子不要求回答,但是,要
用疑问句的形式,疑问句的语气。应改句号为问号。

″怎么能不…呢″ is a rhetorical question which requires no answer but takes the form of an interrogative sentence and carries an
interrogative tone. The full stop should be replaced by a question
mark.

例 **885**

误:请你告诉我明天早上几点出发?

正:请你告诉我明天早上几点出发。

句中用了疑问代词"几",但"明天早上几点出发"是兼语谓语
动词"告诉"的宾语。这是问句形式作宾语,它在大句子里失去了本
身的特征与功能,成为陈述句的一个部分,句尾应当用句号。

This is a pivotal sentence in which ″告诉″ is the predicate verb
to the pivot ″你″. ″明天早上几点出发″ is the object of ″告诉″.
Though with an interrogative pronoun ″几″, it has lost the interrogative feature and function and becomes part of the entire statement. Hence a full stop should be used at the end of the sentence.

3. 感叹号使用不当

Improper use of the exclamation mark

例 **886**

误:玛丽画儿画得真不错!

正:玛丽画儿画得真不错。

这是个感叹句,但说话时并没有带上强烈的感叹语气,句子未尾不必用感叹号。应改用句号。

This sentence is not a typical exclamation with a strong emotional tone. One should use a full stop rather than an exclamation mark.

例 **887**

误:我多么想早点儿去别的大学学习专业啊。

正:我多么想早点儿去别的大学学习专业啊!

这是由"多么……啊"构成的感叹句,以抒发强烈感情为主。句子未尾误用的句号,应改为感叹号。

This is an exclamation in the pattern of ″多么…啊″. It expresses a strong emotion. The full stop at the end of the sentence must be replaced by an exclamation mark.

例 **888**

误:让我们一起热热闹闹地过个节吧。

正:让我们一起热热闹闹地过个节吧!

由"让……吧"构成的带有强烈情感的呼语,句子未尾不用句号,要用感叹号。

The pattern ″让…吧″ also carries a strong emotional tone and should end up with an exclamation mark rather than a full stop.

例 **889**

误:请你把这封信带给安娜!

正:请你把这封信带给安娜。

此祈使句语气缓和,句尾不能用感叹号,应当改用句号。

With a moderate tone, this imperative sentence should use a full stop instead of an exclamation mark.

4. 顿号使用不当
Improper use of the slight-pause mark

例 890

误:为了玛丽的生日,同学们买了蛋糕巧克力糖葡萄酒什么的。

正:为了玛丽的生日,同学们买了蛋糕、巧克力糖、葡萄酒什么的。

由于缺少必要的顿号,使句子产生了歧义。可以理解为买了三样东西,即在"蛋糕""巧克力糖"后分别加顿号。也可以理解为买了五样东西,那就是在"蛋糕""巧克力""糖""葡萄"后各加一个顿号。

This sentence is ambiguous with the absence of the slight-pause mark. To mean three kinds of thing, one should use a ″、″ after ″蛋糕″ and ″巧克力″. To mean five, ″、″is needed after ″蛋糕″, ″巧克力″,″糖″ and ″葡萄″respectively.

例 891

误:你父、母身体好吗?

正:你父母身体好吗?

并列的名词"父""母"字数少,结构简短,没有明显的语音停顿,一般中间不必用顿号。

″父″ and ″母″ are two simple nouns of only one character. When they are in co-ordination, there is no evident pause between them. Thus, it is unnecessary to use a slight-pause mark.

例 892

误:现在我住在北京语言学院、八楼、三层、三一五号。

正:现在我住在北京语言学院八楼三层三一五号。

说明住址的四个词组之间的关系是领属关系,中间不用顿号,句中的三个顿号统统去掉。

The four phrases indicating living address are not co-ordinate to each other. Hence, one should not use the slight-pause mark between them.

例 893

误:北京大学清华大学离北京语言学院不远。

正:北京大学、清华大学离北京语言学院不远。

"北京大学"与"清华大学"两个词组是平列关系,中间应该加上顿号。

"北京大学" and "清华大学" are co-ordinate and must be joined by a slight-pause mark.

5. 逗号使用不当

Improper use of the comma

例 894

误:巴里亚的桌子上放着书,本子,词典,笔,录音机等。

正:巴里亚的桌子上放着书、本子、词典、笔、录音机等。

并列的名词"书""本子""词典""录音机"之间的停顿较短,不必用逗号,用顿号就可以了。

There is only a slight pause between the four nouns ("书","本子","词典","录音机") in co-ordination. The slight-pause mark rather than the comma should be used.

例 895

误:因为你的问题太难了所以我不能马上回答你。

正:因为你的问题太难了,所以我不能马上回答你。

这是由关联词"因为……所以……"构成的表示因果关系的复句。分句与分句之前要有停顿,应用逗号断开。

This is a causative complex sentence formed by "因为…所以

⋯". There is a pause between the two clauses, and it should be indicated by a comma.

例 896

误:他的身体很好像一个运动员。

正:他的身体很好,像一个运动员。

由于该用逗号而没有用,使句子结构不明,句意不清。在"好"与"像"之间加上逗号,改成"他的身体很好,像一个运动员",全句就通顺了。

Without a comma sentence structure meaning becomes unclear. We add a comma between "好" and "像" to make the sentence read smoothly, i. e. "他的身体很好,像一个运动员".

例 897

误:这样的录音比较难,有的地方,我听得懂,有的地方,我听不懂。

正:这样的录音比较难,有的地方我听得懂,有的地方我听不懂。

句子里的逗号用得过多,后两个分句中的"有的地方"后的逗号应当去掉。否则,读起来断断续续,句意搞得支离破碎。

The error lies in an excessive use of comma which leads to a broken sentence. "有的地方" should not be separated from the respective clause by a comma.

6. **冒号使用不当**

Improper use of the colon

例 898

误:阿里,

┅┅┅┅┅┅┅┅┅┅┅┅   谢力 1989. 5. 28

正:阿里:

┅┅┅┅┅┅┅┅┅┅┅┅   谢力 1989. 5. 28

在书信的称呼语后,用逗号不当,应改用冒号。含有注意下边的话的意思。

After the title of a letter, we use a colon rather than a comma to arouse the reader's attention.

二、标号的误用
Errors in the Use of Markers

1. 书名号使用不当
Improper use of the title mark

例 899

误:我们每个人都有基础汉语课本。

正:我们每个人都有《基础汉语课本》。

"基础汉语课本"是一本教科书的名称,由于没有用书名号,看不出词语的性质和作用。应该在"基础汉语课本"前后加上书名号,以标出书名。

"基础汉语课本" is the title of a textbook which must be characterized by the title mark.

2. 引号使用不当
Improper use of the quotation mark

例 900

误:昨天妈妈打来电话说,你学习很紧张,一定要注意身体。

正:昨天妈妈打来电话说:"你学习很紧张,一定要注意身体。"

动词"说"后是引用妈妈的原话,"说"后应改逗号为冒号。引用的话的前后加上引号""。

The object of the verb "说" is a direct speech. Thus, the comma should be replaced by a colon and direct speech must be crowned with the quotation mark.

附录
Appendices

病 句 索 引
SENTENCE INDEX

第一个阶段
Period I

所使用的教材 text-book	序号 number	病　　句 example sentence	页数 page
基础汉语课本	（001）	他今年二十年，我二十一年。	13
基础汉语课本	（002）	一个男人和一个女人教我们汉语。	13
初级口语	（005）	现在我在北京里学习汉语。	15
初级口语	（009）	我9月12日1996年开始学习汉语。	16
初级口语	（010）	现在是5分过12点。	16
初级汉语课本	（011）	她每天学习四点（钟）。	16
初级汉语课本	（012）	我们上午8小时上课。	17
普通汉语教程	（013）	我们只谈了一半小时。	17
普通汉语教程	（021）	今天是10月25天。	20
普通汉语教程	（022）	没关系，你的病一会儿以后会治好的。	20
普通汉语教程	（027）	我们的老师们都是中国人。	22
普通汉语教程	（028）	北京语言学院的外国留学生们很多。	22
普通汉语教程	（033）	要是我没有汽车，我给你我的。	24
现代汉语教程	（034）	我很喜欢我妹妹的两个儿子，我常和他一起玩儿。	24

基础汉语课本　（035）　玛丽和安娜来了，你问问她。　　24

基础汉语课本　（039）　丁力让我在这等他。　　26

基础汉语课本　（042）　你去那儿。　　26

基础汉语课本　（043）　明天早上你去朋友吗？　　27

基础汉语课本　（047）　你等谁人？　　28

基础汉语课本　（048）　谁马老师问问题？　　29

基础汉语课本　（049）　谁是哪国人？　　29

现代汉语教程　（050）　什么你教？　　29

基础汉语课本　（051）　星期天很多人去什么玩儿？　　30

普通汉语教程　（052）　你家有什么口人？　　30

初级口语　　　（053）　对老年妇女什么称呼？　　30

基础汉语课本　（054）　（A 昨天你做什么了？）　　31
　　　　　　　　　　　B 昨天我做写信、洗衣服、
　　　　　　　　　　　看朋友了。

基础汉语课本　（055）　北京语言学院有几个外国留学生。　31

普通汉语教程　（056）　您要几苹果？　　32

基础汉语课本　（058）　请问，这种毛衣多少？　　32

基础汉语课本　（059）　长江比黄河多少长公里？　　33

普通汉语教程　（060）　你是从哪地方来的？　　33

普通汉语教程　（061）　去动物园在怎么地方换332路　　33
　　　　　　　　　　　公共汽车？

基础汉语课本　（062）　这个图书馆怎么书都有。　　34

基础汉语课本　（068）　我想参观一个中国工人的家庭。　36

初级汉语课本　（078）　他给很多帮助我。　　40

基础汉语课本　（080）　刚到北京没给你一封信，请原谅。　41

基础汉语课本　（081）　他一本外文书还图书馆。　　42

基础汉语课本　（082）　我要给阅览室还几本画报。　　42

基础汉语课本　（083）　阿坦克借我一本词典。　　42

基础汉语课本 (086) 同志,给您找五毛钱。 44
普通汉语教程 (091) 请代我问好你的父母亲。 45
基础汉语课本 (093) 我送送你一下儿。 46
基础汉语课本 (094) 他知道那件事,可以给我们讲了讲。 47
普通汉语教程 (095) 我送送你们出去吧。 47
普通汉语教程 (097) 你会什么时候去? 48
现代汉语教程 (099) 我喜欢说汉语,但是我只说一点儿。 49
普通汉语教程 (100) 以后你汉语说得很好。 49
基础汉语课本 (103) 谢力,我用你的自行车吗? 50
普通汉语教程 (105) 请问,这儿能不能啄烟?能。 50
基础汉语课本 (106) 阿里在家吗?他现在不能在家。 51
基础汉语课本 (119) 阿里去图书馆要借一本书。 55
初级汉语课本 (122) 他想想学会打球。 56
初级汉语课本 (127) 秋天不刮风,小下雨。 58
普通汉语教程 (136) 同志,找您两块两毛两。 61
基础汉语课本 (138) 今天我们用了两十五块八毛二。 62
汉语课本 (145) 我一个月多没有接到家里的信了。 64
基础汉语课本 (148) 我还有百多块钱。 65
基础汉语课本 (165) 这些邮票一共五块零毛六分(钱) 71
现代汉语进修教程 (166) 这件大衣二百八十块零八。 71
基础汉语课本 (168) 那张词典是我的。 72
汉语课本 (170) 一年有十二月。 73
现代汉语教程 (171) 我喝了两个杯牛奶,他喝了一个瓶啤酒。 73
基础汉语课本 (173) 我会说汉语一点儿。 74
基础汉语课本 (179) 一些巴里亚的衣服放在箱子里。 77
初级口语 (182) 昨天他不去张老师那儿。 78
初级口语 (183) 我们法语不说得好。 78

医学汉语　　　　　（185）　今天我不有看报呢。　　　　　　　　　79

基础汉语课本　　　（186）　她不会滑冰，我不也会滑冰。　　　　79

初级汉语课本　　　（188）　对不起，我没有去，你们快去吧。　　80

现代汉语教程　　　（189）　他俩没愿意去那儿游泳。　　　　　　80

现代汉语教程　　　（190）　来中国以前，我没有会说汉语。　　　80

现代汉语教程　　　（193）　我每天都没有锻炼身体。　　　　　　81

现代汉语进修教程　（194）　明年暑假他和阿里都没有回国。　　　81

基础汉语课本　　　（197）　那种花漂亮，这种花没有漂亮。　　　82

基础汉语课本　　　（198）　我没有看那部电影了。　　　　　　　82

医学汉语　　　　　（202）　每天八点上课，他常常八点一刻来。　84

汉语课本　　　　　（203）　颐和园不远，但是我们一个就到那儿。84

基础汉语课本　　　（204）　昨天下了课，就他去看朋友。　　　　84

基础汉语课本　　　（206）　香山很远，我们一个半小时就到。　　85

基础汉语课本　　　（207）　我就才知道他是大夫。　　　　　　　85

基础汉语课本　　　（208）　以前常常我去友谊商店买东西。　　　86

初级汉语课本　　　（209）　现在我们跟中国同学常常说汉语。　　86

普通汉语教程　　　（210）　我不常常跟朋友一起吃饭。　　　　　86

基础汉语课本　　　（219）　我过去已经去过她几次故宫。　　　　89

基础汉语课本　　　（221）　已经我们研究了那个问题了。　　　　90

基础汉语课本　　　（226）　你们都学习汉语，他们都也学习汉语。92

科技汉语教程　　　（227）　这个班有十个学生，都不是非洲的，　92
　　　　　　　　　　　　　　还有亚洲的。

初级汉语课本　　　（228）　（A 星期天你都作什么？）　　　　　93
　　　　　　　　　　　　　　B 星期天我都洗衣服、写信、去看
　　　　　　　　　　　　　　朋友了。

基础汉语课本　　　（236）　这个电影太好了，我想看一遍。　　　96

现代汉语进修教程　（237）　他们班上星期去长城了，我们　　　96
　　　　　　　　　　　　　　班下星期还要去。

现代汉语进修教程	（247）	我看画报,也我看杂志。	99
普通汉语教程	（248）	这条裤子很合适不合适?	100
基础汉语课本	（255）	快要下雨,我们赶快回学校吧!	103
基础汉语课本	（257）	快要大风了,快关上窗户吧!	103
普通汉语教程	（258）	现在六点五十五分了,快要音乐会开始了。	104
基础汉语课本	（261）	我们能学好中文一定。	105
现代汉语时修教程	（264）	你一定不告诉他这件事。	105
基础汉语课本	（277）	别叫阿里了,正他准备考试呢。	110
初级口语	（281）	我问只一个问题。	111
现代汉语进修教程	（282）	他们有中文书,英文书,没只有阿文书。	111
基础汉语课本	（289）	你哪个国家来的?	114
汉语课本	（290）	他以上课回宿舍去。	114
基础汉语课本	（291）	丁力以他朋友去大使馆。	114
基础汉语课本	（292）	阿里买来一个录音机从上海。	114
普通汉语教程	（294）	她妈每天以家去工厂早晨六点钟。	115
普通汉语教程	（297）	到了十字路口,从右拐就行了。	116
汉语教科书	（313）	老师讲语法给我们。	121
基础汉语课本	（317）	我们离语言学院,坐331路汽车可以到。	122
基础汉语课本	（318）	那个商店离我们睡觉不太远。	123
汉语教科书	（319）	从他的家离马老师的家很近。	123
基础汉语课本	（322）	那儿往1路车站很近。	124
初级汉语课本	（332）	你这儿作什么?	127
初级汉语课本	（334）	在这个地方你们踢球吗?	128
汉语课本	（335）	去动物园换车在哪儿?	128
基础汉语课本	（339）	请你把这张票给阿里还是巴里亚。	130

基础汉语课本　　（340）　你姐姐是大夫，还是是工程师？　130

基础汉语课本　　（341）　晚上你们看杂技或者看京剧？　130

基础汉语课本　　（344）　我们的教室很大和很干净。　132

初级口语　　　　（350）　上星期我们去几个公园。　134

基础汉语课本　　（353）　我没有看了这本历史书。　135

汉语教科书　　　（354）　我每天复习了一个小时的旧课。　135

现代汉语进修教程　（355）　我和我的朋友喜欢了这个学校。136

基础汉语课本　　（357）　早上我吃早饭了，就来教室了。　136

基础汉语课本　　（358）　巴里亚的衣服放在箱子里。　137

普通汉语教程　　（360）　他的箱子很重，阿里要替他拿着。　138

普通汉语教程　　（375）　谁朋友是英国人？　142

普通汉语教程　　（376）　她有一双非常漂亮布鞋。　143

基础汉语课本　　（377）　我买了一张《人民的日报》　143

基础汉语课本　　（378）　谢力踢足球踢的不错。　143

基础汉语课本　　（381）　这是阿里买来地中文小说。　144

基础汉语课本　　（384）　安娜写汉字写很好。　145

汉语教科书　　　（386）　同学们都积极得参加运动会。　146

科技汉语教程　　（387）　水蒸发的快慢与温度得高低有关。　146

基础汉语课本　　（391）　我们等一会儿再去书店，她吧？　148

基础汉语课本　　（397）　昨天他吃了晚饭，就去朋友那儿。　149

汉语教科书　　　（398）　我们请张老师教我们中国歌，他教　150
　　　　　　　　　　　　　我们。

基础汉语课本　　（399）　你的身体好不好了？　150

基础汉语课本　　（402）　我每天晚上都复习旧课，预习新　151
　　　　　　　　　　　　　课了。

基础汉语课本　　（406）　你给我介绍的那本书我还没有看了。152

现代汉语教程　　（407）　现在玛丽能用汉语跟中国朋友谈了　152
　　　　　　　　　　　　　话。

基础汉语课本	（408）	你是什么时候来北京的吗？	153
基础汉语课本	（410）	明天（还是）你们来，还是我们去吗？	154
汉语教科书	（411）	你去图书馆吗？还是去教室呢？	154
基础汉语课本	（416）	明天你们还有课呢？	156
现代汉语教程	（419）	他们买东西很便宜。	157
基础汉语课本	（426）	现在人等车的很多。	161
普通汉语教程	（430）	那位是教留学生汉语老师。	162
基础汉语课本	（431）	去火车站接朋友人多极了。	162
初级汉语课本	（433）	那本词典是我。	163
初级汉语课本	（434）	那件毛衣不是黄，是绿。	164
汉语课本	（435）	去滑冰多极了。	164
基础汉语课本	（436）	今天晚上的电影是谁的？	165
初级口语	（437）	我们每天上午有课从八点到十二点。	165
基础汉语课本	（438）	我每天下午复习从三点起。	166
基础汉语课本	（439）	他从中学学习法语和英语。	166
基础汉语课本	（449）	这个商店的前没有工厂。	170
初级汉语课本	（453）	这个电影不错，很多看的人。	171
初级汉语课本	（455）	我刚上车，车就开始了。	172
初级汉语课本	（461）	老师让我通知大家明天欢送会。	174
汉语教科书	（463）	这支歌叫名字"社会主义好"。	175
基础汉语课本	（465）	今天上午我们有上课。	175
基础汉语课本	（466）	如果你去上海，可以给我买带来一个录音机吗？	176
基础汉语课本	（467）	我每天早上做很多东西，锻炼身体，去食堂吃早饭，去教室上课。	176
基础汉语课本	（470）	办公楼在学校医院。	177
基础汉语课本	（471）	下雨了，我们别长城去了。	177

初级口语	（472）	您这是五块,找两两毛二分钱您。	178
初级口语	（475）	你买了一本书词典吗?	178
初级口语	（476）	我常常跟同学说中国汉语。	179
医学汉语	（480）	外国留学生的北京语言学院很多。	180
基础汉语课本	（481）	他们在前边我们宿舍打网球。	181
基础汉语课本	（483）	那个我们学院的操场很小。	181
基础汉语课本	（484）	这是一本书新。	182
基础汉语课本	（486）	他是一位我们学校的好老师。	182
基础汉语课本	（493）	星期三和星期六我们每天在礼堂里看电影。	185
初级口语	（495）	我们好久时间不见了。	186
普通汉语教程	（496）	丁力的妈妈工作很忙,她去工厂早上六点。	186
初级汉语课本	（497）	天安门很远离我们学校。	187
基础汉语课本	（502）	他每天早上在教室都跟阿里一起听录音。	188
基础汉语课本	（504）	刚才我听中文广播懂了。	189
基础汉语课本	（506）	星期天我吃早饭就去看朋友。	190
基础汉语课本	（507）	我昨天一天没看他。	191
基础汉语课本	（508）	你告诉他,我来这儿看见他。	191
基础汉语课本	（509）	正在坐前边的是丁老师,坐后边的是马老师。	191
初级汉语课本	（510）	我每天上课二十点(钟)。	192
现代汉语进修教程	（511）	今天下午我给妈妈寄垤了生日礼物。	192
基础汉语课本	（512）	那辆自行车没让人走骑。	193
基础汉语课本	（513）	请你把这张表填完清楚。	193
基础汉语课本	（517）	丁力学习很努力,他英语说不错。	194

基础汉语课本　　（520）　我学得很忙。　　　　　　　　　　195
基础汉语课本　　（522）　他们法文说不很很慢。　　　　　　196
基础汉语课本　　（523）　谢力汉字写不写得很快？　　　　　197
基础汉语课本　　（525）　我送你们出来。　　　　　　　　　197
现代汉语进修教程（528）　刚才我给妈妈寄来生日礼物了。　198
基础汉语课本　　（529）　他出书店去买书了。　　　　　　　199
基础汉语课本　　（533）　明天我们到去参观。　　　　　　　200
现代汉语进修教程（561）　这个故事比较难，我听了八、九次　210
　　　　　　　　　　　　　才听懂。
基础汉语课本　　（567）　这本小说很有意思，我想再看这本　211
　　　　　　　　　　　　　书。
基础汉语课本　　（568）　这些句子很容易，我能翻译一下儿。　212
初级汉语课本　　（569）　今天第一九八六年五月四日。　　　212
初级口语　　　　（571）　他美国的人。　　　　　　　　　　213
初级口语　　　　（574）　你看，这件衣服干净。　　　　　　214
普通汉语教程　　（577）　你们屋子是大不大？　　　　　　　215
基础汉语课本　　（582）　它下雨了，咱们快点儿走吧。　　　217
基础汉语课本　　（584）　他是不英国人，他是法国人。　　　218
基础汉语课本　　（586）　今天不十二月二十七号。　　　　　218
基础汉语课本　　（587）　这支钢笔是弟弟。　　　　　　　　219
基础汉语课本　　（588）　食堂是宿舍旁边。　　　　　　　　219
基础汉语课本　　（589）　他有没自行车。　　　　　　　　　220
普通汉语教程　　（590）　对不起，我现在不有时间。　　　　220
基础汉语课本　　（591）　（A 你有电影票吗？）　　　　　　220
　　　　　　　　　　　　　B 我没有一张电影票。
基础汉语课本　　（592）　明天下午两点半我们有开会。　　　221
普通汉语教程　　（596）　教学楼有图书馆北边。　　　　　　222
普通汉语教程　　（597）　这个教室十张桌子和十把椅子。　　223

基础汉语课本　（598）　你家有口人？　223
普通汉语教程　（599）　玛丽,我们祝你好生日。　223
基础汉语课本　（600）　马教授衣我叫你去吃饭。　224
基础汉语课本　（601）　阿里让我那件事告诉你。　224
初级汉语课本　（602）　请明天晚上你来我这儿一趟。　225
普通汉语教程　（603）　丁力让马上我去。　225
基础汉语课本　（604）　老师让我通知去教室练习汉语节目。225
基础汉语课本　（605）　今天的参观很高兴。　226
普通汉语教程　（607）　谢力让我在操场不等他。　227
初级口语　　　（608）　我学习汉语来中国。　227
基础汉语课本　（610）　现在他们可以会话用汉语了。　228
医学汉语　　　（612）　丁力去火车站了送米希尔。　228
基础汉语课本　（614）　我同屋去商店了一件毛衣。　228
汉语教科书　　（641）　我们要搬到外边这些椅子。　238
普通汉语教程　（643）　我想把美元换了人民币。　239
普通汉语教程　（646）　我已经把本子上写上我的名字了。240
基础汉语课本　（648）　我的作业被作完了。　241
基础汉语课本　（649）　那件衣服已经被洗过了。　241
基础汉语课本　（673）　他被人非常热情。　248
基础汉语课本　（681）　在桌子上放着很多书。　250
基础汉语课本　（683）　座位上放那位同学的衣服。　251
初级汉语课本　（684）　椅子上放在那个同学的书。　251
汉语课本　　　（687）　前两天太热了,这两天更热。　253
基础汉语课本　（778）　他俩一边走了路,一边谈了话。　289
初级口语　　　（789）　先我坐汽车去天安门,再坐车去天坛。293
基础汉语课本　（790）　我先念课文,就作练习。　294
基础汉语课本　（791）　早上我先去友谊商店,中午我再要去　294
　　　　　　　　　　　　友谊商店。

科技汉语教程	(801)	金属不但导电好，而且也导热好。	298
基础汉语课本	(870)	虽然简单，这是一个很好的办法。	323
基础汉语课本	(871)	天气虽然好了，但是注意身体。	323
基础汉语课本	(873)	我们都是加拿大留学生。	325
基础汉语课本	(874)	我的朋友在北京语言学院学习汉语。	325
基础汉语课本	(875)	这里的天气你现在习惯不习惯。	326
初级汉语课本	(879)	你们喜欢不喜欢这种颜色。	327
现代汉语进修教程	(881)	那位先生是法国人，不是 德国人。	327
汉语课本	(882)	你去大使馆呢?还是去国际俱乐 部呢?	327
现代汉语进修教程	(883)	你爸爸在哪儿工作。	328
汉语课本	(886)	玛丽画儿画得真不错!	329
基础汉语课本	(887)	我多么想早点去别的大学学习专业。	329
基础汉语课本	(891)	你父、母身体好吗?	330

第二个阶段

Period II

所使用的教材	序号	病　　　句	页数
text-book	number	example sentence	page
基础汉语课本	(006)	他把那张画儿挂在屋子的墙里了。	15
基础汉语课本	(007)	有一条蛇掉进缸。	15
现代汉语进修教程	(008)	从前有一家里姓姜。	15
基础汉语课本	(015)	原来我是工人，这年我是老师了。	18
汉语课本	(016)	我们上课，他走进教室来了。	18

基础汉语课本　　　（017）　　我们出去时候,外边下着雪呢。　　　　18

基础汉语课本　　　（020）　　从上大学的时候以来,她一天假也　　19
　　　　　　　　　　　　　　　　没(有)请过。

基础汉语课本　　　（024）　　我没有来过这儿以前。　　　　　　　21

基础汉语课本　　　（025）　　三个女孩子们把鲜花送给代表了。　21

基础汉语课本　　　（029）　　除了阿里以外,另的同学们都去　　　22
　　　　　　　　　　　　　　　　东北旅行。

基础汉语课本　　　（037）　　我一听,我就明白了。　　　　　　　25

基础汉语课本　　　（041）　　请你告诉巴里亚来我那儿。　　　　　26

基础汉语课本　　　（044）　　这个商店没有那个商店这么大。　　27

医学汉语　　　　　（045）　　去年的水果产量没有今年的水果　　28
　　　　　　　　　　　　　　　　产量那么多。

基础汉语课本　　　（046）　　那么钱一个钟头数得完数不完？　　28

初级口语　　　　　（057）　　老大爷,您今年几岁了？　　　　　　32

基础汉语课本　　　（063）　　明天早上八点我们出发学校。　　　34

基础汉语课本　　　（064）　　我想明年再旅行中国。　　　　　　　35

医学汉语　　　　　（066）　　溶液在工业、农业、医学上有什么　　36
　　　　　　　　　　　　　　　　重要的应用？

汉语课本　　　　　（067）　　昨天我们访问了一个工厂。　　　　　36

基础汉语课本　　　（070）　　老师常常说我们:"你们学习努力,　37
　　　　　　　　　　　　　　　　进步很快。"

基础汉语课本　　　（073）　　我不太知道中国,我想去看看。　　38

现代汉语进修教程　（074）　他认识这件事的经过。　　　　　　　39

基础汉语课本　　　（087）　　如果接不到你的信,我就不来你那　44
　　　　　　　　　　　　　　　　儿了。

现代汉语进修教程　（088）　我在北京等你,希望你很快去　　　44
　　　　　　　　　　　　　　　　看我。

基础汉语课本　　　（089）　　她已经毕业大学了。　　　　　　　45

基础汉语课本　（092）　我到这儿已经两个月了,生活上还不　46
　　　　　　　　　　　　习惯,我想想我的爸爸,妈妈。

基础汉语课本　（096）　只有有才能的人,才会当大使。　48

现代汉语进修教程　（098）　一个好演员既会跳得好,又会　48
　　　　　　　　　　　　　　唱得好。

现代汉语进修教程　（104）　请你把你的词典借我用用,能吗?　50

现代汉语进修教程　（107）　你把这件衣服洗干净吗?我洗不　51
　　　　　　　　　　　　　　干净。

初级汉语课本　（108）　旧的杂志可能借吗?　51

现代汉语进修教程　（109）　你能去不去参观?　52

基础汉语课本　（110）　你把你的学习方法能不能给我们介绍　52
　　　　　　　　　　　一下儿?

汉语课本　（113）　已经十点了,他可以来吗?　53

基础汉语课本　（115）　我们跟小朋友可以谈话了。　54

基础汉语课本　（118）　我身体不太舒服,今天的晚会我不要　55
　　　　　　　　　　　参加了。

汉语教科书　（120）　以后我们一定应该生产更多的机器。　55

基础汉语课本　（121）　老师说:"你们学习很紧张,还注意　56
　　　　　　　　　　　身体"。

基础汉语课本　（124）　妈妈比五年前旧多了。　57

基础汉语课本　（126）　今年来北京语言学院学习的可能有　58
　　　　　　　　　　　多人。

基础汉语课本　（129）　男要长得好的女朋友,女要求文化　59
　　　　　　　　　　　水平比她高的男朋友。

基础汉语课本　（131）　同学们很高高兴兴地走出教室去了。　60

现代汉语进修教程　（132）　她的房间收拾得干干净净极了。　60

初级汉语课本　（134）　我们的房间有二个书架。　61

基础汉语课本　（135）　下午二点大家在九楼前边集合。　61

初级口语	(137)	我吃了两两米饭。	62
基础汉语课本	(139)	这是五万零零八块钱。(50008)	62
基础汉语课本	(140)	那个大学有十三千人。	63
基础汉语课本	(142)	阿里住院已经十四几天了。	63
基础汉语课本	(143)	这个礼堂坐得下七百、八百人。	64
基础汉语课本	(144)	这课生词我写了九、十遍。	64
基础汉语课本	(146)	今天参加运动会的有三千个多人。	65
汉语课本	(147)	这台机器两多天就修好了。	65
基础汉语课本	(153)	今年那儿的水果产量提高了左右百分之二十。	67
基础汉语课本	(154)	这个大学有两千左右个人。	67
普通汉语教程	(158)	这是二分之三。	69
普通汉语教程	(159)	那是二十三分六。	69
普通汉语教程	(160)	这是百分之九十九点六十四。(99.64%)	69
基础汉语课本	(161)	我刚才吃了半苹果。	70
医学汉语	(162)	我们到中国已经一半年了。	70
基础汉语课本	(163)	我已经学了两半个月的汉语了。	70
基础汉语课本	(164)	一个本子才三十五分。	71
普通汉语教程	(167)	这是三百十五块钱。	72
汉语课本	(169)	一个年有三百六十五天或三百六十六天。	73
基础汉语课本	(174)	他比我一点儿高。	75
初级汉语课本	(175)	哥哥新买的皮鞋一点儿小,送给我了。	75
现代汉语进修教程	(177)	你等我一点儿,我马上就来。	76
基础汉语课本	(181)	我听说过北京一些的情况。	77
现代汉语进修教程	(184)	到北京以后,他立刻不到学校去。	78
现代汉语进修教程	(191)	大家没有知道他俩结婚的事。	80

348

基础汉语课本　　（192）　马老师过去没吸烟,也没有喝酒。　81

医学汉语　　　　（195）　如果没有上课,咱们就一起去医院看　82
　　　　　　　　　　　　丁力。

基础汉语课本　　（196）　加里亚没有去上海就来你这儿。　82

基础汉语课本　　（199）　别说话吧,广播开始了。　83

初级汉语课本　　（200）　时间不早了,大家别再讨论。　83

初级汉语课本　　（201）　昨天晚上十一点才我回到学校。　83

初级汉语课本　　（205）　骑自行车十分钟可以到清华大学。　85

汉语课本　　　　（211）　他常常早上在操场跑步了。　87

普通汉语教程　　（216）　我的朋友曾经学三年英语。　89

现代汉语进修教程　（217）　我不曾经去过那儿。　89

现代汉语进修教程　（218）　我们班曾经不参观过农村。　89

汉语课本　　　　（220）　我在北京语言文化大学的学习　90
　　　　　　　　　　　　已经快要结束了。

基础汉语课本　　（222）　她已经身体好了。　90

基础汉语课本　　（223）　下课的时候都我们去外边休息。　91

基础汉语课本　　（224）　我们都去国际俱乐部,只有阿时去　91
　　　　　　　　　　　　友谊商店。

汉语课本　　　　（229）　她汉语多么说得好啊!　93

现代汉语进修教程　（230）　老师多么工作认真啊!　93

基础汉语课本　　（231）　虽然天气多么冷啊!可是他还是坚　94
　　　　　　　　　　　　持锻炼身体。

现代汉语进修教程　（232）　今天的天气多么很暖和啊!　94

基础汉语课本　　（234）　刚到语言学院以后就上课了。　95

基础汉语课本　　（235）　他们刚是北京大学的学生。　96

现代汉语教程　　（238）　大夫,我还这儿疼。　96

基础汉语课本　　（239）　你借给我的那本书,我没还看。　97

基础汉语课本　　（240）　我喜欢游泳,他喜欢游泳。　97

基础汉语课本　（242）　你去哪儿,我们都也去哪儿。　　　　98

基础汉语课本　（243）　北京的冬天不但很冷,而且也常常　　98
　　　　　　　　　　　　刮风。

基础汉语课本　（246）　最近我们比较很忙。　　　　　　　　99

现代汉语教程　（247）　那里天气很冷,还常很刮风。　　　　99

基础汉语课本　（249）　这个展览很好看极了。　　　　　　　100

基础汉语课本　（250）　公园里的人多极了不多极了?　　　　100

基础汉语课本　（252）　听了医生的话,我决心了锻炼身体。　101

现代汉语教程　（259）　我一定知道他对跳舞不感兴趣。　　104

基础汉语课本　（260）　这些是学过的生词。我一定记住了。104

基础汉语课本　（262）　他说明天可能有事,一定不来。　　105

基础汉语课本　（266）　他想下星期又去一次友谊商店。　　106

基础汉语课本　（267）　这个电影前天我再看了一遍。　　　107

初级汉语课本　（268）　我听不懂,你告诉我再一遍。　　　107

基础汉语课本　（269）　我去买啤酒,咱们一块儿跟他再喝。107

基础汉语课本　（272）　来这儿以后,我跟我的朋友再有联系。108

基础汉语课本　（273）　虽然比较忙,但是再有时间复习。　108

基础汉语课本　（274）　他看完了电影再走了。　　　　　　109

基础汉语课本　（276）　你去看他,他正在什么呢?　　　　109

现代汉语进修教程　（278）　我们早上五点出发的,你可能正　110
　　　　　　　　　　　　在睡觉了。

基础汉语课本　（279）　我在要打电话找你,你来了。　　　110

基础汉语课本　（280）　快走吧,大家已经正等着你呢。　　110

基础汉语课本　（285）　按照他说,下个月我们该去上海　　112
　　　　　　　　　　　　学习专业了。

基础汉语课本　（286）　我们都作作业,按照老师的方法。　113

基础汉语课本　（287）　根据学校的规定,我们早上八点上课。113

基础汉语课本　（293）　他从操场上跑步。　　　　　　　　115

350

基础汉语课本 （295） 车一停,他很快地车上跑下来。 115

基础汉语课本 （296） 老人说:狼小路逃走了。 116

现代汉语进修教程 （298） 他自从上海去广州。 116

初级汉语课本 （302） 当我们来到北京语言学院的时候, 118
热情地欢迎我们。

现代汉语教程 （303） 他不太礼貌对老师。 118

基础汉语课本 （304） 不王不对他很热情。 118

汉语课本 （307） 他对于我们很热情。 119

现代汉语进修教程 （308） 这种药说话有副作用。 120

现代汉语教程 （309） 我们要对于这个问题进行研究。 120

现代汉语进修教程 （310） 他们都对于这件事感兴趣。 120

基础汉语课本 （312） 他们正在讨论一些问题关于汉语 121
语法。

现代汉语进修教程 （314） 来中国以后没立刻写信你们, 121
请原谅!

汉语课本 （316） 玛丽给我告诉明天参观的事儿。 122

基础汉语课本 （321） 古时候有个人住在城里很远的 123
村子里。

现代汉语进修教程 （323） 您从这儿走往北。 124

现代汉语进修教程 （324） 她为了身体不好,每天早上坚持 125
锻炼。

汉语课本 （325） 我以后要为了我的国家贡献力量。 125

基础汉语课本 （326） 我们现在努力学习汉语为了以后学好 125
专业。

普通汉语教程 （333） 他在书包里拿出来一本新书。 128

现代汉语进修教程 （337） 刚才玛丽在我的房间来过。 129

医学汉语 （338） 他们买到了飞机票,座位不错。 129

基础汉语课本 （346） 我们复习旧课和我们预习新课。 132

初级汉语课本　　　（348）　他学习很努力,进步不快。　　　133

现代汉语进修教程　（352）　我一定要记住了这些生词。　　　135

基础汉语课本　　　（356）　昨天晚上杜朗去了国际俱乐部看　136
　　　　　　　　　　　　　　电影。

普通汉语教程　　　（359）　以前我吃了烤鸭,我还想吃一次。　137

基础汉语课本　　　（363）　他们班的同学站着十楼前边。　　138

基础汉语课本　　　（364）　安娜把衣服挂着在墙上了。　　　139

现代汉语进修教程　（365）　我喜欢着我的父亲、母亲。　　　139

初级汉语课本　　　（367）　他在北京的很多地方工作,去年才　140
　　　　　　　　　　　　　　回国。

现代汉语教程　　　（369）　这星期我进城过三次。　　　　　140

基础汉语课本　　　（370）　他在北京大学三年学习过汉语。　141

汉语课本　　　　　（371）　他在八个月里已经有过不少进步。141

初级汉语课本　　　（374）　来中国以前我看过介绍北京的书,　142
　　　　　　　　　　　　　　我的朋友也给我介绍。

现代汉语进修教程　（379）　我们大家都很认真学习。　　　　144

汉语课本　　　　　（380）　我非常地喜欢这个城市。　　　　144

汉语教科书　　　　（382）　不努力发展生产,就不能有幸福　144
　　　　　　　　　　　　　　地生活。

基础汉语课本　　　（385）　这课课文很难,我看得不懂。　　145

高级汉语　　　　　（389）　快下雨了,咱们赶快到那边躲一躲了。147

基础汉语课本　　　（392）　妈妈的病很快就会好。　　　　　148

基础汉语课本　　　（393）　老师布置会场的任务由我们负责的。148

基础汉语课本　　　（394）　运动场上站着很多人的。　　　　148

高级汉语　　　　　（395）　老马的病好多。　　　　　　　　149

基础汉语课本　　　（400）　我分析得完那几个句子了。　　　150

现代汉语教程　　　（401）　明天他俩结婚了。　　　　　　　150

汉语课本　　　　　（404）　下一次旅行,我们不是去上海,就是　151

去广州了。

基础汉语课本	（405）	狼对老人说,他这样做,不是要闷死我了。	152
基础汉语课本	（409）	你们看得见看不见黑板上的字吗?	153
现代汉语进修教程	（412）	她接到信了,一定高兴了吗?	154
基础汉语课本	（413）	要是明天下雨,我就不去美术馆呢。	155
基础汉语课本	（414）	她不在,正在出去呢。	155
现代汉语进修教程	（415）	他只学过两个多月的英语,怎么能看懂英文杂志了。	155
基础汉语课本	（418）	借我看一下杂志你借来,好吗?	157
基础汉语课本	（420）	我想他们的决心完成这个任务。	158
现代汉语教程	（421）	妈妈的希望我有一个好的工作。	158
汉语课本	（423）	王进喜参加开采新油田国家宣布大会战。	159
基础汉语课本	（424）	我还没看完你给我介绍那本小说呢!	160
汉语课本	（425）	工厂领导希望我们给他们的工作意见。	160
基础汉语课本	（428）	昨天的开会进行了五十五分钟。	161
医学汉语	（429）	昨天下了课,我就去看朋友有病的了。	162
现代汉语教程	（443）	在老师和同学们帮助下,他进步很快。	168
现代汉语进修教程	（446）	他们什么时候两个进城的?	169
基础汉语课本	（454）	今天天气很美,不过我必须准备考试。	172
基础汉语课本	（459）	我们好久没见了,没想到你这儿。	173
基础汉语课本	（462）	下一次旅行,我不是去上海,就是广州。	174
初级汉语课本	（468）	早上我开开门一看,外面有很多雨。	176
现代汉语教程	（477）	打架的戏有意思。	179
汉语课本	（479）	广大部分的农民不认识字。	180

汉语课本	(489)	王进喜积极地下决心帮助国家解决 困难，参加开采新油田的大会战。	184
基础汉语课本	(490)	这本小说很有意思，我想看多几遍。	184
基础汉语课本	(499)	在公园他昨天划船划了多长时间？	187
基础汉语课本	(500)	张老师热情地给我们非常介绍了学校 的情况。	188
基础汉语课本	(501)	他们比我们今天早回来一个小时。	188
基础汉语课本	(503)	请你给我们把你的学习方法介绍 一下。	189
基础汉语课本	(505)	中国医生接了他的手指，所以他绣了 "友谊"两个字给中国人民。	190
汉语教科书	(515)	电影里的人说得很快，我不听懂。	194
基础汉语课本	(516)	如果没学好汉语，那么学习专业就很 困难。	194
基础汉语课本	(518)	他打篮球越来越好。	195
基础汉语课本	(519)	由于考试的缘故，大家来了很早。	195
基础汉语课本	(521)	他排球打得很好极了。	196
基础汉语课本	(524)	他来得怎么样？	197
基础汉语课本	(526)	你们快上山去，这里的风景美极了。	198
初级汉语课本	(530)	你在宿舍等我，我马上就进来。	199
基础汉语课本	(532)	你们进去一个一个。	199
基础汉语课本	(535)	同学们看见老师进来了，立刻站上来。	200
基础汉语课本	(536)	我朋友从医院里走过来了。	201
基础汉语课本	(538)	上课了，我们走进去教室吧！	201
基础汉语课本	(539)	我们刚走到校门口，就下雨起来了。	202
基础汉语课本	(540)	我同屋从图书馆借一本中文书回来。	202
现代汉语进修教程	(541)	我的自行车被朋友骑去城里 到了。	202

汉语课本	（542）	解放军战士很快跑过马来了。	203
基础汉语课本	（543）	他跑过宿舍进去了。	203
基础汉语课本	（544）	请你把画儿在墙上挂起来。	204
现代汉语教程	（546）	我听懂了，但是我写不来。	204
基础汉语课本	（547）	老师让我把课文接着念。	205
现代汉语教程	（549）	请你大点儿声，我听不懂。	205
基础汉语课本	（550）	这台洗衣机又大又重，我们抱不动。	206
基础汉语课本	（551）	你说得不清楚，所以我不听懂。	206
基础汉语课本	（552）	你想得起来不起来他叫什么名字？	206
基础汉语课本	（554）	坐那么远，你能不能看得清楚？	207
基础汉语课本	（555）	我把那篇文章翻译得完。	207
基础汉语课本	（556）	我去图书馆看报了半个小时。	208
基础汉语课本	（557）	我在公园里等他了一个小时。	208
基础汉语课本	（558）	他来教室来了一刻钟。	209
基础汉语课本	（559）	昨天上午的会一个小时开了。	209
初级汉语课本	（560）	他没上课两天了。	209
汉语课本	（562）	我以前来过一遍上海。	210
汉语课本	（563）	刚才下了一次雨，凉快点儿了。	210
现代汉语教程	（564）	让他们来这里避雨一下儿。	211
现代汉语教程	（565）	我的朋友住院了，我一次去看了他。	211
基础汉语课本	（566）	我送送你们一下。	211
现代汉语进修教程	（575）	今天天气太好。	214
现代汉语进修教程	（578）	他考试成绩很好，因为他很努力地学习。	215
基础汉语课本	（579）	我最近非常忙学习。	216
基础汉语课本	（581）	谢力和丁力都身体很好。	216
基础汉语课本	（583）	天气刮大风了，把衣服收进来吧！	217
基础汉语课本	（585）	谢力跑得最快的运动员。	218

医学汉语	（594）	这个问题对我们有十分重要。	221
基础汉语课本	（595）	那个班几乎有日本留学生。	222
中级汉语	（606）	叫智叟的一个人。	226
汉语课本	（611）	很多旅游者来这儿开着汽车。	228
普通汉语教程	（613）	以后我们要别的大学学习五年专业。	229
初级汉语课本	（617）	她在柜子里把衣服放。	230
基础汉语课本	（618）	阿里把带回来了录音机。	231
基础汉语课本	（619）	把那棵小树大风刮倒了。	231
基础汉语课本	（620）	黑板把阿里擦干净了。	231
基础汉语课本	（622）	谢力昨天把那个照相机进城买来了。	232
基础汉语课本	（623）	玛丽把安娜给自己的自行车了。	232
基础汉语课本	（624）	我同屋把收音机没弄坏。	233
基础汉语课本	（625）	他把练习不作完，不休息。	233
现代汉语教程	（626）	我把新课在宿舍里预习好了。	233
普通汉语教程	（627）	从书包里谢力把票拿出来了。	233
基础汉语课本	（628）	每天上课的时候，我们都本子拿出来听写。	234
基础汉语课本	（629）	那位先生把提包在座位上。	234
基础汉语课本	（630）	孩子们把门前的堆成一个雪人。	234
基础汉语课本	（631）	我上午要把这篇文章翻译。	234
汉语课本	（632）	放假以后，我们打算去把上海旅行。	235
汉语教科书	（633）	他把那件不愉快的事知道了。	235
汉语课本	（634）	希望你们把这个地方喜欢。	235
基础汉语课本	（635）	大家都把《基础汉语课本》有了。	236
汉语课本	（636）	我们只把排球打了半个小时。	236
基础汉语课本	（637）	我也把北京烤鸭吃过。	236
初级汉语课本	（640）	我写"太"成"大"了。	238
汉语课本	（644）	他把箱子送给我这儿了。	239

基础汉语课本　　　（645）　她把花儿摆上桌子上了。　　　　　240

基础汉语课本　　　（647）　你把一本书放在什么地方了。　　　240

现代汉语教程　　　（651）　这月房租还没被交呢。　　　　　　241

基础汉语课本　　　（652）　北京1949年被解放了。　　　　　　242

基础汉语课本　　　（653）　困难已经被克服了。　　　　　　　242

基础汉语课本　　　（656）　课文已经能被念熟了。　　　　　　243

基础汉语课本　　　（658）　衬衣被洗得很干净。　　　　　　　243

基础汉语课本　　　（659）　汽车被开得太快了。　　　　　　　243

现代汉语教程　　　（660）　你的衣服被送到宿舍里去了。　　　244

基础汉语课本　　　（661）　他的书被放在桌子上了。　　　　　244

基础汉语课本　　　（662）　那些画报被还给图书馆。　　　　　244

普通汉语教程　　　（663）　这个电影两个小时被演得完演不完？245

普通汉语教程　　　（664）　书架里的书被看不到。　　　　　　245

基础汉语课本　　　（665）　这样好的茶杯偏偏他打碎了。　　　245

普通汉语教程　　　（666）　我被收音机醒了。　　　　　　　　246

基础汉语课本　　　（668）　那张画儿让刮掉了。　　　　　　　246

基础汉语课本　　　（669）　那两条鱼叫吃光了。　　　　　　　246

初级汉语课本　　　（670）　一辆自行车被小王搬到外边去了。247

医学汉语　　　　　（671）　那件事被我忘了。　　　　　　　　247

汉语课本　　　　　（672）　外国客人们被工人们热烈欢迎。　247

现代汉语进修教程　（675）　这件事能被他知道吗？　　　　　248

医学汉语　　　　　（676）　那些画被他都卖了。　　　　　　　249

基础汉语课本　　　（677）　自行车被丁力没骑走。　　　　　　249

现代汉语进修教程　（678）　我的自行车被朋友骑去城里　　　249
　　　　　　　　　　　　　　到了。

基础汉语课本　　　（679）　信被寄走了。　　　　　　　　　　249

基础汉语课本　　　（682）　操场上站着运动员，等着比赛。　251

基础汉语课本　　　（685）　巴里亚的箱子里放着了一些衣服。252

初级汉语课本	（688）	虽然课文简单,但是他更看不懂。	253
基础汉语课本	（691）	阿里汉语说得好,杜朗说得最好。	254
汉语课本	（693）	这个地方最安静极了。	256
汉语课本	（694）	这些年人们的生活比以前非常好。	256
现代汉语教程	（695）	我觉得武戏比文戏很有意思。	256
基础汉语课本	（696）	我们学了生词比他们学了生词多。	256
基础汉语课本	（698）	风比刚才小多。	257
基础汉语课本	（699）	他比我多有五块钱。	257
基础汉语课本	（700）	丁力比我来了早教室。	258
基础汉语课本	（701）	我比他来得早一天。	258
基础汉语课本	（702）	她跳得比那个运动员高九厘米。	259
基础汉语课本	（703）	弟弟学中文比他的学习好。	259
初级汉语课本	（704）	我参加工作比他不晚。	260
医学汉语	（705）	我的意见比他的完全不同。	260
基础汉语课本	（706）	一天比一天学的语法多。	261
医学汉语	（707）	他一天比一天学习有很大的进步。	261
基础汉语课本	（708）	这篇作品比那篇没有好。	261
基础汉语课本	（709）	我的词典没有你那么好。	262
基础汉语课本	（710）	我哥哥的身体没有你哥哥那么高。	262
基础汉语课本	（711）	这棵树没有那棵树这么粗。	263
基础汉语课本	（712）	他们没有我们来这么早。	263
基础汉语课本	（714）	她翻译句子不如你翻译的句子准确。	264
现代汉语进修教程	（715）	那个公园不如这个公园那么安静。	264
基础汉语课本	（717）	谢力不如巴里亚说法语。	265
基础汉语课本	（718）	我写的汉字不如他写的好看得多。	265
初级汉语课本	（719）	上海冷不如北京的冬天。	266
初级汉语课本	（720）	这件衣服的颜色跟那件的是一样。	266

医学汉语　　　　（721）　他买了一本书跟我买了一本书不 　266
　　　　　　　　　　　　　 一样。

基础汉语课本　（722）　他借的小说跟我一样好。 　　　267

中级汉语　　　 （724）　我要买一件毛衣跟他的那件颜色 　268
　　　　　　　　　　　　　 一样。

基础汉语课本　（725）　他跑得快极了,跑跟飞一样。 　　268

初级汉语课本　（726）　那个国家的人口比我们国家的人口 268
　　　　　　　　　　　　　 一样多。

初级汉语课本　（728）　玛丽有我高一点儿。 　　　　　269

医学汉语　　　 （729）　这个班的学生有那个班的学生多 　270
　　　　　　　　　　　　　 十个人。

基础汉语课本　（730）　这个游泳池有那么大。 　　　　270

基础汉语课本　（731）　今天大米的产量有去年的(产量) 　270
　　　　　　　　　　　　　 一样多。

基础汉语课本　（732）　这间屋子有那间屋子很大。 　　271

基础汉语课本　（734）　他的发音那么像小王的发音清楚。 272

基础汉语课本　（735）　阿里没像谢力那么喜欢踢足球。 　272

医学汉语　　　 （736）　妹妹像弟弟那么不爱玩儿。 　　272

基础汉语课本　（738）　我们越来越比较习惯这里的生活了。273

现代汉语进修教程 （739）　越来越学习汉语的人多了。 　　273

基础汉语课本　（742）　你把这些东西不是称一称吗? 　　275

基础汉语课本　（743）　站在东门口的那个人就不是阿里吗? 275

初级汉语课本　（744）　我怎么能找到他的家了? 　　　276

基础汉语课本　（745）　你没告诉我,我哪儿知道这件事了? 276

基础汉语课本　（746）　谁都不赞成呢? 　　　　　　　276

基础汉语课本　（747）　他们是坐火车去上海了。 　　　277

基础汉语课本　（748）　我是在路上碰到了老朋友的。 　　277

基础汉语课本　（749）　你是什么时候来中国? 　　　　278

医学汉语　　　　　（750）　是昨天上午欢迎代表团的大会　278
　　　　　　　　　　　　　　举行的。

现代汉语进修教程　（752）　是他们去年夏天在颐和园照　279
　　　　　　　　　　　　　　的相。

高级汉语　　　　　（754）　甚至连他不能回答这个问题。　280

现代汉语进修教程　（755）　他连有急事，也没吃午饭就走了。280

汉语课本　　　　　（756）　冬天到了，树上连一片叶子也没。281

基础汉语课本　　　（757）　医生作了六个钟头的手术，一分钟　281
　　　　　　　　　　　　　　也没休息了。

基础汉语课本　　　（760）　没有人努力学习，所以我们班的同学　282
　　　　　　　　　　　　　　汉语都学得不错。

现代汉语进修教程　（762）　没有钱，不能上大学。　283

基础汉语课本　　　（763）　我们不克服缺点，就我们不能进步。283

基础汉语课本　　　（764）　谁在学习上有困难，谁老师就帮助。283

基础汉语课本　　　（765）　哪个问题没讨论完，咱们就讨论　284
　　　　　　　　　　　　　　什么问题。

基础汉语课本　　　（767）　你念怎么，我就念怎么。　285

基础汉语课本　　　（768）　哪儿有意思，就我们去哪儿玩。　285

基础汉语课本　　　（772）　既阿里不喜欢唱歌，也不喜欢跳舞，287
　　　　　　　　　　　　　　别请他了。

科技汉语教程　　　（773）　在月球上，既有水和空气，生物也　287
　　　　　　　　　　　　　　不能生存下去。

科技汉语教程　　　（774）　圆柱形的容器既使用方便，比较　288
　　　　　　　　　　　　　　美观。

基础汉语课本　　　（775）　巴里亚汉字写得也快也好。　288

初级汉语课本　　　（776）　也小王是你的朋友，也是我的朋友。288

汉语课本　　　　　（779）　听到这个消息，老人一边悲痛，一边　289
　　　　　　　　　　　　　　气愤地离开了那里到别的地方去找

工作。

基础汉语课本　　（780）　小朋友们一边作什么，一边作什么　290
　　　　　　　　　　　　　　欢迎来参观的人？

基础汉语课本　　（781）　一边儿我听录音，一边儿写生词。　290

基础汉语课本　　（786）　这辆自行车又很好又很便宜。　292

基础汉语课本　　（787）　风又刮又大。　292

基础汉语课本　　（788）　愚公决定搬走两座山，又高又大。　293

现代汉语进修教程　（792）　我和我同屋学校一放假，就去　294
　　　　　　　　　　　　　　中国的南方旅行。

医学汉语　　（793）　大脑的工作一停止，生命结束了。　295

基础汉语课本　　（794）　一我作完练习，就去找你打球。　295

初级汉语课本　　（795）　我一吃过晚饭以后，咱们就一起散步。295

初级汉语课本　　（798）　不但北京的冬天很冷，而且还常常　297
　　　　　　　　　　　　　　刮风。

基础汉语课本　　（799）　谢力不但爱打乒乓球，而且巴里亚　297
　　　　　　　　　　　　　　也爱打乒乓球 。

现代汉语进修教程　（800）　马老师不但教我们汉语，　297
　　　　　　　　　　　　　　教玛丽她们汉语。

基础汉语课本　　（802）　现在是春天了，天气不但不暖和，　298
　　　　　　　　　　　　　　反而不冷。

科技汉语教程　　（803）　水变成冰时，不但体积不收缩，　299
　　　　　　　　　　　　　　反而膨胀。

基础汉语课本　　（804）　我不仅能吃中国饭、菜，而且要　299
　　　　　　　　　　　　　　喝中国酒。

基础汉语课本　　（805）　那本书不仅你没看过，而是我也　299
　　　　　　　　　　　　　　没看过。

基础汉语课本　　（806）　不仅他从星期一到星期六工作，　300
　　　　　　　　　　　　　　而且星期天也工作。

科技汉语教程	（807）	肺不仅能吸入氧气，能呼出 二氧化碳。	300
基础汉语课本	（808）	除了外国留学生外，北京语言学 院有中国学生。	300
基础汉语课本	（809）	除了你们班去长城以外，我们班 还去。	301
基础汉语课本	（810）	除了她俩学习中国历史以外， 别的同学学习中国文学。	301
科技汉语教程	（811）	即使昨天晚上七点你去看他， 他还没有从大使馆回来呢。	301
科技汉语教程	（812）	你今天即使不来这儿， 我也要你那儿去。	302
科技汉语教程	（813）	即使明天下雨，我们要去参观。	302
基础汉语课本	（814）	假如接不到你的电话，我那么不到 你那儿去。	302
初级汉语课本	（815）	如果你看过那书，就你给大家 介绍一下。	303
医学汉语	（816）	如果大脑停止工作，生命结束了。	303
基础汉语课本	（817）	要是明天刮大风，就没打篮球。	304
基础汉语课本	（818）	你要是用词典，再到我这儿来借了。	304
基础汉语课本	（819）	要是你不去，就你告诉我一声。	304
基础汉语课本	（820）	要是明天下不下雨，我就不去参观。	304
现代汉语教程	（821）	不管学习上有什么困难，但是我们 应该努力克服。	305
基础汉语课本	（822）	不管天气不好，她都要去颐和园。	305
现代汉语教程	（823）	冬天不管怎么冷，小王都坚持锻炼。	306
基础汉语课本	（824）	不管今天怎么再忙，我都要把这个 材料看完。	306

现代汉语教程　　　（825）　不管明天下雨不下雨，咱们都去　　307
　　　　　　　　　　　　　　　游泳了。

基础汉语课本　　　（826）　不论每天没有时间，我们都要看报。　307

基础汉语课本　　　（827）　不论明天你来，我们都去参观。　　307

基础汉语课本　　　（828）　不论这个问题十分难，我们都要解决。308

基础汉语课本　　　（829）　不论你们去哪儿，我们也去。　　　308

基础汉语课本　　　（830）　同学们只要努力，就一定学好汉语。308

基础汉语课本　　　（831）　只要学好汉语，就要有决心。　　　309

科技汉语教程　　　（832）　只要什么生物，就离不开空气和水。309

基础汉语课本　　　（833）　我们只要一起想办法，这件事才能　309
　　　　　　　　　　　　　　　办好。

基础汉语课本　　　（834）　只要学好汉语，就学专业不难了。　309

基础汉语课本　　　（835）　只有坐飞机去，今天晚上才到上海。310

基础汉语课本　　　（836）　只有努力学习，学习好中文。　　　310

基础汉语课本　　　（837）　只有七千美元，我才能买汽车。　　310

现代汉语进修教程　（839）　雨越下越很大。　　　　　　　　　311

基础汉语课本　　　（840）　你学习越刻苦，学习得好。　　　　312

基础汉语课本　　　（841）　越我们讨论，越问题清楚。　　　　312

基础汉语课本　　　（842）　今天的生词越多越难。　　　　　　312

初级汉语课本　　　（843）　这个故事很有意思，我越听越好。　313

基础汉语课本　　　（844）　我不是想她来，就是她姐姐来。　　313

基础汉语课本　　　（845）　明天上午我们不是去图书馆，就是　313
　　　　　　　　　　　　　　　去阅览室了。

汉语课本　　　　　（846）　他告诉我他不是星期六来，就是星　314
　　　　　　　　　　　　　　　期日。

基础汉语课本　　　（847）　下一次旅游，不是我去桂林，就是　314
　　　　　　　　　　　　　　　去昆明。

基础汉语课本　　　（848）　我们班的教室不是大，就是他们班　314

的教室大。

基础汉语课本　（849）　我想与其《红楼梦》，不如　　　　315
　　　　　　　　　　　　　《水浒传》。

基础汉语课本　（850）　既然你去过长城，就你给我们介绍　315
　　　　　　　　　　　　　一下长城的情况。

基础汉语课本　（851）　既然我家里不想我，我不回国。　　316
基础汉语课本　（852）　既然他的身体不太好，不可以来上班。316
基础汉语课本　（853）　既然你病了就不想去旅行。　　　　316
基础汉语课本　（854）　既然这些是学过的生词，所以我　　317
　　　　　　　　　　　　　记住了。

基础汉语课本　（855）　既然你请我，然而我一定去。　　　317
基础汉语课本　（856）　人们所以把粽子扔到江中喂鱼，　　318
　　　　　　　　　　　　　不让鱼吃屈原的身体。

基础汉语课本　（857）　因为冬天就要到了，他所以　　　　318
　　　　　　　　　　　　　要进城买棉大衣。

基础汉语课本　（858）　因为报纸重要消息很多，他都看了。318
科技汉语教程　（859）　因为天坛公园里的回音壁以奇妙的　319
　　　　　　　　　　　　　声音现象，所以吸引了很多游人。

科技汉语教程　（860）　因为由于他每天锻炼，所以他的身体　319
　　　　　　　　　　　　　不错。

科技汉语教程　（864）　尽管他每天来上课，但是身体不好。　321
科技汉语教程　（865）　尽管月球上有水，但是在温度很高　321
　　　　　　　　　　　　　时，水就会变成气体。

科技汉语教程　（866）　尽管这个工作很困难，他完成了这　322
　　　　　　　　　　　　　个工作。

初级汉语课本　（868）　尽管他家很难找，我就找到了。　　322
基础汉语课本　（869）　尽管他每天锻炼身体，他跑得很慢。322
基础汉语课本　（872）　但是他没来过中国，虽然他对中国　324

		的情况还是很了解的。	
普通汉语教程	（876）	长城多么雄伟啊。	326
普通汉语教程	（877）	开会了，别说话了。	326
初级汉语课本	（878）	那个地方好极了，咱们怎么能不去呢。	326
初级汉语课本	（880）	以前你看过京剧吗。	327
初级汉语课本	（889）	请你把这封信带给安娜！	329
现代汉语进修教程	（892）	现在我住在北京语言学院、八楼、三层、三一五号。	330
现代汉语教程	（893）	北京大学清华大学离北京语言学院不远。	331
基础汉语课本	（894）	巴里亚的桌子上放着书，本子，词典，笔，录音机等。	331
基础汉语课本	（895）	因为你的问题太难了所以我不能马上回答你。	331
高级汉语	（896）	他的身体很好像一个运动员。	332
基础汉语课本	（897）	这样的录音比较难，有的地方，我听得懂，有的地方，我听不懂。	332
基础汉语课本	（898）	阿里，………　谢力 1989.5.28	332
基础汉语课本	（899）	我们每个人都有基础汉语课本。	333
基础汉语课本	（900）	昨天妈妈打来电话说，你学习很紧张，一定要注意身体。	333

第三个阶段
Period III

所使用的教材	序号	病　　句	页数
text-book	number	example sentence	page

高级汉语	（003）	作者想自己不够爱情自己的妻子。	14
高级汉语	（004）	结婚以后他们很恩情。	14
汉语课本	（014）	特别是刚才毕业的大学生，失业是个大问题。	17
高级汉语	（018）	祥子小的时失去了父母。	19
高级汉语	（019）	开始的时，林道静想自己的丈夫很不错。	19
高级汉语	（023）	刚结婚以后，他们很幸福。	20
汉语课本	（026）	我还有几个朋友们要来这儿学习。	22
高级汉语	（030）	今天的节目演得真好，观众们都热烈地鼓掌。	23
高级汉语	（031）	人民们对这新生事物表现了极大的兴趣和热情。	23
高级汉语	（032）	阿里你别着急，咱们等你。	23
基础汉语课本	（036）	那个领导不怕我们给自己提意见。	24
高级汉语	（038）	祥子没有办法，他只好卖他自己的力气了。	25
现代汉语进修教程	（040）	他在这儿里的生活非常愉快。	26
基础汉语课本	（065）	去年暑假我们旅游了西藏。	35
汉语课本	（069）	我决定了参加足球比赛。	37
现代汉语教程	（071）	我说他了，下星期学习第三本书。	38
高级汉语	（072）	昨天我们见过面，我知道他。	38
高级汉语	（076）	每次他去朋友家，他总是告诉一两件有意思的事情。	40
现代汉语进修教程	（077）	他对杏仙告诉，他要走了。	40
高级汉语	（079）	他常常帮助我，我要给他一个感谢。	41
现代汉语教程	（084）	我问他去看电影，他立刻答应了。	43
高级汉语	（085）	他们经常没有钱，但是不轻易问	43

		朋友帮助。	
高级汉语	（090）	昨天我见面我的朋友了。	45
高级汉语	（101）	胜利是不轻易得到的。	49
汉语课本	（102）	太晚了，不会他来了。	50
高级汉语	（111）	在十天内，你们可不可以造好箭？	52
高级汉语	（112）	如果你没有钱，不可以结婚。	53
高级汉语	（114）	可以你的词典借用一下儿吗？	53
高级汉语	（116）	我们痛痛快快地可以玩几天。	54
高级汉语	（117）	学校同意他能够上二年级吗？	54
汉语课本	（123）	今天天气暖和，很合适到山里去玩儿。	57
汉语课本	（125）	她们俩的年纪一致。	58
高级汉语	（128）	她觉得自己的丈夫很私人。	58
高级汉语	（130）	他们离婚的理由是女不喜欢男，男也不喜欢女。	59
高级汉语	（133）	这件工艺品做得细细致致。	60
高级汉语	（141）	她们俩个今天晚上也动身。	63
现代汉语进修教程	（149）	中午我复习了两多小时。	66
高级汉语	（150）	我有几中国朋友。	66
高级汉语	（151）	我还有几多百块钱。	66
现代汉语进修教程	（152）	他们学校有几十八个国家的学生。	67
高级汉语	（155）	他们到北京整整一年左右了。	68
高级汉语	（156）	为什么你第一天、二天没来？	68
高级汉语	（157）	他朋友在北京语言学院第二系第一年级学习汉语。	68
高级汉语	（172）	我认识那位人。	74
高级汉语	（176）	今天的面条煮点儿硬了。	75

高级汉语	(178)	让她们来这里避雨一点儿。	76
高级汉语	(180)	他们两个应该作让步一些。	77
高级汉语	(187)	你一定不拒绝我的要求。	79
高级汉语	(212)	他希望你以后常常也来玩儿。	87
高级汉语	(213)	我以后往往来看望你。	87
高级汉语	(214)	他们往往去旅游。	88
高级汉语	(215)	他曾经在中国住了两年。	88
高级汉语	(225)	大家为他学习上的进步都感到高兴。	91
高级汉语	(233)	他的房间多么干干净净啊！	95
现代汉语进修教程	(244)	愚公说："我死了以后有儿子， 儿子死了也有孙子……"	98
高级汉语	(245)	他的中文水平提高得很快，甚至 鲁迅的小说能看了。	99
现代汉语进修教程	(253)	我恐怕天要下大雨了。	102
高级汉语	(254)	我恐怕他要生病了。	102
现代汉语进修教程	(256)	我们已经快要毕业了。	103
高级汉语	(257)	你究竟去天津学习专业吗？	103
高级汉语	(263)	你放心，我不一定会忘记给你买书。	105
高级汉语	(265)	一年来我的汉字一定写得比以前好。	106
现代汉语进修教程	(270)	他照了几张相后，再不照了， 留下几张明天照。	108
汉语课本	(271)	他要永远留在她身边，不再走了。	108
高级汉语	(275)	明天再是星期天了。	109
高级汉语	(283)	只努力学习，才能取得好成绩。	111
高级汉语	(284)	按照天气预报，明天有大雨。	112
高级汉语	(288)	地主逼林道静住在一起跟一个有 钱的人。	113
高级汉语	(299)	我自从1986年学习汉语。	117

高级汉语	（300）	自从明天起,我要在清华大学学习 专业。	117
高级汉语	（301）	当我学习上遇到困难,就请老师帮 助我。	117
现代汉语进修教程	（305）	我已经对大家通知了。	119
高级汉语	（306）	京剧对他俩很感兴趣。	119
汉语课本	（311）	对于去南方旅行的路线,我想听听 大家的意见。	120
高级汉语	（315）	在端午节的时候,为了给神鱼感谢, 人们把粽子扔到江里去。	122
高级汉语	（320）	阿里去学校比较远的地方照相。	123
高级汉语	（327）	来往的汽车很多,向公路上跑着。	126
汉语课本	（328）	玛丽,今天是你的生日,我们表示 向你祝贺。	126
现代汉语教程	（329）	那条小路两旁都是树,我们常常 晚饭后,沿着小路。	126
高级汉语	（330）	您沿这条路一直往前走。	127
现代汉语教程	（331）	他的汉语水平提高了由于朋友的 帮助下。	127
高级汉语	（336）	明天下午在两点我去找你。	128
高级汉语	（342）	诸葛亮叫船上的士兵大声喊叫和 擂起鼓来。	131
高级汉语	（343）	每一事物与周围其他事物都联系 着和互相影响。	131
高级汉语	（345）	我去他家和他来我家。	132
汉语教科书	（347）	群众的欢迎,可见这个工厂生产 出来的无线电质量很好。	133
高级汉语	（349）	她每天下午打球、跑步,然而身体	134

越来越好。

现代汉语进修教程	（351）	楼下有了一个人叫你。	134
高级汉语	（361）	李波拿很多东西走进宿舍里去了。	138
高级汉语	（362）	我的姐姐以前曾经在学校里教 着书。	138
高级汉语	（366）	人民的生活水平提高着。	139
高级汉语	（368）	祥子没上大学，他对社会上的事情 不感兴趣。	140
高级汉语	（372）	他开始过工作不久，又没有工作了。	141
高级汉语	（373）	我过去知道过这件事情。	142
高级汉语	（383）	我汉语说得不够流利，还差地远呢。	145
高级汉语	（388）	这次我们所休息的地方很安静。	146
高级汉语	（390）	让我们高高兴兴地过个节。	147
基础基础课本	（396）	这件事我们都知道了，你别再说。	149
高级汉语	（403）	我正想看书，忽然有人在敲门了。	151
高级汉语	（417）	大家汉语学得好呢。	156
高级汉语	（422）	他说的话，大家很感动。	159
高级汉语	（427）	外面下雨很多。	161
高级汉语	（432）	凡是老师都喜欢他。	163
基础汉语课本	（440）	对日常生活，水十分重要。	167
高级汉语	（441）	工业各部门无论在产品的产量、 质量和品种都跃进了一大步。	167
汉语课本	（442）	考试方法还要看学生在困难上 解决问题的水平。	168
基础汉语课本	（444）	参加劳动和社会活动中，他们两 个人的感情越来越深了。	168
现代汉语进修教程	（445）	小王帮我买了一本《家》书。	169
高级汉语	（447）	他个子很结实。	170

现代汉语进修教程　（448）　他一起抚养这个孩子。　　　170

高级汉语　　　（450）　经过一年的努力,使他的汉语水　171
　　　　　　　　　　　　平提高了。

高级汉语　　　（451）　在学习上给了我很大的帮助。　171

高级汉语　　　（452）　运动员走进会场的时候,热烈地　171
　　　　　　　　　　　　鼓掌。

高级汉语　　　（456）　她的丈夫要她在家里办家务。　172

高级汉语　　　（457）　他天天在田里做工作。　　　173

汉语课本　　　（458）　这种情况没有使工人失望,反而　173
　　　　　　　　　　　　提高了他们的精神。

现代汉语教程　（460）　我已经完了今天的作业了。　174

现代汉语进修教程　（464）　屈原投汨罗江自杀死了。　175

高级汉语　　　（469）　如果不听父母,就要挨骂。　177

汉语教科书　　（473）　这本小说的内容又丰富又生动,　178
　　　　　　　　　　　　因为这是作者写自己的经历事儿。

现代汉语进修教程　（474）　这个问题我们一定要解决它。　178

汉语教科书　　（478）　她是唱歌学院的学生。　　179

高级汉语　　　（482）　第二天下起大雾漫天。　　181

高级汉语　　　（485）　请给我二十只那快船。　　182

汉语课本　　　（487）　他们化他们的悲痛为力量。　183

汉语课本　　　（488）　他们也亲切地照顾我。　　183

高级汉语　　　（491）　请你替问你的父母亲好。　185

汉语课本　　　（494）　好像田地可能是很肥沃的。　186

高级汉语　　　（498）　在家乡因为没有办法过日子,　187
　　　　　　　　　　　　他就十八岁跑到北京来了。

高级汉语　　　（514）　我听懂明白你的话了。　　193

高级汉语　　　（527）　你常常到我这儿去帮助我,我很　198
　　　　　　　　　　　　感激。

高级汉语	（531）	安娜不在,她回去美国了。	199
高级汉语	（534）	一个月之内,你一定寄来我那本	200
		新书。	
现代汉语进修教程	（537）	刚才我看见丁力跑山下去了。	201
高级汉语	（545）	桌子上太乱了,你包上来这些	204
		东西吧。	
高级汉语	（548）	太晚了,咱们还爬山得了(liǎo)吗!	205
现代汉语进修教程	（553）	五道口剧场坐得下坐得不下	206
		一千人?	
高级汉语	（570）	我和你哥哥都是我们学校的篮球	213
		队员,他今年几岁了?	
高级汉语	（572）	这是很贵,有便宜的吗?	213
汉语课本	（573）	虽然他们住在一个富国,但是他们	214
		是很穷。	
高级汉语	（576）	我认为他们夫妻生活不是幸福。	215
高级汉语	（580）	尽管他不学习努力,他的考试成绩	216
		还可以。	
高级汉语	（593）	等你没有时间,我再来。	221
高级汉语	（609）	阿里出去了穿上衣服。	227
高级汉语	（615）	每当见到朋友的时候,她总是有很	229
		多事告诉。	
高级汉语	（616）	祥子想买一辆新的拉车。	230
高级汉语	（621）	人们把粽子扔了在河里,好让鱼吃	231
		粽子,不吃屈原的尸体。	
现代汉语进修教程	（638）	阿里挂这张地图在那张世界地	237
		图旁边了。	
高级汉语	（639）	你扔果皮进垃圾箱里(边)。	237
高级汉语	（642）	人们都叫做她孟姜女。	238

高级汉语	(650)	我的钱包被丢了。	241
汉语课本	(654)	房子是怎么被卖掉的？	242
高级汉语	(655)	大家的意见正在被研究中。	242
现代汉语进修教程	(657)	这些旧习惯早该被改了。	243
高级汉语	(667)	他被人骗。	246
高级汉语	(674)	家长是重要的人，每件重要的事情被他负责解决。	248
高级汉语	(680)	屈原被鱼拉回尸体。	250
高级汉语	(686)	他连最简单的汉字也写不好，复杂的汉字写不好。	252
高级汉语	(689)	这个城市建设得更加美了。	253
高级汉语	(690)	这个商店的商品越来越更加丰富了。	254
高级汉语	(692)	他家养的花都不错，特别是水仙花美丽。	255
高级汉语	(697)	他小时候比你淘气了。	257
现代汉语进修教程	(713)	吃的饭不如在家，但是还行。	263
高级汉语	(716)	小王不如小马安排作息时间。	265
汉语课本	(723)	我也希望你跟白求恩大夫对技术一样精益求精。	267
高级汉语	(727)	天坛有大同那么有名。	269
高级汉语	(733)	安娜很像她妈妈那么漂亮。	271
高级汉语	(737)	你买的自行车不像我这么结实。	272
高级汉语	(740)	车越来越开得快了。	274
高级汉语	(741)	雨越来越下了。	274
高级汉语	(751)	阿里不跟他的朋友一起去日本的。	279
高级汉语	(753)	我连想也没有用，就回答出来了。	279
高级汉语	(758)	这儿一点也一切没变，都跟从前一样。	281

高级汉语	（759）	他没有钱,甚至一分钱找不到。	282
高级汉语	（761）	因为她明天就要回法国去了。我今天不能去看她。	282
高级汉语	（766）	你什么时候方便,什么时候我就来看你。	284
高级汉语	（769）	这件毛衣的样子不是不好看,而是颜色不好。	286
高级汉语	（770）	她不是是北京大学的学生,而是是清华大学的学生。	286
高级汉语	（771）	他既跳远也跳高都不会,你教教他吧。	287
汉语课本	（777）	上课的时候,我们边儿听边儿说。	289
高级汉语	（782）	他一方面抓紧时间学习,一方面记生词。	290
高级汉语	（783）	老师一方面指出我们学习上的一些问题,一方面肯定我们的成绩。	291
现代汉语进修教程	（784）	他喜欢一方面吃饭,一方面看报。	291
现代汉语进修教程	（785）	在中国的五年里,一方面我要学好汉语,一方面要学好专业,一方面了解中国的建设情况。	291
高级汉语	（796）	阿里在这次比赛中,不但给我们拿到名次,而且自己取得好成绩。	296
现代汉语进修教程	（797）	他不但会说汉语,而且认识很多中国朋友。	296
高级汉语	（823）	冬天不管怎么冷,小王都坚持锻炼。	306
高级汉语	（824）	不管今天怎么再忙,我都要把这个材料看完。	306

高级汉语	（838）	什么事只有下功夫去做，就能成功。	311
高级汉语	（849）	我想与其《红楼梦》，不如《水浒传》。	315
基础汉语课本	（855）	既然你请我，然而我一定去。	317
现代汉语进修教程	（856）	人们所以把粽子扔到江中喂鱼，不让鱼吃屈原的身体。	318
高级汉语	（861）	因为我考试不及格，因此我不能毕业。	319
高级汉语	（862）	因此这儿不能游泳，由于水太深。	320
现代汉语进修教程	（863）	由于他对这儿比较熟，但是还走了一个小时。	320
高级汉语	（867）	尽管学习怎么忙，他每天还是坚持看报。	322
高级汉语	（884）	丁力最喜欢足球，他怎么能不来呢。	328
高级汉语	（885）	请你告诉我明天上午几点出发？	328
高级汉语	（888）	让我们一起热热闹闹地过个节吧。	329
高级汉语	（890）	为了玛丽的生日，同学们买了鲜花蛋糕巧克力糖葡萄酒什么的。	330

责任编辑:贾寅淮
封面设计:王 博

汉语病句辨析九百例

主 编 程美珍

副主编 李 珠

＊

@华语教学出版社

华语教学出版社出版

(中国北京百万庄路 24 号)

邮政编码 100037

电话:010-68320585

传真:010-68326333

网址:www.sinolingua.com.cn

电子信箱:hyjx@sinolingua.com.cn

北京外文印刷厂印刷

中国国际图书贸易总公司海外发行

(中国北京车公庄西路 35 号)

北京邮政信箱第 399 号 邮政编码 100044

新华书店国内发行

1997 年(大 32 开)第一版

2009 年第四次印刷

(汉英)

ISBN 978-7-80052-515-5/H・696(外)

9 - CE - 3227P

定价:35.00 元